JIM PICKRELL'S PERSONAL GUIDE TO SANTA MONICA, WITH LOS ANGELES AND SOUTHERN CALIFORNIA

Hotels, Restaurants, Museums, Beaches, Movie Studios, Surfing, Hiking and Travel Tips.

JIM PICKRELL

Jim Pickrell's Personal Guide to Santa Monica, with Los Angeles and Southern California (v2.6)

Contents

Introduction

Santa Monica is one of the top destinations in the world. Tourists come year around, even when it's too cold to visit the beach. Hi Tech and Entertainment businesses are also flocking to town, in pursuit of the good life and perfect weather.

Enjoying the beach and restaurants in Santa Monica is enough for a vacation by itself, but it's also the ideal base for exploring Hollywood and Los Angeles.

For many visitors, Southern California is all about Disneyland and Universal Studios, and that's sad, because there is so much to do here. LA is an outdoor place, and there are opportunities for outdoor and sports activities everywhere. There is architecture, history, food, museums, shopping, science and education, but most people have no idea where to start. That's what this book is for.

I will show you the best things to do and see throughout the LA area, using Santa Monica as your base. The best restaurants. The best hostels and hotels. The best beaches. The best museums. The best fine dining and places for people watching. The best taco trucks.

I will also include ideas of things to do. Architecturally notable buildings. Factories for guitars and Sriracha hot sauce, and a hundred other things you might not have thought of.

I will include a bit of history, a little bit of culture, and I'll even give some suggestions of side trips to places like Palm Springs and Tijuana.

I am assuming that you have access to Yelp and TripAdvisor, so you can look up any particular restaurant, hostel or hotel and see what the reviews are like. I'm not going to try to duplicate this. I'll just mention a few that like best.

I'm going to give you all the advice and helpful suggestions that I would give if you were a friend coming to visit me in Santa Monica.

Links and Maps

A well-equipped traveler should always have an iPhone or smart-phone with service that works. I don't know how I could even travel without my phone.

I've included web links and maps wherever they seemed to be helpful. The maps are live links, so if you are online, means click to see the online Google map. Where available, I have also included links to websites for all places listed here. The live links only work in the electronic version.

20 Fun Things to do While Visiting Santa Monica

Here is a list of some ideas of things that you can do while using Santa Monica as a base for exploring Southern California.

Visit the Santa Monica Beach

Watch people, then go down to the beach and go for a swim. It isn't really necessary to go anywhere. You can have a great time on the beach here right in front of town. It's a huge, clean and generally safe sandy beach, with no rocks or hazards. It's amazing that a beach can be right here in the middle of the city and still never be even close to full.

Rollerblade to Venice

Rollerblade or bike from Santa Monica to Venice along the paved beach path. The Venice boardwalk is filled with shops selling everything from T-Shirts to medical marijuana licenses. If you brought your skateboard, there are some good spots. Have lunch in Venice and then rollerblade or bike back.

Take the train to Downtown LA

Santa Monica now has a train to downtown. See the Bradbury Building, where Blade Runner was filmed, visit the Broad Museum, the famous Maya theater, and have dinner at Suehiro, a family style Japanese restaurant, or Philippe's, the inventor of the French Dip Sandwich.

Eat Korean BBQ

The Korean population in LA is large, and the food choices excellent. There are so many good places in Koreatown, it's hard to count. One of the best is Soot Bull Jeep, which offers wood charcoal BBQ right at your table. You will smell like BBQ at the end, but the food is the best.

Learn Trapeze

There is a trapeze school on the Santa Monica Pier. They welcome new students. This may be the best chance you will ever have to swing on a flying trapeze.

Visit the Magic Castle

Wander the halls of this large Victorian mansion, and enjoy a dozen or so magic shows, some up close and personal by individual magicians, some in one of the large theaters. They serve dinner.

Surfing Adventure

Visit Zuma J or one of the other surf shops in the area. They can sell or rent you a board, and anything else you need, and they can hook you up with lessons if you need them.

Amoeba Records

Buy a vinyl LP at Amoeba in Hollywood. It's the best record store on planet earth. They have CDs too, and often have shows of current bands. If you are into music, this is the place.

Movie Studios

Instead of a theme park, why not tour a real movie studio? Sony and Warner Brothers have tours. You can also get into some of the other studios if you come for the taping of a TV show.

Hollywood Bowl

Go to a concert at the Hollywood Bowl. Famous groups from the Beatles to Monty Python have played here, and there's something fun almost every day of the week. Seating is outdoors and picnics are allowed, so stop by Trader Joe's on the way and get some snacks and beverages and bring the picnic basket.

Huntley Hotel

Go up the glass elevator of the Huntley Hotel to the hotel at the top, and have dinner. The view of Downtown Santa Monica, the beach and Malibu is amazing, and the food is too.

McCabe's Guitars

Catch a music show at McCabe's, probably the world's most famous guitar store, for acoustic people anyway. Many well-known acts play their 100 seat theater. They also sell guitars, banjos and assorted stringed instruments. Free guitar pick and a cup of coffee with every visit.

Third Street Promenade.

There are street musicians, stands, and lots of shops, restaurants and movie theaters all along 3rd street and the surrounding area.

Go fishing for Yellowfin Tuna

Boats go out from Marina del Rey and from Oxnard. The fish is sushi quality, and large. An amazing fishing experience.

Vasquez Rocks

Captain Kirk of the Enterprise fought countless aliens on these rocks. Westworld is filmed here too. When you see it, it's going to look very familiar. Around every rock outcropping, you will expect to see a man in a rubber lizard suit, ready for battle.

Taylor Guitar Factory Tour

The best guitars are still made in the US. It's a two-hour drive to get there, but if you are interested in seeing how guitars are made, it's worth the trip.

Labrea Tar Pits

You can see the original tar pits, and in the Paige Museum see the skeletons of giant sloths, mammoths, and sabre toothed tigers that used to live in this area. It's a small but amazing exhibit. The LA County Art Museum is right next door in the same park, and the Petersen Auto Museum is just across the street.

Santa Monica Summer Pier Concerts.

Depending on the band, some concerts may have 20,000 people or more in the audience, most on the sand. The best thing to do is to pack a picnic, take along a blanket, and make an evening of it.

Zuma Beach in Malibu

This is the site where they filmed the end of "Planet of the Apes". That's the scene where the astronaut (Charlton Heston) sees the ruined Statue of Liberty sinking into the Pacific and realizes that apes have taken over Earth. Contemplate the impending fall of mankind. Then, have a picnic and go surfing or swimming at one of California's best beaches.

Helicopter to Catalina Island

Take a boat or a helicopter out to Catalina Island and spend the day. Swim or scuba dive or hike in the hills or just have dinner at one of the many restaurants. Consider taking the helicopter at least one way. It may be the best chance you will get to ride a helicopter.

Long Beach

See the Aquarium, the Queen Mary, the Battleship Iowa, ride over some very high bridges, then wander the quaint downtown area and have dinner. There is also an aquarium at San Pedro. Long Beach is fun.

Paddle Boarding

The best facility is the UCLA Aquatic Center, but there are private rental shops all along the beach, and in the harbors at Marina del Rey and Oxnard too.

Mulholland Drive

Mulholland Drive rides the crest of the Hollywood Hills. There are amazing views in both directions. Visit the Griffith Observatory in Griffith Park, and check out the view over the city. When you are done, go to Thai Town and have dinner at any one of the amazing Thai restaurants along Hollywood Blvd.

Drive a Harley to the Rock Store

Rent a Harley Davidson from the dealer in Marina del Rey and drive it up to the Rock Store, in the hills above Malibu, for a pulled pork sandwich and a beer. On Sundays Harley owners congregate here.

Beach Volleyball

Many of our country's Olympic volleyball players got their start on the beach at Santa Monica. You can play with the pros, or play with your friends. There are lots of beach volleyball courts, and they are free.

Sriracha Tour

Take a trip out to Irwindale and get a tour of the Sriracha hot sauce factory. The product is excellent and the tours are free. On the way back stop for dim sum at Ocean Star Seafood in Monterey Park.

Joshua Tree National Park

Take a road trip to Joshua Tree and hike in the desert. It's an amazing area, about two hours by car from Santa Monica, but well worth the drive. Then visit nearby Palm Springs for dinner.

Tijuana and Mexico

A three hour drive gets you to Tijuana. Food is good, people are nice, and it will add a little adventure to your trip. Border formalities are minimal, though there is usually a line coming back. Stay a night or two at the Rosarito Beach Hotel, an expansive resort built in the 1920's. Have lobster for dinner at Puerto Nuevo, a half dozen quail eggs for breakfast at El Nido, and a margarita as Hussong's..

Movie Extra

Sign up with Central Casting and be and extra for a few days. See filmmaking from the other side. This is much better than a tour bus, and you get paid and fed too. Think how much better a story that will make for the friends back home.

Horseriding in the Paramount Ranch

Go for a horse ride through the old Paramount Ranch in the hills above Malibu. It's a beautiful area, most of it park.

Some advice….

Santa Monica is the best area to stay

Why would you want to come to the LA area and not stay at the beach? Hollywood has major name recognition. The most interesting architecture is downtown LA. Anaheim has Disneyland. But that doesn't mean you need to stay in these places. The weather is better, the neighborhoods safer, and everything cleaner closer to the beach. It would cost you just as much to stay in a gritty part of town where there is nothing to see. If you stay in Santa Monica you can walk out of your hotel in the morning and see the beach. That by itself is enough to justify using Santa Monica as a home base for your visit to Southern California.

Hollywood Walk of Fame - Skip

When friends visit from out of town, I tell them to skip Hollywood and Vine and the "Walk of Fame" with the stars in the sidewalk. People think they will see movie loos, but the studios are all far from this location, in Culver City or Burbank. All you will see here is tour busses and tourists. If you want to see relics of old Hollywood, go to the cemetery and look for famous names. It's actually pretty interesting, and there are guides. If you want to see a movie studio go to Sony in Culver City and do the tour. Or sign up to see a TV Show being filmed, which will get you on a real movie lot to see real production.

Universal Studios and Disneyland - Skip

I hate standing in line, and that's about all you do at these theme parks. If you have kids along, you may have no choice, but there are so many other things to do that are so much more fun. They are expensive and the food is horrible. For me, riding in a little train, watching fiberglass mannequins turn left and right mimicking some scene from a movie, is completely boring.

For much less money you could ride the helicopter to Catalina, go for a hot air balloon ride, or take a scuba lesson. Rent a limo for a couple of hours. Eat at the nicest place in town and see a show. Go to Oxnard and rent a Jet Ski. That's a lot more better than spending the day waiting in line at Universal Studios.

If you want to see a theme park, try Magic Mountain or one of the local water parks. They won't have movie tie-ins but the rides are more fun.

Facts and Numbers

If you start in Downtown LA and head west until you hit the sea, you will be in Santa Monica. It is an independent city, but is surrounded on three side by Los Angeles. To the north is Pacific Palisades, to the east is Brentwood and West LA, to the south is Venice and Marina del Rey. On the west is the beach and the Pacific Ocean.

Santa Monica was the starting point of Route 66, the cross-country highway. This has been replaced by Interstate 10, which starts in Santa Monica, goes through Hollywood and Downtown, then heads east through Nevada, Arizona, and winds all the way to Chicago.

Santa Monica is a small town. The population is about 92,000. The town is a square almost three miles on a side, with a total area of 8.4 square miles.

Santa Monica has an average of 310 days of sunshine a year. The average high temperature ranges from 64 in January to 71 in August, though summer temperatures in the 80's and 90s are not unusual. In Winter nights temperatures in the 40's and even high 30's are possible, but frost is virtually unheard of.

95% of Santa Monica residents are high school graduates and 65% have a bachelors or better. Of those with a bachelors, 21% have a masters, 11% a professional degree and 6% doctorates. In the LA area, only Beverly Hills ranks higher.

The median age of Santa Monica residents is 40.5. Of 92,000 residents, 53,000 are employed. The median household income is $76,000. The average property value is $1.03 million.

While hotels and restaurants are the most visible businesses, they are only a small part of Santa Monica's economy. Professional services, health care, legal, education, and information technology are the dominant employment categories. Software is big business in Santa Monica. Hotels and food service represent only about 5% of employment.

History

Before the Spanish

In prehistoric times, Southern California was savanna, vast grassland and woods populated by mastodons and mammoths, giant sloths, saber tooth tigers and dire wolves and wild horses.

Indians appeared on the scene perhaps 20,00 years ago. Global cooling during the ice ages meant that ocean water was tied up in glaciers that covered much of North America. As water levels dropped, people were able to walk across to North America from Siberia. For this reason, Indians should have an ethnic kinship to the residents of Mongolia.

It is hard to lay blame, but arrival of the Indians coincided with the extinction of all the large ice age mammals. The hairy elephants, sabre toothed tigers and giant sloths vanished, but their skeletons can be seen in the La Brea Tar Pits in Hollywood.

The most advanced Indian cultures were in Peru and Mexico. California Indians were technologically far behind. Small in number, the Tongva, Chumash and other local tribes were hunter gatherers who didn't know about farming or keeping livestock. They didn't have the wheel, metals, pottery, and didn't construct permanent stone or brick buildings. They lived in a style that we would associate with prehistoric hunters, with stone age tools and culture.

The Chumash had a unique style of planked canoe, the "tomol", which allowed them to freely travel between the mainland, Catalina and the Channel Islands. Fish was a major part of their diet, as were otters, seals, and chestnuts.

The Indians made excellent baskets, either of the "coiled" type, or the "spined" type.

Coiled baskets are shaped with a spiral of three slender rods of juncus rush, wrapped and sewn together with split strands of the same material. They would just spiral round and round until the shape of the pot was built.

"Twined baskets" were woven by twisting weft strands around rigid warps that radiated from a central point like spokes on a wheel. "Twined baskets" include leaching basins, sieves, fish traps, cradles, and water bottles. Most were made from whole juncus rush stems or split tule (bulrush).

The Chumash house, or "ap", was round and was built like a very large upside-down basket. It was made by setting willow poles in the ground in a circle. The poles were bent in at the top, to form a dome. Then smaller saplings or branches were tied on crosswise. To cover the outside, bulrush or cattails were added in layers starting at the bottom, each row overlapping the one below. Like shingles on a roof, this thatched covering kept out the rain. For air circulation a hole was left in the top, which was covered with a skin when it rained. In good weather the cooking was done outside, but when it rained a fire could be lit in the fire pit in the center of each house. This also provided warmth. The houses were 12-20 feet in diameter. The chief's house was up to 35 feet across.

Since the Indians had no agriculture and no domestic animals, the populations in California were extremely small, limited by the amount of fish and game they could catch. The total population of Chumash and related tribes between Santa Monica and Santa Barbara is estimated by some to be about 18,000, but may have been far less. Many numbers are published by people with political axes to grind, but in fact, there was no census, no cemeteries or churches to keep records, and the numbers really are not known. Based on the food production, with no livestock and no farming, it doesn't seem like the population could have been very large.

Spanish Period

Columbus arrived in the new world in 1492. A few years later, Cortés and his Spanish soldiers conquered the huge Aztec empire in Mexico with lies and treachery backed by horses and guns. The Aztec king Moctezuma made Cortés his guest in his palace. Cortes repaid the favor by holding him captive and demanding the surrender of his armies. There were many adventures, battles, and much treachery by the Spanish, but in the end, they were able to win.

The Spanish laid claim to the entire New World. From this time, the history of California, is the history of Mexico.

The huge wealth won by Cortes and other Conquistadors was an inspiration to later generations of Spanish visitors, who spent the next hundred or so years exploring and subduing North America up to the Oregon border, hoping to find another city full of gold.

The conquistadors were followed by missionaries and priests, who built a trail of missions from Mexico City all the way up the coast to Oregon.

Spanish explorer Francisco de Ulloa named California after a mythical land "California", supposedly a Caliphate governed by black Islamic Amazon women. So "California" comes from the word "Caliph". The story comes from a 1510 work *The Adventures of Esplandián*, by Spanish writer Garci Rodríguez de Montalvo. The mythical kingdom of California was said to be a remote land inhabited by griffins and other strange beasts, and rich in gold. Of course, Ulloa didn't believe any of this, but he liked the name. Ulloa's surveys show California as an island, and it is show that way on Spanish maps up to the 1700's.

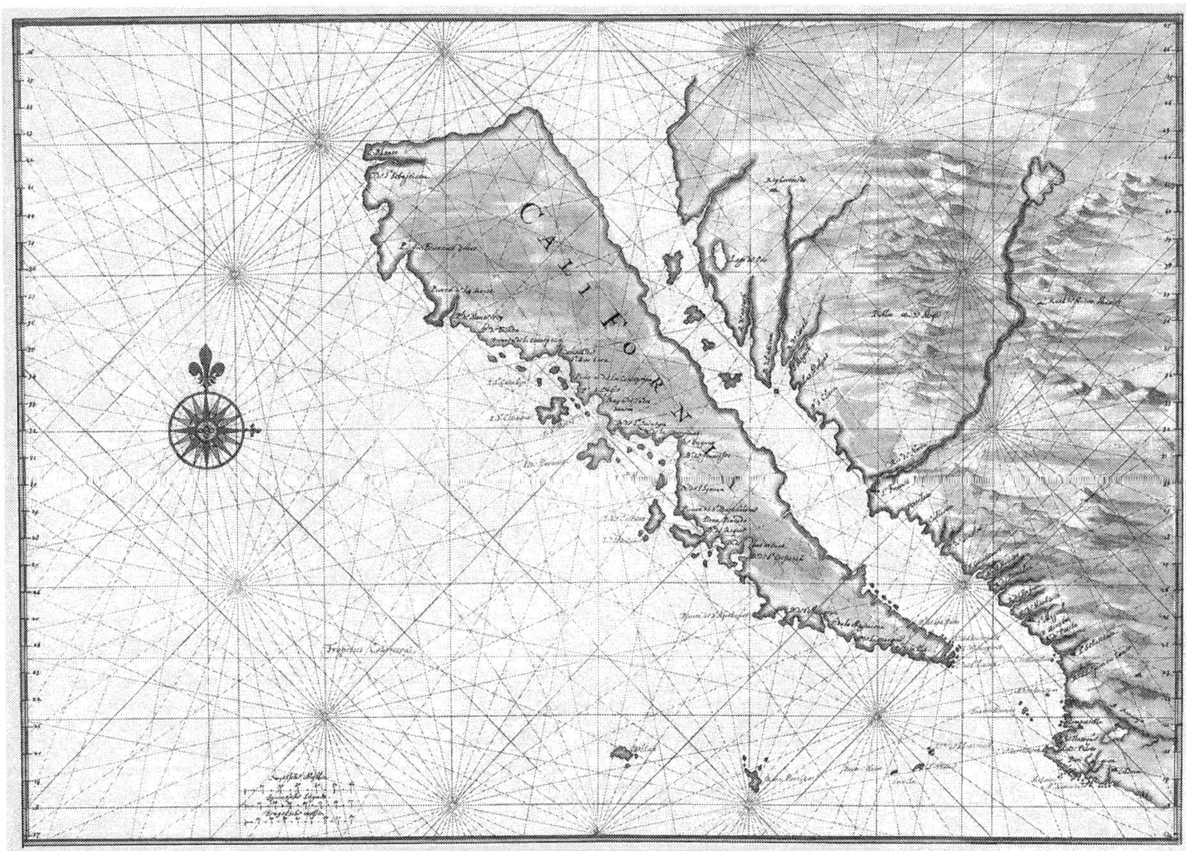

The Spanish considered California a wasteland. The local Indians were small in number, and had neither agriculture nor gold. For the Spanish, California was the far end of the world. So, colonization was left to the church.

The early missions in Baja California were established by members of the Jesuit order supported by a few soldiers. Most of the mission were built with the best of intentions, to bring Christianity and civilization to the local inhabitants, but on a practical level, the missions meant a lot of work for the Indians, with little or no pay.

The line between government and church was a blurry one. In many areas of Mexico, the church was also the government, and the king of Spain controlled the Spanish church.

The Jesuits were a monastic order that encouraged education. The Jesuit order was founded in 1540 by Ignatius Loyola, a Spanish soldier.

When the Spanish arrived in California there was little if any opposition to them. The Jesuits and other groups simply moved in and started organizing the missions, with little thought to land ownership.

After a power dispute between Charles III of Spain and the Jesuits, Charles resolved III of Spain resolved to expel the Jesuits from all of their dominions. The Spanish followed the example of the way that France had shut down and liquidated the Templars a few years before. They acted by surprise, arresting all the Jesuits and shipping them back to Spain, and from there into exile to Italy in 1767.

The operation was a total success. 678 Jesuits, including 11 from Baja California and California, were sent to Italy, a country most of them had never seen before. The properties of the Jesuits were confiscated and auctioned off. Most of the missions were taken over by Franciscan and later Dominican friars. Both of these groups were under much more direct control of the Spanish monarchy.

Junipero Sera, an idealistic Franciscan monk from Majorca, came to Mexico in about 1749, as an educator and missionary. He was already there when the Jesuits were expelled in 1767. Serra established his first mission in San Fernando de Velicatá in May 1769. Moving further north, he founded another mission in San Diego, first of nine missions he created in what is present-day California, that July. Serra spent the rest of his life building missions up the coast of California, from San Diego to San Francisco.

The Franciscan order differed from the Jesuits, in their emphasis on poverty and evangelization. When Junipero Sera first arrived in Mexico, he decided to walk from Veracruz to Mexico City, because he felt riding horses was an unnecessary luxury.

Sera saw his duty was to bring Christianity to the Indians, as well as the benefits of education and modern farming technology. Sera envisioned the missions as a utopia based on Franciscan principles. His honesty, hard work and austere lifestyle won him respect on all sides. The Catholic church canonized him in 2015.

In California, successful missions were built at places like San Diego, Santa Barbara, and San Francisco. Missions at San Luis Obispo and San Gabriel are still standing today, and can be visited.

Yet the Spanish themselves never arrived in large numbers, and the inhabitants remained mostly Indians.

Mexican Independence

In the early 1800's, Spain was conquered by France under Napoleon. Unable to protect their own homeland, the Spanish lost credibility in the colonies.

Mexico declared independence from Spain in 1822.

Yet independence was not a solution to Mexico's problems. The country gradually descended into chaos and civil war.

The missions of California were nationalized and the Franciscans ejected in 1834-1836. Much of this land was then handed over to politically well-connected people who made huge profits.

By 1846 the Mexican government had already had 40 presidents. That's nearly two presidents a year in the first 24 years of its existence.

The Mexican government did not place a high priority on California. For them it remained far from the center, with no gold and few people.

Mexican American War

In 1848, the United States invaded Mexico with the objective of "liberating" Texas. The American army that entered Mexico included many of the same military men who fought in the civil war a few years later, on both sides.

Jefferson Davis, later president of the Confederacy, supported the war under the theory of "Manifest Destiny", the belief that the United States was destined to rule North America.

Ulysses Grant, later leader of the Union forces that crushed the Confederacy, opposed the war as aggression against an almost defenseless enemy without any good reason.

The Mexicans, under Santa Ana, spent almost as much time fighting with each other as they did fighting the invaders. Their army collapsed almost immediately. The American quickly captured Veracruz and Mexico City. It was a disaster for the newly independent country, now only 24 yes old.

California, Santa Monica, and the area that is now the states of Nevada, New Mexico, Arizona, and Texas all were taken as booty by the United States at the end of the war.

California Statehood

It was only a year later, in 1849, that John Sutter found gold in the San Francisco area, and the gold rush was on. An estimated 50,000 would be miners came to California, hoping for instant wealth.

California became the 31st US state in 1850. By the census this same year, California had a permanent population of only 7,500 people, who were quickly overrun by those who had come to participate in the gold rush.

It was gold that brought the immigrants, but it was farming that convinced them to stay. From orange and lemon groves in the Los Angeles area, to grapes, dairy, rice and vegetables in the Sacramento valley, California had some of the richest farmland in the world.

California was a free state and supported the north in the Civil war. Slavery was banned in the State Constitution.

Transportation to California at this time was by ship, a long voyage, or by wagon train. For mail, there was the pony express.

The transcontinental railway came to California in 1869, only a few years after the end of the civil war. Coast to Coast transportation was reduced to a few days, and California economically became part of the United States.

The pace of immigration to Santa Monica and California in general increased dramatically.

Santa Monica Founded

The northern sections of Santa Monica were originally part of the Rancho San Vicente and the Rancho Boca de Santa Monica, which belonged to the Sepulveda family, who got it from the Mexican government for basically nothing. They sold 38,409 acres to Nevada Senator John Jones and Robert Baker for $55,000. They subdivided the property and created the town of Santa Monica, on July 15, 1875. The lots were put on sale for $75 to $500.00, at auction, and some prices went even higher. The tradition of land speculation in Santa Monica started early, and hasn't slowed down since.

The city electorate went to the polls in November 1886 and voted 97 to 71 to incorporate Santa Monica. In 1905, the town had reached a population of 7,208.

When the Southern Pacific Railroad arrived at Los Angeles, a controversy erupted over where to locate the seaport. Santa Monica's pier was built, and for a while Santa Monica was touted as the port of Los Angeles. San Pedro (Long Beach) eventually won out, and Santa Monica became a beach town, instead of the commercial port of Los Angeles.

Developer Abbot Kinney bought the southern area of Santa Monica and named it Ocean Park in 1895. He built an amusement park and residential project. A race track and golf course were built on the Ocean Park Casino. After a falling out with his partners he focused on the south end of the property, which became Venice.

Piers and amusement parks were hugely popular in the early 1900's, and at one point, Santa Monica had five of them. Only one survives today.

The Ocean Park Pier burned down in 1912. In its place was Fraser's Million Dollar amusement pier, which claimed to be the largest in the world at 1250 feet long and 300 feet wide. The pier housed a spacious dance hall, two carousels, the Crooked House fun house, the Grand Electric Railroad, the Starland Vaudeville Theater, Breaker's Restaurant and a Panama Canal model exhibit. It too burned within the year.

Douglas Aircraft

Donald Wills Douglas, Sr. founded the Douglas Aircraft Company in 1921, with his first plant on Wilshire Boulevard. He built a plant in 1922 at Clover Field (Santa Monica Airport), which was in use for 46 years. In 1924, four Douglas-built planes took off from Clover Field to attempt the first aerial circumnavigation of the world. Two planes made it back, after having covered 27,553 miles in 175 days, and were greeted on their return September 23, 1924, by a crowd of 200,000.

The Douglas Company (later McDonnell Douglas) kept facilities in the city until 1975. The entire facility was demolished and removed by 1977. This area is now Santa Monica Airport.

Wartime production at Douglas Aircraft grew to over 40,000 workers. Facilities were located at the current Santa Monica Airport. It was the beginning of the rise of Santa Monica as an aerospace and tech center. The airplanes built in Santa Monica were at the forefront of modern technology at that time.

1920's and 1930's

This was a period of massive growth. In the 1920's many of Santa Monica's landmark buildings were constructed, including the Miramar Hotel, Casa del Mar, and Henshey's Department Store (Now Barnes and Nobles).

Comedian Will Rogers bought a substantial ranch in *Santa Monica Canyon* in 1922. In his will, a large portion of the estate was left to the public, and it became the Will Rogers Park.

In 1928, Will Rogers sold a parcel with two large houses on the beach at the base of the bluffs to William Randolph Hearst, who then gave it to his girlfriend Marion Davies. This property is now the site of the Annenburg House, a public beach club and swimming pool. It is open to the public today.

By this time many of the familiar buildings from the Third Street Promenade had already been built, as shown in a postcard from 1927.

By 1930 the population of Santa Monica had reached 30,000.

Los Angeles hosted the Summer Olympics, which were held in Memorial Coliseum, which had been constructed 9 years earlier. This was in the middle of the worldwide depression, so no other cites had applied to host the Summer Olympics. About half those who attended the 1928 Olympics, were able to attend in 1932 due to financial problems.

The Olympics were a big success for Los Angeles. Posters urged fans to take Route 66 to see the competition. By limiting construction and using existing venues, the games profited more than a million dollars, which was a lot of money at that time.

In the 1930's, Santa Monica became a center for illegal offshore gambling. Customers would board ships located just offshore, where liquor and gambling laws were not enforced.

This is the period described by author Raymond Chandler, who calls Santa Monica "Bay City" in his classic detective novels.

In the 1930's, the Santa Monica City Hall, Post Office, and Santa Monica High School were built as WPA projects. They were designed in a style that was part Deco, part California, and remain landmarks today.

In the next decades Santa Monica continued to grow.

Route 66

The highway from Chicago to Santa Monica was authorized in 1926. Initially it consisted of a number of local highways and roads, many of them still just gravel. The whole highway wasn't completed and paved from end to end until 1938.

Santa Monica was the final stop in Route 66. Thousands of American cruised the new highway, which became the most important highway to the west coast of the US. The original route of Route 66 went down Santa Monica Blvd, right into the middle of downtown Santa Monica, ending at the intersection with Ocean Ave., in front of the spot where the Kingshead Pub and Sushi Roku are located today.

In the 1940's, war traffic boosted the importance of Route 66, and many sections were upgraded in the name of national defense.

Route 66 started in Santa Monica, on what is now Santa Monica Blvd, and inspired the song of the same name.

Interstate 10, the Santa Monica Freeway, was completed in 1966, replacing Route 66 as the main route to Chicago from LA.

Civic Auditorium

The 3,000-seat Santa Monica Civic Auditorium opened in 1958. From 1961 to 1968 the Academy of Motion Picture Arts and Sciences held its annual Oscar awards ceremony there. Performers over the decades include: André Previn, Dave Brubeck, Pete Seeger, Ella Fitzgerald, Tony Bennett, Joan Baez, Bob Dylan, Jimi Hendrix, David Bowie, Elton John, Ray Charles, Arlo Guthrie, The Beach Boys, The Carpenters, Bill Cosby, Jonathan Winters, Bob Hope, Allen Ginsberg, The Rolling Stones, T. Rex, Led Zeppelin, Ramones, The Clash, Buzzcocks, Public Enemy and countless others.

The Auditorium has been landmarked but is currently in a limbo state. Developers who want to tear it down and put in a hotel have been able to get the auditorium closed, but resident opposition is large. It remains a live issue today.

Surfing Safari

In the early 1960s, surfing was imported from Hawaii, and caught on in a big way. Local bands like the Beach Boys, Surfaris, and Dick Dale became national hits, and there were a long string of beach party and surfing movies that planted Southern California in the public imagination.

The earliest surfers rode big heavy Hawaiian style long boards, but as time passed, smaller boards became popular. It's easier to get up on a big board, but once you are up, a small board is much more maneuverable.

Santa Monica is a nice beach, but isn't really optimal for surfing because the wave roll straight into the beach and the break is pretty short. Serious surfers often opt for places like Zuma where the rides will be longer. Yet the importance of surfing in the development of Santa Monica was huge, and surfing remains as popular as ever today.

Promenade and Mall

In the late 1950's many cities were seeking to revitalize their downtown shopping areas, that were suffering from competition from Malls. Chamber of Commerce president and J.C. Penney general manager Ernest Gulsrud first proposed closing Third Street to cars in 1959.

The project finally went forward in 1965. Traffic was closed on third street and the pedestrian way was built in it's path. Originally it was called the "Santa Monica Mall". It included including retail areas and several large free parking lots on 2nd Street and 4th Street.

Yet the Mall was a modest success, compared to other areas such as Westwood that were booming with foot traffic. The Santa Monica mall had inexpensive shops selling T-shirts and used books, and wasn't generating the kind of traffic the city was hoping.

The city decided further investment was needed. After a two-year, $10-million renovation, the Santa Monica Mall was reopened in 1989 as the "Third Street Promenade". Several new multiples movie theaters attracted visitors, free parking made it easy, and afterwards it was hoped that they would patronize local restaurants and shops.

At that time the Westwood area in front of UCLA was the nightlife center of the Westside of LA. Several first run theaters and dozens of restaurants were all popular. At night the streets were jammed with cars full of teenagers cruising, and the sidewalks were full of pedestrians. However, after a 1988 drive by shooting, the police decided to clamp down on Westwood. Traffic barriers were erected to stop "cruising", and parking rates were raised. The result was that all those people who used to visit Westwood, started coming to the Promenade. By 1991, Westwood was a ghost town.

The Promenade project has been a huge success, and helped change Santa Monica from a sleepy beach community, into a major regional shopping and entertainment center. Between 1988 and 1998, taxable sales in the city grew 440%, quadrupling city revenues.

Not everyone is in love with the changes that the Promenade brought. Smaller local hardware stores, bookstores and thrift shops have been replaced with big name stores like GAP and Banana Republic.

Quality bookstores like Hennessey and Ingalls and the Midnight Special have been priced out by high rents. Local diners like Nate's, Penguin's and Zucky's are long gone.

Santa Monica Place

The original Santa Monica Place mall was built at the south end of the Third Street Promenade, two blocks from the Santa Monica Pier.

Local architect Frank Gehry designed the mall. It featured a three-story main hall, with shops on both sides on all three levels, and elevators and escalators at both ends and the middle, which formed a center court. A food court was on the ground level facing the Promenade, where many inexpensive food stands, such as "Hot Dog on a Stick" were located. Popular stores included Macy's, Robinsons-May, Radio Shack, Eddie Bauer, B Dalton Books, Walden Books, GameStop, and Speedo Swimsuits. Large parking lots with abundant free parking were built on the north and south sides.

Mall chain Macerich purchased the mall, and immediately began planning expansion. Their main proposal was to increase the height and add high rise condominiums, which got much opposition from local residents.

A second proposal eliminated most of the height increase, and all of the condominiums, and attempted to create an open feeling by removing the roof over the common areas. The central atrium was enlarged and made round. The look for the mall was redone, with grey, steel and cement being the predominant colors. Many find it cold and uninviting.

The mall closed for about two years while the reconstruction was in progress, and during that time, most of the tenants either moved or went out of business.

The anchor tenants were replaced by Nordstrom, Bloomingdale's, and an ArcLight Cinema. The mall's other shops include Tiffany & Co., Louis Vuitton, Burberry, Emporio Armani, and Diane Von Furstenberg, giving the mall a very different feeling than it had before.

The food court was moved up to the third floor. In order to get there, customers take the escalator path that requires them to walk all around the mall twice. Few bother. The food court is usually empty.

There is much discussion now of the future of Santa Monica Place. The shops aren't popular with local people, and the mall is not nearly as busy as the Promenade, which is only steps away.

Planners from Starbucks recently estimated they believed that 20% of the nation's malls will close by the end of the decade. Because the land is so valuable, especially now that the new train has arrived next door, so many people expect Macerich to come back with a new plan for more development at this location, probably with new proposals for high rise development.

Santa Monica for Renters Rights

In 1978, Santa Monicans for Renters' Rights (SMRR) was formed by Yannatta Goldway, Derek Shearer, Dennis Zane, and Reverend James Conn with support from Tom Hayden and Jane Fonda. A strict rent control ordinance passed in 1979 and SMRR achieved a council majority in 1981. Unhappy apartment owners complain about the "Soviet Republic of Santa Monica."

Santa Monica City Council is currently dominated by Santa Monicans for Renter's Rights. All council members are members of SMRR, and most had SMRR support in the elections.

Santa Monica currently has the highest rent levels in the LA area, and tourism is at an all-time high. Santa Monica is something like 80% renters. Many residents believe, without rent control, most of the original residents of Santa Monica would be forced out. Santa Monicans for Renters Rights is seen as the only organization that will help local people stay in their homes.

The biggest political issue in Santa Monica today is development. Plans to allow the Miramar Hotel, Wynn Hotel, and other local sites to build skyscrapers with minimal parking is highly controversial.

Papermate opened its Santa Monica factory in 1957. The plant produced 600 million ballpoint pens in 1971 and closed in 2005. Plans to build a million square foot development at the Papermate site were successfully challenged by "Residocracy", a resident group, but the initiative they proposed calling for voter approval of all new construction over three stories, was defeated a year later.

Today, all of the members of the Santa Monica City Council are members of SMRR, and all generally agree on the goal of keeping rents affordable. There is much disagreement on the subject of development among SMRR members. Some feel development is the future, others prefer things as they were twenty years ago.

Planning Your Trip

When to go

Santa Monica is nice to visit most any time of year. If you're planning to go swimming at the beach, then summer is going to be the best, but summer in Santa Monica lasts longer than it does in other places.

Airline flights and hotels will be tight around major holidays such as Thanksgiving or Christmas. Hotels consider summer to be the high season, and generally will charge more in Summer than they do in winter.

Climate

The temperatures in Santa Monica or nearly always comfortable. In the summer it seldom gets above 90°. In winter it's very low it's rare to get below 50°. Many people wear shorts year around.

Temperatures in Southern California vary a lot even with and short distances. The closer you are to the water, the more moderate the temperatures. In the summer Downtown LA and Pasadena will be 5° to 10° warmer than Santa Monica, and they will be colder in the winter. Temperatures are even more extreme as you move further inland to places like Lancaster or Barstow.

Rain is fairly rare. Santa Monica, and in fact all of Southern California, is basically desert. The oasis of trees and grass in Santa Monica is made possible by wells and by large scale diversion of water from other areas such as the Colorado river.

When it does rain, the water falls in torrents. It's like someone dumped a bucket of water on your head. It's very different from the month after month of drizzle you get in places like Seattle. There are usually a few rainy days in February and you might get a day or two of rain in November or December. The rest of the year it's just sunny day after sunny day.

Holidays

Holidays in California are pretty much the same as in other American cities.

Christmas

Dec 25. Virtually all businesses are closed Christmas day and many the day before. In fact, most are closed the entire period from Christmas to New Year's Day. If you are looking for food on Christmas, try Norms or look for Chinese places or Jewish delis.

New Year's Eve

Jan 31 is a holiday for most. People like to get together for parties and welcome the new year. Many restaurants double their prices and require advance reservations, which usually isn't much fun. Better to spend time with friends.

Easter

The week leading up to Easter is often a school holiday. Spring Break isn't such a big thing in California as it is in some other tourist destinations, since the Summer weather hasn't really arrived yet.

Halloween

Oct 31 isn't really a proper holiday at all, but it is widely celebrated. Most people go to parties with friends, or go out to a local pub. Costumes are popular. There is a big parade in West Hollywood which has many good costumes and is fun. Businesses do not close for Halloween.

Thanksgiving

Always held on the fourth Thursday in November. Most businesses are closed Thursday and Friday. This is considered a "family" holiday. Most people stay home and eat Turkey dinner with friends and family.

Presidents Day

Third Monday in February. This is a public holiday. Most people don't care much about the holiday, but are happy to have the day off from work. Stores and restaurants will be open.

Labor Day

First Monday in September. This is a public holiday. Most people don't care much about the holiday, but are happy to have the day off from work. Stores and restaurants will be open.

4th of July

This is a public holiday. Most people have the day off and go to the beach, to parties with friends, or to watch public fireworks at Marina Del Rey or other locations all over town.

St Patrick's Day

March 17. This is not a proper holiday at all. Many people wear something green and go to their local Irish pub for a beer.

Cinco de Mayo

May 5. This is even less of a holiday than St. Patrick's Day. Even Mexicans don't celebrate Cinco de Mayo. It is the anniversary of a victory of Mexico over the French. The actual national holiday for Mexican independence is in September. However, many people in Santa Monica go to local bars and drink tequila or Mexican beer to celebrate.

Packing

Temperatures in Santa Monica or moderate most of the year, so you will want to pack casual clothes that are appropriate for spring or summer.

Temperatures are warming enough for swimming about half the year, so you may want to bring your swimsuit.

Southern California is an informal place. Many people in the Tech and movie industries wear shorts year around. Suits and formalwear are usually reserved for bankers, lawyers, and people attending funerals.

Heavy winter clothing and raincoats will get no use at all and can be left at home.

I always spend a lot of time agonizing over what to take with me when I travel. I usually find I have taken more than I need. Here are some suggestions:

- Pack as light as you can.
- Don't go on a shopping spree before your trip. You can have fun shopping in LA.
- Dress for Spring and you'll probably be fine. A windbreaker or sweater will be useful for cooler evenings.
- Wear comfortable walking shoes.
- Dress clothes are not a necessity unless you really have in mind going to some specific black-tie events. My closet is full of nice wool blazers and suits I never wear.
- Socks and underwear are your primary need. Extra coats and suits and winter clothes will not get used much.

Check the weather report before you go. Santa Monica has a very mild climate, but in winter it could be cool or rainy.

Sample Packing List

Here's what I would take for a one-week trip

Wear on the plane:

- Long sleeve T-shirt
- Rainproof windbreaker
- Long cotton pants or jeans
- Underwear and socks
- Practical comfortable shoes

Carry-on Suitcase:

- Seven pairs underwear
- Seven pairs socks, low-rise, they take less space
- Two T-shirts or polo shirts
- One pair shorts
- One pair sandals
- Bathing suit and towel.

Personal needs:

- Toothbrush
- Toothpaste
- Shampoo (in checked bag only)
- Suntan Lotion (in checked bag only)
- A couple of disposable razors (in checked bag only)

Note that if you were carrying everything on hand luggage in the cabin, you're probably best to leave the liquid products such as suntan lotion and shampoo at home. Razors too. It's not worth the hassle of trying to get them through security. These are available and inexpensive anywhere you go.

Leave at home

Things you should not bring:

- Multiple pairs of shoes. They are heavy.
- Excessive numbers of pairs of pants and jackets.
- Ski parkas, heavy raincoats and heavy boots. You will not have any occasion to wear them, unless you are actually going up to the mountains.
- Weapons, drugs, or anything that might get you in trouble.
- Liquids over 4 ounces, or knives of any kind. If you must take them, put them in your suitcase and check it.
- Large, heavy items of any kind.

Transportation

Air Travel

Most visitors come to Santa Monica and LA by airplane, unless they live in California.

Buying Air Tickets Online

Buying tickets for air travel has become a game. Two people sitting next to each other on an airplane might have paid completely different prices for their tickets, and there are often large price differences between airlines.

When looking for tickets I usually start with Kayak.com to get any idea of the prices. I will double check on Travelocity or other sites, but there usually aren't any surprises. If Southwest flies the route I'm looking at, you have to look at their site directly, since they do not participate in Kayak.com.

There are certain airlines I won't fly on, including Volaris, Sprit and Air Pakistan. These are silly airlines with fairly random safety records and a penchant for surprises like $100 charges for hand luggage or a requirement that you show up for your plane three hours before takeoff (Air Pakistan). I just don't want to deal with these kind of problems, so I refuse to even look at these carriers.

When you compare prices, be sure to include baggage fees, and change fees if you think that will be an issue. Some airlines will give you a free checked bag if you have their credit card. Most airlines charge more if you buy a ticket at the airport.

Airports

There are several Airports in the LA area. LAX is the closest to Santa Monica, and it's where most visitors arrive. Burbank Airport is smaller and easier to deal with, but it is a 45-minute drive away. John Wayne airport in Orange County is more than an hour away, and Ontario airport is even further. Burbank and John Wayne are much better run and easier to get in and out of, but they are pretty far from Santa Monica. Unless you get some kind of amazing deal at one of these other airports, LAX is going to be your best bet.

LAX Airport

https://goo.gl/maps/3jCWVZZ95p12
1 World Way, Los Angeles, CA 90045
lawa.org
(855) 463-5252

Lax can seem bewildering the first time you arrive, but in fact the layout is very simple. The main road through the airport is shaped like a giant "U", with the top facing east and the International Terminal at the bottom. Departures are on the second floor. Arrivals and baggage retrieval are on the first floor. Vans and cars usually pickup on the first floor, except for Uber and Lyft, which are limited to assigned spots on the second floor. There are signs posted for hotel vans, rental company vans, and the shuttle to Lot C where you can catch buses to other parts of town.

International flights usually arrive at terminal B, which has the offices for most of the international airlines. This terminal is also called the "International Terminal" or the "Tom Bradley Terminal". All the other terminals have numbers.

The terminals themselves are generally very disorganized. The main cause is security, which was added as an afterthought. X-ray machines, walls and barriers, and lines where people wait to get searched, all have been improvised and with a little thought to convenience or common sense. I have flown into many airports. LAX is without a doubt the most disorganized airport I have ever seen.

Customs and immigration are located in the international terminal. It may take a half hour to an hour to collect your bags, get your passport stamped, and make it to the sidewalk.

Major Airlines can be found at these terminals:

Southwest: 1

Aeroméxico: 2

United: 7-8

Delta: 2-3

Alaska: 6

Jet Blue: 5

Frontier: 5

Spirit: 5

Air Canada:6

WestJet: 6

American: 4-5

International airlines are almost all at terminal B.

Restaurants

Food at the airport is generally mediocre and very expensive. Fast food restaurants like McDonald's that have cheap menus in other parts of town won't have them here. Instead, they will try to sell you some kind of meal combination for $8 or $10.

The best thing you can do is bring your own food with you. A $3 sandwich from Subway is much better than anything you can buy at the airport.

If you really need to eat, Panda Express in the international terminal is not too bad. They serve hearty combinations of Asian inspired food with rice and noodles for about eight dollars. Real Food Daily upstairs in the international terminal has decent food, but is expensive.

Changing money

Most Americans have never seen any kind of currency other than dollars. If you go to an average bank branch and ask them to exchange your euros, rubles or yen, you might as well be showing them slices of green cheese from the moon. They will look at you, look at your bank notes, consult Google to see what your Canadian dollars or English pounds are supposed to look like, and then call a manager to ask for advice.

The exchange rates for cash at the airport will be terrible. Exchange at hotels is even worse, if you can get them to do it. Commissions may exceed 10% to 15%.

The best option is to use a cash machine card, and withdraw cash when you arrive. Bank of America operates ATM machines on both levels at every terminal at the airport. Cash machines at the airport will charge you a fee, but it will still be much cheaper than travelers checks or attempting to exchange currency at one of the exchange windows at the airport.

If you cannot arrange an ATM card that will work in the US, your best second choice is to bring dollars in cash, or travelers checks denominated in dollars from a bank that has branches locally, so you don't get killed with fees when you try to cash them.

Airlines

Alaska Airlines

Alaska airlines is the biggest carrier on the West Coast of the United States. They recently purchased Virgin, and got even bigger. They have a reputation for good quality service, however, more and more they seem to be playing the same games as other airlines, trying to squeeze extra money out of passengers for carry-on bags and other fees. Currently Alaska allows one carry on and one personal item. Checked bags are $25 each.

Virgin Airlines

Virgin used to run a lot of flights up and down the coast, with excellent service, but they just got bought out by Alaska, so they are gone.

American Airlines

American Airlines offers a large number of flights around the US and overseas, especially to Latin America. American permits one carry-on that fits in the overhead bin, and one personal item. American charges $25 for the first bag, $35 for the second bag. International flights, first class tickets, and those with special credit cards will get one back for free.

United Airlines

United Airlines offers scheduled flights all over the United States and overseas too. Prices are often quite competitive, but management has set their sights on providing the worst and most annoying service possible. They nickel and dime passengers until the frustration level gets so high that passengers choose some other airline. There is a rumor that they will start charging for in flight restroom use, but that's not yet. United charges $25 for the first checked bag and $35 for the second. Ticket changes are $200. Phone reservations are $25. You can take a checked bag for free if you have their credit card.

Delta Airlines

Delta is a traditional American flag carrier. Delta offers reasonable priced flights from any other parts of the country. There doesn't really seem to be much that distinguishes Delta from other similar carriers like American or United. You are allowed one carry-on and one personal item. Checked bags are $25 for the first and $35 for the second.

JetBlue

JetBlue is a moderately priced carrier that tried to break the airline pricing system by offering lower fees and comfortable leather seats. Pricing on JetBlue varies a lot depending on how much advance notice you have. You will get the best price if you book a couple of weeks or a month in advance. You are allowed one carry-on and one personal item. Checked bags are $25 for the first and $35 for the second.

Southwest Airlines

This company has tipped over the apple cart for many carriers. You get two checked bags for free, reservations are changeable, and ticket prices are usually cheap, with a few days notice.

Southwest allows two checked bags on all flights, with additional bags $75 each.

Southwest Airlines has major hubs in Las Vegas and Phoenix, San Francisco and Oakland. Flights from other parts of the country will frequently involve a stop at one of these places.

Southwest doesn't have reserved seats. They just up at boarding time, and passenger scramble for the seats. I don't like this much, but that's how they do it.

Southwest Airlines does not participate in reservation systems such as Kayak or Travelocity. If you want to find out the availability of Southwest airlines flight to Los Angeles, you have to go to their website and check.

One of the big plusses of Southwest Airlines is that they offer two bags checked for free. They also allow you to change tickets without penalty, but sometimes this works better than others. If you want to another flight the same day, they will usually let you do this with no penalty. If you change the date they will charge you the difference in fares.

I think it's always worth checking Southwest airlines to see what kind of ticket offer they have available on your travel dates.

Air Canada

Other than a nice red color scheme, Air Canada seems about the same as any US based airline. I have flown on Air Canada several times. Services was always good and prices competitive. One time they did lose my luggage. You are allowed one carry-on and one personal item. Checked bags are $25 for the first and $35 for the second, for flights from Canada to the US.

British Airways

England's flag carrier offers excellent service and competitive rates for worldwide travel. If you're coming from Europe it's worth checking to see what they offer. Flights from the UK to the US get one bag free, $51 for the second.

Air Tahiti

Air Tahiti has regularly scheduled service between Tahiti and Paris, with a refueling stop in Los Angeles. If there are seats available, you can often get them for very cheap. Air Tahiti has clean new planes and excellent service. I would choose them over most other airlines, if tickets are available. One bag is included with an international ticket. Upgraded tickets get a second bag, otherwise there would be a charge. One carry-on and one personal item are allowed.

Air France

France's flag carrier offers fine service and good food in trans-Atlantic flights. They also code share with Delta. If the prices are right, Air France can be an excellent choice for travel to California. One carry-on and one personal item are allowed. Economy passengers get one checked bag, with the second one $80 online or $100 at the airport.

Lufthansa

Germany's flag carrier offers excellent service and good food, although pricing is often a few dollars more than other carriers, depending on your destination. Lufthansa also owns Swissair. Service on both airlines is excellent. Economy passengers on Lufthansa from Europe to the US get a carry-on, personal item and one checked bag, except cheap tickets from Scandinavia which get a carry-on but no free checked bag. From Scandinavia, a checked bag is $60 extra online or $100 at the airport.

Norwegian

Norwegian Airlines is a rock-bottom price airline with nickel and dime charges for absolutely everything.

Some passengers consider dealing with airlines like Norwegian or Volaris to be like a game. If you learn the rules and play carefully, you can often get tickets for about half what anybody else would be charging. A normal ticket includes a carry-on but you have to pay extra for overweight baggage or for a checked bag. The formula for the charges is complicated so it is best to confirm with Norwegian and pay for the bag when you buy your ticket. They charge by the kilo for overages so it might be a good idea to put anything heavy like books or laptops in your coat pockets, if they will fit. It may sound funny but it might save you money. In fact, if you look online, you can find companies that sell trench coats with very large pockets for just this purpose. Really.

SAS

Scandinavian Airlines claims to be the flag carrier of about half a dozen countries, but flies mostly through Copenhagen. Service is about equivalent to the other major European flag carriers. Due to competition with Norwegian, SAS is now selling cheap tickets with no checked bag included. It's impossible to tell from their website what the luggage charges are, so my best guess would be $110 per bag, which is what they charge premium ticket passengers for extra bags. Best to confirm and pay for any desired checked bag, when you buy your ticket.

Aeroflot

More and more, Aeroflot is offering flights between various European destinations in the United States. Prices are very aggressive.

It used to be that Aeroflot flew tired old Russian military airplanes, but these days they are flying mostly new Boeing jets. I have only flown on Aeroflot once, but I thought it was great.

With visa restrictions, many countries have to go through an elaborate visa process to visit Russia, and it can cost $100 or more, but you don't need a visa to stop over for a flight. So, if you can book an Aeroflot flight with a 24 hour stopover in Moscow, this would be a very cheap way to get a short visit to Moscow, especially if it saves you money on the flight as a whole.

Aeroflot includes one carry-on and one checked bag with economy tickets.

Turkish Airlines

Turkish Airlines is on a campaign to capture a large portion of the European airline market, following the model of Emirates.

As part of this plan, they have purchased many new airplanes, provide excellent food and service, and their pricing is very aggressive.

I have flown on Turkish airlines a couple of times, and service was generally very good. The food was nice, the planes were nice, everything was excellent.

A few years ago, when I was caught in Cairo during the 2011 Arab Spring revolution, the people from Turkish Airlines were very kind to provide an evacuation flight to Istanbul, which is how I got out of the country. That was nice of them.

Turkish Airlines allows carry-on plus TWO checked bags on flights to the US.

LAX Airport Transportation

Transportation at the airport is not efficient. Transit is blocked by airport authorities who want everyone to bring their own vehicle. Every car that is left at home, is $10 a day lost to the people who own the parking lots. They can't ban you from using transit, but they do their best to make it inconvenient. We will show you how to work with the situation.

Train to the airport

LAX has banned the Green Line train from downtown from coming into the airport. The nearest stop is Aviation station, two miles away. The train comes to an abrupt halt, and passengers must board a shuttle to get to the airport.

Aviation/LAX station

https://goo.gl/maps/oWq4uhnzwMH2

11500 Aviation Boulevard, Los Angeles, CA 90045

Aviation station is the closest the airport would let the train come. If you are coming from the airport, catch the free shuttle from the airport to the green line station, which has a stop in front of each terminal.

The LAX story is that they would have to rip up the runway to complete the train route to the airport. A quick look at the map (see link below) shows that this is not true. In cities that support transit, such as Seattle, Zurich, or Tokyo, the train station is in the airport. Someday, when corrupt officials are removed from the airport administration, the train line will be completed, and the train will come right into the airport.

Bus to the airport

LAX has banned busses from the airport. Buses must go to Lot C, a parking lot about a mile from the airport, and passengers take a shuttle to/from the airport.

LAX Lot C Bus Terminal

https://goo.gl/maps/TVVbW2ak9UC2

96th St & Sepulveda Boulevard, Los Angeles, CA 90045

This is the bus terminal that serves the airport. If you want to take a bus into town, catch the shuttle labelled Lot C, which has a stop in front of each terminal.

The LAX official explanation is that allowing busses into the airport would cause traffic problems. The reality is that they would rather have you bring your car and park in one of the paid lots. New York's La Guardia and SeaTac have bus terminals are right inside the airport. Traffic is reduced with busses.

Uber/Lyft to the airport

For many years LAX banned both Uber and Lyft. Drivers who entered the airport would be arrested or given tickets for a thousand dollars by LAX airport police.

Eventually a deal was made where both companies can pick up riders at the airport, but drivers are only allowed to pick up riders on the top level (departures) at posted stops. They pay a $5 fee for each ride they pick up. If you want to catch a ride, take your bags and call Uber or Lyft from one of the stops on the top level of the airport.

A ride to Santa Monica will cost around $20-$25 including the surcharge.

Taxi to/from the airport

There are taxi lines on the ground level in front of each terminal. A taxi ride will typically cost about $45 though sometimes coupons are available which will bring the price down to as low as $25.

Airport Limo Vans

Several companies offer Airport vans. There are stops in front of each terminal. They leave for Santa Monica about every half hour, and serve other areas too. They will usually take a half dozen or so passengers in a single area and drop them off wherever they want to go.

Prime Time Shuttle

https://www.primetimeshuttle.com

Super Shuttle

https://www.supershuttle.com/locations/losangeleslax/

Riding in shuttles sometimes can be frustrating, as they circle around and around the airport looking for additional riders. In the past I have spent up to an hour circling, until I threw a tantrum and demanded that they take me home or let me out.

The cost to Santa Monica is about $20. For two or more people, Uber or Taxi will be cheaper.

Driving to Santa Monica

If you are coming from somewhere else in the western United States, driving to Santa Monica may be an option.

Factors that will help you decide are: Do you wish to have a car while you're in California? What are the rental options? How long does it take to drive? How much gas will you burn on the way?

Driving from Las Vegas

From Las Vegas the distance is about 280 miles. It takes about five hours if the traffic is clear. If your car gets 20 miles per gallon you are going to need about 14 gallons of gas each way, at an average of three dollars per gallon, and that will be $42 each way.

Compare this to the time and cost for flying. An advance reservation ticket from Las Vegas to LA will average about $70.

The flight only takes about 45 minutes. It seems like as soon as the plane gets to altitude it starts to descend. However, when you figure the hassles of getting to the airport, checking in, getting through security, and then getting out of the airport at your final destination, the time savings is at best an hour.

The drive through the desert is pretty boring, but it's handy to have a car in Los Angeles, so visitors from Nevada usually drive.

Driving from San Francisco

From the Bay Area, the distance is about 250 miles, and travel time is about five hours, very similar to Las Vegas. The inland drive is a bore, but it's nice to have a car when you arrive in Los Angeles.

As an alternate, you can take the coastal route from San Francisco to Los Angeles. This drive is absolutely beautiful, and it is something everyone should at least once. On the downside it takes about 11 hours. So, if you are in any kind of hurry, you will take I5 south.

Driving from Seattle

From Seattle, the distance is about 1300 miles, and the drive takes about 22 hours on the inland route.

If you get 20 MPG that's 65 gallons of gas at three dollars a gallon, costing almost $200 each way. Airline tickets typically cost between $90-$150 each way. This means driving usually isn't worth it unless you really just want to experience the drive.

Driving from anywhere else

From other places like Chicago, Dallas, or the East Coast, driving is absolutely not worth it. It will be much cheaper to fly and then rent a car.

Train to Santa Monica

You can find train prices and schedules on the Amtrak website:
https://www.amtrak.com/tickets-reservations

I love trains, and I ride then whenever I can. I like to see the countryside, I like to get up and walk around while I am traveling, and I enjoy meeting other travelers on the way.

Unfortunately, in the United States, Amtrak doesn't make it easy for you. In fact, I often get the feeling the only reason they offer train service passenger train service between Los Angeles and other cities is because they are legally required to do so. It doesn't seem like they are marketing things in a way that is designed to fill the trains with passengers.

For example, if you want to take a train from Seattle to Los Angeles, it takes about 36 hours for $155. However, this is for the privilege of spending 36 hours in a seat. You don't get any bed, you don't get a room, you don't get in the shower and you don't get any breakfast.

Book a cabin and a bed and you're looking at more like $682 each way.

What this means is that riding the train is an option only for people who have lots of time and absolutely don't care what it costs.

The train that runs along the coast is the "Coast Starlight". Don't take any of the other trains, which will cost more and take the inland route with stops and train changes.

In my opinion, a train ticket should cost less than an equivalent air ticket. From Chicago or New York, riding a train really truly only makes sense if you are very excited about the train trip itself, and do not care about time or money.

Bus to Santa Monica

Greyhound

https://www.greyhound.com

Santa Monica used to have a Greyhound bus station, but this was removed years ago. You can still take busses to/from the downtown LA station. Fares are great. Greyhound is trying a little harder than Amtrak to make their pricing competitive, but the 48-hour trip from Chicago could be a bit of an ordeal. Greyhound now offers Wi-Fi on their busses, which could help pass the time.

Sample fares to LA:
Chicago 48 hours $120
Phoenix 7 hours $28
San Francisco 6 hours $19
Las Vegas 5 hours $10
Exact fares depend on dates and advance purchase.
Detailed information about Greyhound is found on their website:

Green Tortoise

www.green tortoise.com

Green Tortoise is the old hippy camping bus. They sometimes run bus tours up and down the coast or out to Las Vegas and Grand Canyon. They have an old double decker bus that is built out as a camper and they do various tours. They also have hostels in San Francisco and Seattle. If their schedule at all matches your travel dates this could be a lot of fun.

StarLine
CitySightseeing
Hop-On, Hop-Off
GET REA
COLLECTION
363
VECTOR
OPERATED BY
STARLINE TOURS
PSC #227 TCP #227
macy

Getting Around

Walking in Santa Monica

Santa Monica is walkable. That's one of the wonderful things about it, and why it makes the best possible place to stay while visiting Southern California.

Santa Monica is a rectangle roughly 3 miles x 3 miles. This means you should be able to walk from any place in Santa Monica to any other place in Santa Monica in an hour. If you are staying in the Downtown Santa Monica area, almost everything you need is right there within walking distance, from hotels to beach, from food to shopping.

Car in Santa Monica

Most local people get around my car pretty much all the time, except when they are going short distances or they can walk or ride a bike. Los Angeles is not a public transit friendly place. Distances are far and transit is slow. Some important destinations such as the airport don't even admit transit. Santa Monica is walkable, but nobody walks in LA.

If you do drive in Santa Monica, make sure you have some arrangement for parking at your hotel. Most hotels have inadequate parking and their rates are completely silly.

The mall and public lots along 3lrd street have 1 ½ hour free parking while you visit.

There is a huge parking lot in front of the Civic Auditorium which has moderate rates. This is where all the lawyers and their clients at the courthouse park.

Beach lots are a little more expensive but allow all day parking.

Almost anything will be cheaper than parking at your hotel.

Bicycling in Santa Monica

The same things that make Santa Monica good for walking also make it good for bicycling. Most of Santa Monica is pretty flat and the weather is always good.

If you're going to be in Santa Monica for a while your best option is probably to buy a used bicycle off of Craigslist. You should be able to get something decent for $50 or so, or something really nice for a few hundred.

If you are only going to be in town for a few days, then rental is going to be your best option. There are half a dozen companies downtown and on the beach that will be happy to rent to a bicycle for $6 to $8 an hour or $15-$20 per day.

Sea Mist Rentals

1619 Ocean Front Walk · (310) 395-7076

http://www.seamistrentals.com

Located on the boardwalk just south of the pier. Bike $7 per hour. Tandem $14. Rollerblades $7/hour.

Jays Rentals

https://goo.gl/maps/ovfr2qt3HBL2

1501 Ocean Front Walk, Venice, CA 90291

jaysrentalsvb.com

(310) 392-7306

This rental shop is right at the start of the Venice Boardwalk. They have bikes, blades, boards and wetsuits. Bike $6/ hour. Surfboard $10/hour and up. Rollerblades $8/hour. They rent other beach equipment, check their website for pricing.

1 hour surf lesson, with suit and equipment, $70.

Venice Bike and Skate

https://goo.gl/maps/TKDs3XQNz8q

21 Washington Blvd, Venice, CA 90292

venicebikeandskates.com

(310) 301-4011

Located on Washington at the South end of the Venice Boardwalk, this shop is almost on the beach. Bikes $8/hour $20/day. Mountain bike $10/hour. Blades $8/hour.

Santa Monica Beach Bicycle Rentals

1428 4th St · Santa Monica CA 90401

(310) 428-5337

www.smbikerental.com

Located just off the Promenade, this bike show has plenty of bikes for rent for about $16 a day.

Santa Monica Bike Center

1555 2nd St (in the parking garage)· Santa Monica CA 90401

(310) 656-8500

www.smbikecenter.com

Public Bike Rental

https://goo.gl/maps/jfNDfbRjWDS2

117 Broadway, Santa Monica, CA 90401

http://public-bike-rental.business.site/

117 Broadway just off Ocean

Rent a beach cruiser for $16, a bike with gears for $20, or a tandem bicycle for two people for $40 per day. This is a shop, not a public facility.

Open 9:00-8:30

Perrys Cafe and Rentals

930 Pacific Coast Hwy, Santa Monica CA 90401

(310) 260-1114

http://www.perryscafe.com

This business is well connected within the City of Santa Monica. They have scored several super convenient beach locations on City land, and use the opportunity to overcharge tourists. They also got the city to chip in $10 million to pay for their bike sharing scheme. That explains why there are no bike sharing kiosks near the Perry's locations on the beach.

Bike rental here $10/hour (other places are $6-$8).

Bad, overpriced food is also available here. You could have dinner in the nicest restaurants in town for what you pay for circus food at Perrys.

Breeze Bike Share

1631 Colorado, Santa Monica CA 90404

https://santamonicabikeshare.com

(310) 828-2525

The city sponsors the "Breeze" bicycle rental system, which most locals call the "Hulu bicycles", because sponsorship from Hulu helped start the system..

When a bike share system-was originally proposed for Santa Monica, Trek bicycles offered to support the system and manufacture the bikes in Santa Monica. The city instead opted to put Perry's beach bicycle rentals in charge, and gifted them $10 million to get things started.

The Chinese made Breeze bicycles were purchased by the city for $2000 each. They have GPS tracking devices for billing purposes. Charges are 12 cents a minute, $7 minimum charge, $25 a month, or $99 per year. The annual charge may seem like a good deal, but you could buy a good used bicycle for the same amount.

Locations for pickup up bikes are convenient, but if you want a bike for all day, you may be better going to a more traditional rental place. There are other options too, such as the new "Bird" electric scooters, which cost $1+15 cents a minute, and may be cheaper for short rides.

Metro Bikeshare (Los Angeles)

In Venice, the City of LA offers a bike share system that is much cheaper than the Santa Monica "Breeze" system. Rentals are $3.50/half hour or $7 per day. You can pay with the same "Tap" card that is used for the Metro transit system.

The downside with this system, is that that bikes have to be returned to one or another of the rental stations. If your ride ends in Venice this should not be a problem.

Bicycle stations can be found at

- Venice Circle, north side.
- Four locations along Rose Ave

- Three locations on Lincoln
- Two locations on Abbott Kinney

A full list of pickup stations can be found at https://bikeshare.metro.net/stations/.

Rollerblades

The same places that rent bikes often rent rollerblades. This is big fun. Rollerblading is very similar to ice skating or roller skating. If you have done either, it's going to be really easy. If not, there's a bit of a learning curve, but this is the best chance you will ever get. The path along the beach is pretty flat, which makes it easy, and there is no car traffic, so it is safe, and the weather is always good for rollerblading. This is super fun. I'd suggest to put this on your bucket list.

Bird Electric Scooter

A new company called "Bird" is offering electric scooters that you can use to ride around Santa Monica. This company's service is similar to the city sponsored bike sharing system. Bird scooters are found all around Downtown. Riders can reserve/unlock one using a smartphone app. Each ride costs $1 plus 15 cents per minute. A typical ride should only take a few minutes, and may be less than taking the bus. At the conclusion of a ride, the user can leave the scooter at their destination and lock the scooter using the app. Accounts are prepaid using a credit card.

If you haven't done this before, you can download the app. The app will show you a map that shows where all the Bird scooters are found. It's very similar to the map from the Uber app.

If you see one of the scooters and have an iPhone, take a picture of the bar code on the handlebars of the scooter, and your phone will take you directly to the spot where you can download the app. It's super easy.

The bird scooters have only been open for a short time, but they became an immediate hit. You will see people riding them around town all the time. The app will show you where to find a scooter near you.

For more information, check their website: http://www.bird.co (note that it's .co, not .com).

Metro Train

If you have ever seen the movie "Roger Rabbit", then you may be aware that Santa Monica and Los Angeles were once served by a widespread rail transit system called the "Red Car".

The Red Car system was closed and the tracks ripped up in the early 1960s, with financial support from General Motors. At the time, most local residents were in general agreement with the decision, but in hindsight, it seems to have been a bad choice.

Metro Transit has reconstructed the train line down the exposition right of way from Santa Monica to downtown, at a cost of $2 billion per mile.

Travel time is about an hour and the fair is about $1.50. The route they have chosen is a strange one, through Culver City and USC. The real cost of travel is closer to $10 per ticket, but the remainder is covered by subsidies.

It is a good way to get to downtown, but the train isn't really useful for getting around Santa Monica, because it doesn't go anywhere anyone would want to go. Instead, it goes past a number of large proposed construction sites such as the former Parker pen factory, which is being turned into a gigantic office and residential complex and the Bergamot Station, where a large hotel and office complex is proposed. Corruption raises its ugly head again. A ore useful route would have been down Santa Monica Blvd, where the old Red Car ran, to UCLA, Beverly Hills, Hollywood, Koreatown, and then downtown.

Still, residents are very happy to have the new train line. Twenty years from now we will probably get the Santa Monica Blvd. route too.

Tickets are purchased from vending machines, located at major stations. The system works with a "tap" card which can be charged up and then used to purchase rides by "tapping" on the sensor on the entrance gate.

Big Blue Bus

Santa Monica's Big Blue Bus provides service throughout the city and to nearby destinations such as UCLA and downtown. The base bus fare is $1.25.

Everyone loves the big blue bus, but there have been a number of controversies lately about the construction of bus stops that cost millions of dollars and offer no shelter from sun or rain. They seem to be purely decorative.

Airport Via Big Blue Bus

https://www.bigbluebus.com

Service from Santa Monica to the airport goes to the airports lot C. The purpose of this is to create enough inconvenience that you will choose to either take a taxi or take your own car and park it in one of the airport parking lots.

From Lot see there are shuttles going to the airport. Time for the trip is about an hour and a half, compared to a half hour by car.

RTD/LA Metro

https://www.metro.net

Service from Santa Monica to downtown or Beverly Hills or Hollywood is usually via RTD/LA Metro, the Los Angeles bus system. Local bus stop about every two blocks and take forever to make the trip. Express busses will save at least a half an hour and are still very slow.

Free Ride Electric Bus

http://thefreeride.com/santa-monica.php

The city sponsors free electric shuttle busses that will take you around Santa Monica for free, if you can figure out where to find them. I've seen them parked near "Hot Dog on a Stick" and behind the Shutters hotel, and sometimes I've seen the cruising Ocean. Sometimes I see them parked in Vons parking lot, just chilling. If you see one, don't feel shy about flagging it down and taking a ride.

There's no fare, but it's nice to tip the driver a dollar or two. For pickup, text location to (please allow 10-15 minutes for pick-up) 310-895-9204.

Uber and Lyft

Ridesharing has created some really excellent opportunities for people who choose not to drive. The charges for Uber and Lyft are about the same, and vary from week to week and from hour to hour depending on specials.

The supply of Uber and Lyft cars in Santa Monica is huge. You should never have to wait more than a few minutes. If Uber is offering surge pricing your best option is to cancel and immediately call Lyft. If that doesn't work, cancel, wait 10 minutes, and then try again.

Fares inside Santa Monica should be $3-$7. The airport is about $20, Hollywood $15-$20, and downtown $20-$25 or more depending on traffic. Uber and Lyft at the Airport are only allowed at posted "Ridesharing" stops on the upper level. They do not come down to the "arrivals" area.

Double Decker Tourist Bus

There are a number of companies that operate tour busses around Santa Monica and the LA area. Starline allows on and off privileges, which could provide a fun and informative way to get around town. They have an office on the pier (see pier section).

Car Rental

Santa Monica is a big tourist destination, so there are lots of car rental places. You can get on any of the big online websites and check for rates. It is highly competitive. Make sure that the rates include all of the side charges, big because some of the rental companies like to play a lot of games with the charges.

There are many good rental companies. I usually rent from Enterprise. They have three different locations in Santa Monica, the rates are reasonable, the people are friendly, and they have weekend specials with prices for about $10 a day that are hard to beat. Note that the weekend special usually doesn't work in the summer.

There are a couple of things that you can do to save money.

- Avoid airport rentals. Figure at least $10 extra per day if you pick up at the airport.
- You can often cut your rental bill nearly in half by providing your own insurance. Check and see whether your regular current insurance will cover you when you're driving a rental. Many do. You have to ask.

- If that doesn't work, check and see if your credit card covers rental car insurance. Many do. The best thing to do is make no assumptions, call the number on the back of your credit card and ask them, if you pay for a rental with this credit card, will they cover the insurance for you?

Insurance is a huge source of profits for car rental companies. Preparing your own insurance in advance will save you a lot of money.

Camper Van

Some friends of mine came this past Summer from Austria and rented a converted van from "Jucy Rentals" and drove it all over California and Nevada. The vans are sort of the equivalent of the old VW Westphalia Camper, but the layout is different. The top goes up, so you have a sleeping space on the roof. The kitchen is in the back. They said it was great. This is not the cheapest way to travel – It's probably cheaper to get an economy car and stay in motels – but it allowed them to visit Yosemite and other parks where motels might not have been available.

Jucy Camper Rentals

https://goo.gl/maps/MEDQK9G2UmA2
11992 Hawthorne Blvd, Hawthorne, CA 90250
jucyusa.com
(424) 456-4830

Motorcycle

Motorcycle fans will enjoy riding in California. The weather is good for motorcycles year around. You can rent Harleys at two shops in Marina Del Rey. They will be in good condition but they cost $100 or more per day, so it's more expensive than renting a car. You need a motorcycle license or endorsement to drive in California.

Bartel's Harley-Davidson

https://goo.gl/maps/kACTtLriBrm
4141 Lincoln Blvd, Marina Del Rey, CA 90292
bartelsharley.com
(310) 823-1112

Route 66

https://goo.gl/maps/kwu2ji2eSoP2
4161 Lincoln Blvd, Marina Del Rey, CA 90292
rt66mc.com
(310) 578-0112
This Harley rental place is associated with the dealer next door. They also have scooters and a repair shop.

Eagle Rider Motorcycle Rentals

https://goo.gl/maps/UBCrPS76EG32
4110 Lincoln Blvd, Marina Del Rey, CA 90292
http://www.eaglerider.com/harley-rentals
(310) 302-1239
Chain renting a wide variety of motorcycles; some locations offer guided tours, sales & service.

Rae's
Restaurant
aily Breeze
uy your
ily Breeze
here

Restaurants and Shops

For its size, Santa Monica has more restaurants than any city I've ever seen. There is something for almost every taste. Unfortunately, as the town becomes more and more popular and more tourists arrive, the less expensive places are gradually getting forced out.

Ethnic food in terms of American and Mexican is generally very good, and there are quite a few Italian restaurants too. Those in search of more exotic fare such as Chinese, Japanese, Ethiopian, or Korean may wish to look in other more ethnically diverse neighborhoods.

I'm going to group the restaurants by area and then I will make note of a few favorites. I will also include shops and sights in each area.

Third Street Promenade

https://goo.gl/maps/71KnfmZimEN2

3rd Street, Santa Monica

downtownsm.com

3rd St. in Santa Monica has been blocked off and converted to a pedestrian walkway, which is now called the "promenade". It's hugely popular. Friday and Saturday nights it's practically wall-to-wall people, and in the daytime, the area is jammed with shoppers.

Most of the shops on the promenade are the same shops you would expect in any mall across America, such as Gap, Urban Outfitters, Adidas, Banana Republic.

There are a lot of restaurants too, though as the rents go up and the national chains move-in, the eating choices have gotten a lot less interesting.

The City of Santa Monica licenses musicians and street performers. In theory, I like the idea of having street musicians, but a lot of them are just annoying. Now that the City has stepped in, they are annoying musicians with licenses.

Dancing on the Promenade

On weekends you often see dance groups on the promenade. They also need to get licenses from the city. Especially on Sunday afternoons, you will often see swing, blues, tango, and salsa groups. Dance is an audience participation event. Bring your dancing shoes and join in the dancing.

The groups that put on the dances all have websites or at least Facebook pages. The group pictured here are the blues dancing group "

Farmer's Market

Every Wednesday local farmers come to Santa Monica to sell their vegetables and other groceries. The market is on Santa Monica Blvd. where it crosses 2nd and 3rd streets. There are no farms within any reasonable distance of Santa Monica, but still they do have a lot of fresh vegetables that are better than you can get anywhere else. Many come from Venture or from the Central Valley up in the direction of Sacramento. The market ends around noon. On other days the market also appears on Main Street or Pico.

Apple Store

https://goo.gl/maps/WAeWmQ6gmtv

1415 3rd Street Promenade, Santa Monica, CA 90401

apple.com

They got too busy for the location up the street, so Apple moved into this new, gigantic glass barn. An army of T-shirt uniformed Apple staff generate more sales per square foot than any other store in the country.

The building itself has design problems. It is an echo chamber. It is the noisiest store I have ever seen.

If you have problems with your Apple product, bring it in here to be repaired at the "Genius Bar". It is often advantageous to make an appointment in advance, or come first thing in the morning and try to set an in-person appointment for later in the day.

Apple has an open network, so if you need to do some really big file uploads or downloads, you can try and use their Wi-Fi.

Urban Outfitters

https://goo.gl/maps/TnXhCg9731w

1440 3rd St, Santa Monica, CA 90401

urbanoutfitters.com

This fun shop combines clothing, shoes, fun T-shirts and a wide variety of collectible and silly merchandise. There are lots of silly books, Games, vinyl LPs, Atari video games, greeting cards, and lots of other fun stuff.

Dump Trump

Santa Monica has long had a reputation for leftist politics, causing angry landlords to call it the "Soviet Republic of Santa Monica". These days you will often see the "Dump Trump" folks out on the Promenade selling inspirational bumper stickers. Location and hours vary.

McDonald's

https://goo.gl/maps/gTqT9TzteBG2

1540 2nd St, Santa Monica, CA 90405

mcdonalds.com

There is little to say about McDonald's. The menu and the prices are about the same anywhere. However, in the city where high-end gentrified bistros have pushed out almost all of the inexpensive local places, it's nice to have at least one place in town where you can still buy something for a dollar. This McDonald's, nestled between the mall and the entrance to the pier, must be one of the busiest in the country. If your budget for lunch is three dollars, this is probably the place. Open 24 hours.

Stefanos NY Pizza

https://goo.gl/maps/dDRxPnG8ZCK2

1310 3rd St, Santa Monica, CA 90401

stefanosnewyorkpizza.com

Located in front of the AMC Multiplex, this slice pizza place has surprisingly good food at very reasonable prices. There is nice seating out front with a view of people walking by on the Promenade.

Slices of pizza $3.50 to $4. Two slices of pizza and a fountain drink or $8.25. A chicken Parmesan submarine sandwich with a fountain drink is $10.

Puzzle Zoo

https://goo.gl/maps/HaaKAizKJvK2

1411 3rd Street Promenade A, Santa Monica, CA 90401

puzzlezoo.com

This very fun toy store sells games, dolls, and all kinds of fun toys. This is definitely a good place to come in and wander around. Fun shop.

Sur la Table

https://goo.gl/maps/YXREh7i4vYP2

301 Wilshire Blvd, Santa Monica, CA 90401

surlatable.com

This wonderful kitchenware store has pots, pans, coffee machines and everything else you might need for your kitchen. The home base is in Pike Place market in Seattle. It's not cheap, but it's really fun to just wander around and look at all the toys.

Originally, they wanted to have a cooking school here in the back, which seemed like a pretty good idea, but the city shut them down. Such a shame. Not sure what the logic was. So, they took the kitchen area and converted into a sample counter for Nestle coffee machines.

Johnny Rockets

https://goo.gl/maps/rFfPyf42dL52

1322 3rd Street Promenade, Santa Monica, CA 90401

johnnyrockets.com

This fun retro 50s theme restaurant has burgers, milkshakes and apple pie. Everything is good. Burgers are about eight or nine dollars.

Everytable

https://goo.gl/maps/6neXqHjPQfC2

1315 3rd Street Promenade #201, Santa Monica, CA 90401

everytable.com

(424) 296-1620

This food court spot isn't even a restaurant. It's just a couple of wall refrigerators full of sandwiches and salads. They are inexpensive and surprisingly good. Everything is take out, but there are plenty of places to sit upstairs in the food court second floor, or outside in the Promenade. This is one of the least expensive eating options in Downtown Santa Monica, and it's surprisingly good. They're located in the semi complete food court across from the AMC multiplex.

Cabo Cantina

https://goo.gl/maps/o44dRbm9jMF2

1240 3rd Street Promenade, Santa Monica, CA 90401

cabocantina.com

In the neighborhood that is full of Mexican restaurants, this is definitely the worst. It's interesting, because from the outside it looks very inviting. Tropical palapa decor and multiple signs advertising 2-for-1 happy hour specials, music and a constant hubbub of people in various levels of intoxication, it looks like it ought to be a pretty good time.

It's basically a tourist trap. The two-for-one drinks are expensive, and if you aren't paying attention, when you ask for a regular margarita, they will give you the super expensive Cadillac margarita in a goldfish bowl style glass. I would expect a regular margarita to cost about five dollars, but if you order one here you will get two, and they will charge you about $25.

When I complained they told me that the cadillac margarita is the regular margarita. Baloney. I just sent the drinks back.

I think this is a scam aimed at tourists, and I think management is in on it. They did this to me twice and I refuse to ever go back again.

If that were not enough, the margaritas are terrible.

If you do decide to try the happy hour, I suggest to stick to the Mexican beers, which are also two for one.

If you're looking for Mexican food there so many better choices in Santa Monica, such as El Cholo, Tacos Por Favor, Lare's, Gilbert's, La cabana, the list goes on and on. Cabo Cantina is the absolute bottom of the list, even below Taco Bell, which is actually closed.

Locanda del Lago

https://goo.gl/maps/n3CX8q7ZVp42

231 Arizona Ave, Santa Monica, CA 90401

lagosantamonica.com

In my opinion this is one of the best Italian restaurants in Santa Monica. Unfortunately, the prices keep creeping up and it has gotten kind of expensive. The pizzas here are particularly good. It's a little cheaper if you shop at happy hour. My favorite is a peperoni pizza with a Peroni beer. The ham and rocket pizza is good too.

Starbucks Third and Wilshire

https://goo.gl/maps/nt4hmL9LmpA2

308 Wilshire Blvd., Santa Monica, CA 90401

starbucks.com

The Starbucks has more character than most of the other Starbucks in the area, perhaps because of the colorful crowd wondering around the third street promenade and overflow from the Barnes & Noble 's bookstore. This franchise Starbucks actually belongs to Barnes & Noble 's. Barnes and Nobles recently removed all the public electrical plugs from the bookstore and the Starbucks, to prevent laptop users from staying too long. It's annoying. If you need a charge for your laptop or phone, go elsewhere. They closed the bathrooms too.

Barnes and Nobles

1201 3rd St, Santa Monica, CA 90401
stores.barnesandnoble.com
(310) 260-9110

There used to be a half dozen general bookstores in this neighborhood, including the Midnight Special, Borders, Hennessey and Ingalls, B Dalton, as well as a number of independent used bookstores. Now there is just this one, and the newly opened Book Monster.

Barnes and Nobles is a pleasant store with good selection of books. You know they are under a lot of pressure from Amazon, but if you are in Santa Monica, and you need a book today, this is probably your best bet. Support Bookstores! Buy Books!

Monsieur Marcel

https://goo.gl/maps/NmQr2SDZYTF2

1260 3rd Street Promenade, Santa Monica, CA 90401

mrmarcel.com

This fun French place is in an island in the middle of the third street promenade. They have fun sandwiches and charcuterie and glasses of wine. Many things are half price between 3 and 6 PM. This is my friend Graham 's favorite restaurant.

Bruxie

https://goo.gl/maps/FKDughAcexn

1412 3rd Street Promenade, Santa Monica, CA 90401

bruxie.com

This new chain has taken the chicken and waffles concept and converted it to high-end fast food. I haven't had a chance to try yet but it looks good. The main downside is the thumping rap music that gives me a headache. I'm not going to go in this place until they turn the music down.

Hummus Bar Express

https://goo.gl/maps/7uaMCUmpZfu

1333 3rd Street Promenade, Santa Monica, CA 90401

hummusbarexpresssantamonicaca.com

(310) 260-1994

My Israeli friend Nui claims this place has the best humus and falafel this side of Tel Aviv. I prefer Z Garden, but this one is good too. If you are looking for good falafel and other Mediterranean food on the Promenade, this is your best choice.

Chipotle

https://goo.gl/maps/oLR6vWhWogS2

1218 3rd St, Santa Monica, CA 90401

chipotle.com

This local branch of the national chain offers fine large burritos. You can choose from beef, chicken, or pork, and they have salads too. It's very good and the cost is reasonable.

Stefano's Pizza

https://goo.gl/maps/Q1MxRyNnPp92

1310 3rd St, Santa Monica, CA 90401

stefanosnewyorkpizza.com

You don't expect much from a slice pizza place attached to an AMC multiplex movie theater, but in fact the slice pizza here is quite good. Large slice are about four or five dollars. There is pleasant outdoor seating along third street promenade.

Lemonade

https://goo.gl/maps/AhnHL2gJsYG2

301 Arizona Ave, Santa Monica, CA 90401

lemonadela.com

The lemonade café on Abbot Kinney in Venice has long been very popular, with good food and reasonable prices. They have sandwiches, salads, and of course lemonade. Get a tray get in line, pick out the things that you want, and pay at the register. The atmosphere is clean, healthy, and cheerful. Everybody loves this place.

This branch just off the Promenade is new but should be successful, because there is so much foot traffic. Moderately placed priced. Recommended.

Trastavere

https://goo.gl/maps/AMEx9MBRJGC2

1360 3rd Street Promenade, Santa Monica, CA 90401

(310) 319-1985

This genuine Italian restaurant is a branch with the original in Italy. It used to be called "Trilussa", and before that it was a bank. The food is very good, and the tables out front are excellent for watching people on the Promenade.

Ocean to 2nd St

This is the area between the Promenade and Ocean Ave. It's almost wall to wall restaurants, plus a few hotels.

Book Monster

https://goo.gl/maps/JxyRn4521vQ2
212 Santa Monica Blvd, Santa Monica, CA 90401
http://www.bookmonster.com/store/main.aspx
(424) 238-8576

This newly opened bookstore offers both new and used books. Prices reasonable. I bought one book here so far, a science fiction novel, for $3.50. Seems reasonable. Support Bookstores! Buy Books!

Del Frisco's Grille

https://goo.gl/maps/qCtwcQB8SjJ2
1551 Ocean Ave Suite 105, Santa Monica, CA 90401
delfriscosgrille.com

Located right across the street from the entrance to the Santa Monica pier, with indoor and outdoor seating, the location of this restaurant is hard to beat.

In my opinion the best food option our steaks are steaks, though they are in the $30-$40 range, which is more than I usually want to pay.

I often get dragged here in the evening to have glasses of wine and drinks at the bar by groups of friends who enjoy the atmosphere and don't really care what anything costs.

The Bungalows

https://goo.gl/maps/dVpBS9kcjAk

101 Wilshire Blvd, Santa Monica, CA 90401

thebungalow.com

This outdoor club is attached to the Miramar Sheraton Hotel, on Wilshire just off Ocean.

If you are looking for a nice place where you can sit outside drink have a beer, and enjoy the party scene under the palm trees, then this is the place. It's like somebody's giant outdoor Hollywood party. The music is good and there's always lots of people.

The downside is that the drinks are really expensive. There's no cover, but a basic beer is about $9, and mixed drinks start at $12 for a well gin and tonic.

I love the ping-pong table. There's no charge. Just come in and wait your turn to play. There's also a pool table.

You can depend on a fairly good party going at the Bungalows most any night of the week.

Britannia Pub

https://goo.gl/maps/Mb4a8y5xunJ2

318 Santa Monica Blvd, Santa Monica, CA 90401

britanniapub.com

This English themed bar has been here for decades and is popular with tourists and locals alike. It's located about a half block off the Promenade on Santa Monica Blvd.

The bar is narrow and long, which is not really an optimum shape, and has an upstairs which doesn't get used a lot but is available if you can't find a place to set downstairs.

Prices are not cheap, with beers averaging about $6-8, but they do have a happy hour with drink and food specials.

Britannia is a regular stop on the Santa Monica pub crawl. Often at some point in the night, a horde of people will appear, like a flash mob. Half hour later the group leader will raise his arm and say "OK we're going to the next place". As quickly as they appeared, the mob will vanish.

About five nights a week, they have karaoke, which is fun. KJ's Star, Studebaker and Laura are all super nice.

I have had many fun evenings here.

Sushi Roku

https://goo.gl/maps/DCfBSKanAkK2

1401 Ocean Ave, Santa Monica, CA 90401

innovativedining.com

(310) 458-4771

This mediocre and overpriced Japanese restaurant is not very interesting. The location is great, and a lot of people have no idea what real Japanese food is, so it does just fine. If you really want Japanese food, head over to Sawtelle and try most anyplace in the area.

Joe's pizza

https://goo.gl/maps/ZBu63idAMdu

111 Broadway, Santa Monica, CA 90401

joespizza.com

This is a nice stand where you can buy slices of pizza, mostly for takeout, but they do have a couple of tables. Good.

Blue Plate Taco

https://goo.gl/maps/KbskCa14EoE2

1515 Ocean Ave, Santa Monica, CA 90401

blueplatesantamonica.com

Attached to the front of the shore Hotel on Ocean Avenue, this restaurant is always busy in the evening. To be honest I've never tried their tacos. Great location. Often busy.

800 Degrees Pizza

https://goo.gl/maps/EHNQnCbbhNz

120 Wilshire Blvd, Santa Monica, CA 90401

800degreespizza.com

The gimmick here is thin crust pizza cooked in a woodfired oven that is supposedly at 800°. Get in line, point to the toppings you want on your pizza, pay at the register, and they will bring the pizza to your table. Pizza here is very, very good.

This restaurant is part of a chain with other locations in places like Las Vegas.

In the evening there is a large overflow from the Bungalows across the street. People come rolling out of the Bungalows, hungry, and wander straight into 800 Degrees across the street.

Ma'kai Restaurant & Lounge

https://goo.gl/maps/1ZfQYuJUQFQ2

101 Broadway, Santa Monica, CA 90401

makailounge.com

I've never actually seen anybody eat here but in theory they do have a food menu with "Pan Asian" cuisine. Mostly it's a bar. It gets busy in the evening. Drinks are expensive.

Hi Ho Cheeseburger

https://goo.gl/maps/AgxXvPJuxa32

1320 2nd St B, Santa Monica, CA 90401

hiho.la

This new restaurant on Second Street offers a very nice burger and fries for $10. The same people own Sugarfish, a popular sushi place across the street and down the block. There are only about three entrée options: plain burger, cheeseburger, and veggie burger. You can get it with fries or salad. The pie is very good. Fries are crunchy and very good. Beer and wine are expensive.

Tender Greens

https://goo.gl/maps/MooX8B7oZ342

201 Arizona Ave, Santa Monica, CA 90401

tendergreens.com

This chain restaurant offers various kinds of salads. I'm not a big salad eater, and I find the dressings kind of bland, so it's not for me. However, if you are looking for salads, this might be a good choice. They often have coupons.

Thai Dishes

https://goo.gl/maps/d5UrwouUQ8P2

123 Broadway, Santa Monica, CA 90401

thaidishessantamonica.com

This is the oldest Thai restaurant in the Santa Monica area. They used to have a really cheap take out window up on Third Street, but that is long gone. These days entrées are about $13-$16, with a fairly standard Thai restaurant menu. Food is good, though almost double what you would pay for the same thing in Thai-town. Their rent must be astronomical.

Sugarfish

https://goo.gl/maps/5hh6WdEEygo

1345 2nd St, Santa Monica, CA 90401

sugarfishsushi.com

This small high-end sushi bar on 2nd Street has great food and is popular. Pricing is expensive.

Meat on Ocean

https://goo.gl/maps/HYMpcZqr8fn
1501 Ocean Ave, Santa Monica, CA 90401
meatonocean.com

This nice restaurant is a recent addition to the line of restaurants and hotels along Ocean Avenue. It offers entrées such as Chilean soon Seabass $45, New York steak $48, and a variety of other states by weight for roughly 3 dollars per ounce. Cheeseburgers are $18 and a meatball sandwich is $19. French fries or eight dollars. You get the general idea. It's really nice inside.

Misfit

https://goo.gl/maps/4MN6JCHi6kD2
225 Santa Monica Blvd, Santa Monica, CA 90401
themisfitrestaurant.com

This is currently one of the most popular bars in Santa Monica. If you want to have a couple of drinks in a lively atmosphere, this is probably the place.

Before it was the Misfit, this was super fancy French restaurant with a big oyster bar. When the Misfit moved in, the place already had a great look. The management of the misfit added good food and nice beverages, and started packing the people in.

The specialty here are the "handcrafted" drinks. I guess every bar pretty much has handcrafted drinks, but at the misfit the drinks are unusually good. Even the will gin and tonic (made with Ford's gin) is far above average. During happy hour most drinks or six dollars and they often have some kind of food special too. At 7 o'clock happy hour is over and drink prices double, but the people keep streaming in. It's almost always busy.

The management here also owns "Ingo's Tasty Diner".

BOA

https://goo.gl/maps/ZEZ7ZnqwzWs

101 Santa Monica Blvd, Santa Monica, CA 90401

boasteak.com

(310) 899-4466

Very nice restaurant selling steaks and drinks.

1212 Santa Monica

https://goo.gl/maps/8tt1bnb31eF2

1212 3rd Street Promenade, Santa Monica, CA 90401

1212santamonica.com

Replacing Monsoon, which was long a favorite of mine, this trendy new restaurant looks pretty cool inside, but it's not nearly as cool as Monsoon used to be. Monsoon had Indonesian style decor with a two level restaurant with a large indoor courtyard in the middle and a dance room upstairs in the back which used to have Salsa dancing. The feeling was Pacific Rim, almost Tiki. The new place removed all the aged wood and made it high tech and grey.

The menu offers high end California cuisine and expensive but tasty drinks. I liked the old Monsoon menu a lot better.

The name is odd, because the name sounds like an address, but it's wrong. 1212 is the street number, but it's on 3rd street, not Santa Monica Blvd, so that could be confusing.

The outdoor tables are super nice and give you a chance to watch people walking back-and-forth on the third street promenade.

North Italia

https://goo.gl/maps/HpEj73JvYUr

1442 2nd St, Santa Monica, CA 90401

northitaliarestaurant.com

This is a nice looking chain Italian restaurant has a very open feeling and above average prices. Main courses average $12-$25, but drinks are expensive and will quickly blow any budget. The menu out front of the restaurant lists their dishes but has no prices, which is a hint. It used to be a Buca di Beppo. The food looks pretty good, but I haven't tried it yet.

Subway

https://goo.gl/maps/dDPqN8dCt9v

1551 Ocean Ave #145, Santa Monica, CA 90401

order.subway.com

Next-door to McDonald's, this is another option for very cheap lunch. The $2.99 sandwich special is a most excellent deal. There are about ten Subway restaurants in Santa Monica.

Subway uses a lot of highly processed bologna style meats, and soft squishy bread that resembles oversized hotdog buns, but somehow they are still pretty tasty. You can get better sandwiches at Bay Cities, or at Von's, or a variety of other good places, but it's going to be hard to match that price.

Ivy at the Shore

https://goo.gl/maps/jw9itS5jMum

1535 Ocean Ave, Santa Monica, CA 90401

theivyrestaurants.com

This high-end restaurant serves an old-school menu and has been here for decades. It's considered one of the best in town, and the location is very nice. The Ivy has another branch in LA. They have all the menus online, but with no prices. If you have to ask, you can't afford it.

The Fig

https://goo.gl/maps/Q345KNQf3ZM2

101 Wilshire Blvd, Santa Monica, CA 90401

figsantamonica.com

Located on the ground floor of the Miramar Hotel, next to the pool, this restaurant is pricey but popular. Locals like the weekday happy hour between 5 and 6 PM. It used to be that everything on the menu was half-price, which was great. These days they have severely restricted the happy hour list, but it's still very popular.

Favorite items include Jidori chicken, cheese plates, and wine. The atmosphere at the side of the pool is very nice. Great place to relax.

The name of the restaurant comes from the giant fig tree right outside the main entrance to the hotel. It's a local landmark.

Hillstone

https://goo.gl/maps/Nw66DFg6p1y

202 Wilshire Blvd, Santa Monica, CA 90401

Located in: Emeritus College

hillstonerestaurant.com

This moderately expensive American eatery makes a fine French dip sandwich and other traditional favorites.

Prices are above average, but the food is good. Wine and drinks are expensive and will blow any budget.

It used to be called Huston's and now it's Hillstone. Why the name change? I am told that if a chain of restaurants has more than a certain number of branches with the same name, then they are obliged to put the calorie count on the menu. So, to avoid this requirement, Houston's change the name of this restaurant to Hillstone.

Probably a good thing too. If customers realized that many of the dinners here have 2000 calories or more, they might reconsider, and go to the "Tender Greens" salad shop down the street instead.

Chez Jay

https://goo.gl/maps/ZLQMnPQo1Cr

1657 Ocean Ave, Santa Monica, CA 90401

chezjays.com

For fifty years or more this diner/bar has been a local Santa Monica favorite. They serve burgers, steaks, and salads, though it is really mostly drinking place. Prices for beer and drinks or a little bit above the average, but you pay for the location.

My friend Bob likes to tell me how this and that and the other famous person used to come here all the time, back before this place became famous. I don't know. I've never seen anybody famous here, but it is a lively bar scene most every night of the week.

The Independence

https://goo.gl/maps/t3uQdVcjtft

205 Broadway, Santa Monica, CA 90401

independencetavern.com

This pleasant bar right next to the mall and the third street promenade has nice drinks and good if somewhat pricey food. During happy hour they will usually have a good food offering, such as a burger or fish and chips for six dollars. I go here from time to time.

Kings Head

https://goo.gl/maps/htuP3MirfqJ2

116 Santa Monica Blvd, Santa Monica, CA 90401

yeoldekingshead.com

This British theme tavern was here long before Santa Monica got really popular. At that time prices were a bit high and there was always a lot of beer spilled on the floor that made your shoes kind of stick to the floor and gave the whole place that distinctive stale beer smell.

It's still like that, but prices have gone up and there are more people. The main improvement is that they don't allow smoking any more. Fish and chips are decent if oily. The chicken pot pie is amazing. Rarebit is fine but expensive for cheese toast. Guinness beer is the same as anywhere else, and at about nine dollars, it's pricey.

In the evenings the Kings Head is filled with tourists, and the intoxication level is usually pretty high. Dart games are fun, though when people get really drunk and are throwing sharp objects, it may be dangerous.

There is also a British shop next door that sells Mint Sauce, Colman's mustard and other imported goods.

Cava

https://goo.gl/maps/sZJVuH8t8Ut

1318 2nd St Suite A, Santa Monica, CA 90401

cava.com

This restaurant looks very nice from the outside. Wood, chrome and light colored bricks interior, and a stainless cafeteria food line. The name in Spanish means "cave". Their advertising says they have healthy bowls with a Mediterranean twist. I can't actually tell what kind of food they serve. Haven't tried it yet.

Uovo

https://goo.gl/maps/kA2zCyRCxxr

1320 2nd St Ste A, Santa Monica, CA 90401

uovo.la

I believe this is the Italian word for egg. It claims to be a pasta restaurant. Looks very dark from the outside. Same owners as Sugarfish. I haven't tried it yet.

4th to Lincoln

Downtown is mostly restaurants, with a few hotels and other businesses. This is roughly the area between the Promenade and Lincoln.

REI

https://goo.gl/maps/ZDm3XFHEwd52

402 Santa Monica Pier, Santa Monica, CA 90401

rei.com

Recreational Equipment Incorporated is a Seattle based coo-op that sells camping equipment as well as clothing, bikes, and expedition equipment.

Long ago they used to make all their own hiking equipment and raincoats and many consider them to be absolutely the top and quality. Today everything is made in China. It looks fancier, with lots more stitching in the jackets and fancier styles in the shoes, but the quality and durability are way down.

Still, for outdoor gear, this is by far the best place in Santa Monica. Staff are helpful and knowledgeable.

In particular, I have had very good luck with the bicycle department. If you need a repair or some parts, they are great. If they don't have what you need they will order it. You might pay a dollar or two more than you would online, but for this price you know you are buying the right parts and you get helpful advice. It's worth it. These people are really helpful and know what they are doing.

Bay Cities

https://goo.gl/maps/NKwduUwvEZ52

1517 Lincoln Blvd, Santa Monica, CA 90401

baycitiesitaliandeli.com

(310) 395-8279

Long considered the best sandwich shop in Santa Monica, this Italian Deli often leads lists of the "Best Restaurants in Santa Monica", beating out fancy places that cost ten times as much.

Go up to the sandwich counter and order the sandwich you want, and they will make it up. They make their own bread, and it's very good.

Next to the sandwich counter, there is a hot food counter where you can get Meatballs, Parmagiana, and various daily specials.

I like to get a couple sausages in tomato sauce ($1.75 each) and a small loaf of bread ($2) and make my own sandwich.

Glass doored refrigerators in the back have a wide selection of drinks.

Seating in front on concrete benches and tables along Lincoln is adequate, but that's not what brings people here.

At lunchtime, there are always big lines. That's how you know it is good. Closed Mondays.

Umami Burger

https://goo.gl/maps/qCgNj1QTbcD2

525 Broadway, Santa Monica, CA 90401

umamiburger.com

(310) 451-1300

Umami is the meaty flavor that is derived from vegetable proteins, soy sauce, or miso. this restaurant has taken that word as their theme and created a small chain of tasty designer burger restaurants. Burgers are very good. They also have a happy hour.

Baja Fresh

https://goo.gl/maps/G1fZH4Kv4gC2

720 Wilshire Blvd, Santa Monica, CA 90401

bajafresh.com

(310) 393-9313

This clean and friendly Mexican place has tacos, burritos, salads, and a variety of other lunch options. Food is generally very good, a notch or two above what you would expect from Del Taco. Prices are reasonable. Order at the register and they bring it out to you.

Hi De Ho Comics

https://goo.gl/maps/9xVQZDJa9852

1431 Lincoln Blvd, Santa Monica, CA 90401

hidehocomics.com

(310) 394-2820

The old shop on Santa Monica Blvd. was very cool. This new location is larger, almost a warehouse, and even more cool. They have comic books, figures, games, and a very fun collection of T-shirts.

Goodwill

https://goo.gl/maps/FXJxW62p5Mv

524 Santa Monica Blvd, Santa Monica, CA 90401

goodwillsocal.org

(310) 393-1400

Thrift shop. Mostly clothes but they do have some housewares, appliances, and books.

Santa Monica Library

https://goo.gl/maps/Pbpj9K8N5pF2

601 Santa Monica Blvd, Santa Monica, CA 90401

smpl.org

The Santa Monica library is a wonderful resource for residents and visitors alike.

There are some strange things about the design of the building. The central area is a large courtyard which is pleasant and airy, but which doesn't seem to have much connection to the buildings primary purchase purpose as a place to keep books. And there are two large star stairways leading to the second floor, right next to each other, which does not seem to have been thought out carefully. There are conference rooms and lots of computers where you can use the Internet, though you need to get a library card to do this. It is not clear to me why they need to restrict the usage The Internet with passwords, since anyone can use it anytime they want as much as they want.

My biggest complaint about the library is if they don't have that many books. If you walk over to 3rd St. Promenade and go to Barnes & Noble's, the selection is much larger and generally more interesting.

Also odd is the refusal of the library to allow anyone to donate books. If you give the library a book, even one that people want to read and isn't in stock, they will put it in the library store and sell it for a dollar. In my opinion a library that wants to have the best possible collection should actively solicit donations of books.

Philz Coffee

https://goo.gl/maps/6Qj7XcmWRPT2

525 Santa Monica Blvd, Santa Monica, CA 90401

philzcoffee.com

This very popular coffee shop has top and quality but is almost amusing in the way they attempt to personalized experience. On entrance you stand in line. The barista will introduce him/herself and custom make your cup of coffee, even if it is just drip. Prices are a little above average, but it's always busy.

Yogiyo Korean Barbecue

https://goo.gl/maps/p2ZoAUmsAgy

510 Santa Monica Blvd, Santa Monica, CA 90401

yogiyokbbq.com

This pleasant hole in the wall place offers bibimbap, kbbq burritos, kimchi fried rice, and other favorites, all at reasonable prices. It's cheerful and quick. Note that this is not the kind of Korean barbecue that has a barbecue in the middle of your table. It's fast food.

Jamba Juice

https://goo.gl/maps/ouSVkQHmiyG2

331 A Santa Monica Blvd, Santa Monica, CA 90401

locations.jambajuice.com

A local favorite for people love fresh squeezed juices with a healthy edge. They make smoothies and mixed fresh juices. If you are looking for bottled juices check out Trader Joe's or Costco.

Sake House

https://goo.gl/maps/pr8QKPdcFe32

401 Santa Monica Blvd, Santa Monica, CA 90401

sakehousesantamonica.com

This California style sushi restaurant is generally popular, especially at happy hour.

Benihana

https://goo.gl/maps/fny41e2Vhbp

1447 4th St, Santa Monica, CA 90401

benihana.com

People either love or hate Benihana. They serve steak, chicken and seafood stir-fried at your table. While they are cooking, the chefs tell jokes and do a bit of a knife tossing show.

Basic dinner comes with one or two entrées, some fried rice, soup and or salad, and ice cream for dessert. They also have some sushi choices. Everybody seems to expect that from a Japanese restaurant.

Lunch is the best deal at Benihana. You get the same thing as you do at dinner, for about $12. My friends and I come here frequently.

Frito Misto

https://goo.gl/maps/W4A1LEScoEA2

601 Colorado Ave, Santa Monica, CA 90401

frittomistoitaliancafe.com

"Mixed Fried" is the translation of the name of this popular Italian restaurant. You can select your pasta and your sauce and they will with it up for you. Frito Misto has long a local favorite. Moderately priced.

Ninjin

https://goo.gl/maps/4N99gcDqt5t
607 Colorado Ave, Santa Monica, CA 90401
ninjinsushi.com

The name of this small Japanese eatery is means "carrot" in Japanese. I don't think I have any carrots on the menu, so I don't know where the name comes from. It's fairly close to the center of downtown Santa Monica and yet somehow off the beaten path. The menu includes various traditional Japanese items as well as sushi. If you're in the mood for some medium priced Japanese food, this might be a good place to try.

Harvelles

https://goo.gl/maps/76EnUmm4e6H2
1432 4th St, Santa Monica, CA 90401
harvelles.com
(310) 395-1676

This blues club is located on 4th street, just a block off the Promenade, there is no better place to go for a musical evening out. Drinks are a little bit expensive, and there is often a cover charge, depending on the band. But that's always the case when you have live music.

The managers come from Liquid Kitty, a favorite dive In West LA, which was known for wild Karaoke nights and events like the "Punk Rock BBQ" that had a fan base from all over town. They have promised to keep Harvelles true to it's Blues traditions.

Super Food Café

https://goo.gl/maps/JxHbUK2awnQ2

530 Wilshire Blvd, Santa Monica, CA 90401

superfoodcafe.org

The small restaurant has had various names over the years, but offers coffee and sandwiches and other nice food with organic and vegan options.

7/11

https://goo.gl/maps/WvEbcGuygPM2

630 Wilshire Blvd, Santa Monica, CA 90401

7-eleven.com

Sometimes 7-Eleven is the only place that's open, and when it is, it can be a lifesaver.

The shop itself is immaculate and clean. All snack foods are fine, but you couldn't get me to eat those hotdogs, they look like they've been rolling over there under the hot lights for days. Out in the parking lot homeless people mumble to themselves or flail at the sky fighting unseen demons.

Federal Express

https://goo.gl/maps/Wu88UssMTwD2

601 Wilshire Blvd, Santa Monica, CA 90401

local.fedex.com

This used to be a Kinko's copies, but Federal Express bought out the chain. If you need to make some copies, or you need to send a package by Federal Express, this is the place.

Soka Gakkai

https://goo.gl/maps/dTKWDQmkKvj
606 Wilshire Blvd, Santa Monica, CA 90401
sgi-usa.org
This is the West Coast headquarters of a large and well organized Japanese Buddhist religious group. Their practice involves peace, respect, and meditation. I am not an expert on their religious beliefs, but they are genuinely nice people and good neighbors.

Tocaya Organica

https://goo.gl/maps/gNiphrF1MyP2
507 Wilshire Blvd, Santa Monica, CA 90401
tocayaorganica.com
(424) 268-8219
This new California style Mexican restaurant offers tacos and burritos with a "healthy" edge. Prices are reasonable, in the $8-12 range. It became almost instantly popular as soon as the doors were opened.

Panera Bread

https://goo.gl/maps/9tJfRkKrUhD2

501 Wilshire Blvd, Santa Monica, CA 90401

locations.panerabread.com

Formerly Polly's Pies, this bakery has coffee sandwiches soups and all kinds of tasty bakery items. They have refillable coffee, salads, soup, and other light meals. The biggest downside is, their Internet connection is totally worthless, so if you plan on coming in here to do some work on your laptop, be sure to bring your mobile phone and be ready to set up tethering.

Wahoo's Fish Tacos

https://goo.gl/maps/8RZ52YqmsGH2

418 Wilshire Blvd, Santa Monica, CA 90401

wahoos.com

I love this Hawaiian/Mexican taco place. Tacos, burritos, salads, all are very good. Hawaiian influence shows with the shredded Kalua pork and the Mr. Lee's hot sauce, would you have to ask for. It's kind of like Korean chili paste, but a little sweeter. Really good stuff.

Dinner is about $6 to $10. Pay at the counter and they bring the food to your table. They have happy hour from 3 to 6 with beer for about $2.

This is one of the most reasonably priced places near the Promenade and the food is generally pretty good. I particularly like the big salad with Hawaiian pork, but everything is good.

Musha

https://goo.gl/maps/YgjEMhP48ap

424 Wilshire Blvd, Santa Monica, CA 90401

musha.us

Many Japanese people consider this to be the best Japanese restaurant in the Santa Monica area. Musha has yakitori grilled chicken kebabs and things like that as well as beverages. Be forewarned: this is not a sushi shop. No sushi here.

P F Chang's

https://goo.gl/maps/XBqziyLr2xR2

326 Wilshire Blvd, Santa Monica, CA 90401

pfchangs.com

This chain restaurant offers a good but somewhat westernized version of Cantonese and Mandarin cuisine. The food is good, but in my opinion it's not nearly as good as you would find in Monterey Park. The happy hour is popular.

T-Mobile

https://goo.gl/maps/qgzcy32fQk32

335 Wilshire Blvd, Santa Monica, CA 90401

t-mobile.com

If you need a new phone, this is the place. Verizon and AT&T have shops down the street closer to Lincoln.

T's Thai

https://goo.gl/maps/is1V4gDMs9M2

1215 4th St, Santa Monica, CA 90401

santamonicatsthai.com

This small local hole in the wall is pleasant and inexpensive. I'm still partial to Thaitown, but this spot is nice. Lunch specials are a good value.

Panini Kebab Grill

https://goo.gl/maps/QwcAqQB8R3N2

312 Wilshire Blvd, Santa Monica, CA 90401

paninikabobgrill.com

A new addition to the neighborhood this Middle Eastern Kabab joint became popular as soon as the doors opened. Panini sandwiches, kebab plates, and other dinners are all good sized and reasonably priced. The appetizer combo, with three kinds of hummus, two other dips, and a couple of stuffed grape leaves, is very good. And the all day long $2.49 mimosa special is as good as a happy hour, but all day long.

Fisher Lumber

https://goo.gl/maps/fJBFfrpvyan

1600 Lincoln Blvd, Santa Monica, CA 90404

fisher-hardware.com

(310) 395-0956

This traditional lumber store and hardware store has anything you might need, as long as it involves tools, nails or wood. Good shop, reasonable prices.

Vons Broadway

https://goo.gl/maps/KBD2cUYMkzT2

710 Broadway, Santa Monica, CA 90401

local.vons.com

(310) 260-0260

Grocery store that is a member of the Safeway chain. The Pavilions on Montana, the Vons on Wilshire, and the Vons on Broadway have the same owner and the same prices and merchandise.

TJ Maxx

https://goo.gl/maps/wewfaHeVPJE2

1251 4th St, Santa Monica, CA 90401

tjmaxx.com

This nationally franchised national chain of home and clothing stores sells stuff that other stores were unable to sell. The deals are very mixed. Some stuff is really cheap and some stuff is as much as Nordstrom's. I almost never buy clothes here, I prefer Ross, but the kitchenwares section is good, especially for wine glasses and pans, and it's also a pretty good place to buy covers for your phone.

Santa Monica Mall (Santa Monica Place)

https://goo.gl/maps/XMCsEj3hW2y

395 Santa Monica Place, Santa Monica, CA 90401

santamonicaplace.com

They describe themselves as "Contemporary open-air mall since 1980 with luxury-brand shops, plus a food court & a movie theater."

Located just off the freeway between second and fourth Street, the Santa Monica mall has been a major feature of Santa Monica life for about 40 years. The original mall was designed by renowned local architect Frank Gehry, and it is his most classical and traditional design project.

Everyone liked it.

As property values rose, owners of the mall tried to get permission to knock down the mall and replace it with high-end condominiums. Massive opposition from local residents caused the city Council to reject this idea.

As the years went by, the owners of the mall observed that the third street promenade, just across the street, had many more visitors than the mall itself, and they decided the solution was to open up the mall. So, they ripped off the roof, created a giant open round courtyard in the middle and got an entire new set of stores.

Gone is Frank Gehry's original design, along with the bookstores, the cheap clothing shops, and the inexpensive ground level food court. GameStop and RadioShack departed, as did the moderately priced Macy's department store.

They were replaced with Tiffany, Swarovski, Gucci and the like.

Outdoor malls have worked well in places like "The Grove" in Hollywood, but somehow they missed the mark here.

Part of the problem is the design theme of concrete and grey metal. It probably seemed contemporary and high tech in sketches, but in person it's impersonal and cold. It doesn't invite people in.

Part of the problem is the crazy arrangement of escalators, which they seem to have designed to force you to walk through the whole mall to get to the food court on the roof. So nobody bothers.

Part of the problem is the poor selection of shops. They are too expensive and don't sell anything that I want.

I live only a few blocks away, and I have never ever purchased anything in any of the new stores at the Santa Monica mall.

However, there are a few good restaurants and a nice Arclight movie theater.

The Curious Palate

https://goo.gl/maps/RDQ3gvniYhD2

395 Santa Monica Place, Santa Monica, CA 90401

thecuriouspalate.com

Located on the top floor of the mall next to the Arclight Cinema, the "Curious Palate" has very good food, though it is a bit on the expensive side. Three gourmet tacos will run you about $14. They also offer wine, beer, burgers, pasta, and salads. Everything is good.

Sonoma wine garden

https://goo.gl/maps/gbbxqwRtRBL2

395 Santa Monica Place #300, Santa Monica, CA 90401

sonomawinegarden.com

This very pleasant outdoor bar located on the roof of the mall is not it is not cheap, but it's a nice place to relax and have a glass of wine. I suppose it's fair that they charge for the location.

Beers $8 to $10, cocktails $12 to $14, pizza $20, kale salad $14, hummus $9, grilled salmon $26. Happy hour is from 3 to 6, Monday through Friday, and offers modest reductions on the price of wine and beer. Sometimes they'll have a really great late night happy hour, sometimes none at all. You just have to check with them and see what the current policy is. For a glass of wine in the afternoon in the outside rooftop garden this place is very nice.

Cheesecake Factory

https://goo.gl/maps/mbn8CJYXto72

395 Santa Monica Place, 3rd Floor, Santa Monica, CA 90401

thecheesecakefactory.com

This national chain is based in the Los Angeles area, but the Santa Monica branch is fairly new. Located on the third floor of the mall near the escalator, this restaurant has an enormous menu of everything from meatloaf to Chinese chicken salad. Prices are above average, but so is the portion size, and the food is generally amazing. They also have many kinds of cheesecake, their signature dish..

Entrée prices range from about $14 to about $20. Drinks and wine are very good here, but a little bit on the expensive side, and there is no happy hour.

Sbarro

https://goo.gl/maps/zs3S9bAbjQH2

395 Santa Monica Pier, Santa Monica, CA 90401

sbarro.com

This slice pizza place is part of a chain found in malls and airports across the country. As fast food goes, it's fairly good. A slice of pizza is about four dollars. They also have salads and drinks.

Johnny Rockets

https://goo.gl/maps/wMJpzkA9Wq32

395 Santa Monica Place, Space 3-A, Santa Monica, CA 90401

johnnyrockets.com

The original Johnny rockets, a burger bar with 50s music, was really great.

The mall version, with just a counter and no restaurant or music, is somewhat less interesting, but still not too bad. A basic burger is about seven dollars more with cheese or bacon, and fries and milkshakes are separate.

The burgers and milkshakes are generally pretty good, and you can take them outside and find a nice place to sit down and eat.

I prefer the sit-down place in the Promenade.

Great Khan's Mongolian Grill

https://goo.gl/maps/LxsPXd8bapz

395 Santa Monica Blvd, Santa Monica, CA 90401

greatkhans.com

This is one of those places where you fill up your plate with meat and vegetables, and then hand it to the gentleman at the giant grill who will stir-fry it with their special Mongolian sauce.

I have never been to Mongolia, so I don't know if they really eat anything like this.

However if you load your plate you can get an awful lot of food. If your goal is to eat as much protein as possible, for a fixed price, this may be your best bet.

Bazile (Nordstroms)

https://goo.gl/maps/rUftmGkpkMK2

220 Broadway, Santa Monica, CA 90401

shop.nordstrom.com

Instead of the usual Nordstroms Café, this Nordstrom's has a trendier place called "Bazile", with lots of "small plates", which means, expensive and small servings. It's not nearly as good as the Nordstrom Nordstrom's café in other stores. Menu items include tomatoes and cheese, eight dollars, lobster macaroni $20, French dip $15, asian chicken salad $15.

True Food Kitchen

https://goo.gl/maps/rS599WdX1j42

395 Santa Monica place #172, Santa Monica, CA 90401

truefoodkitchen.com

This restaurant on the ground floor of the mall, which claims to offer healthy farm to table cuisine, was an almost instant hit when it opens. It's much larger than it looks from the outside. They offer an extensive wine list and a popular collection of general American cuisine such as salads and sandwiches.

Santa Monica Pier

The pier is one of the most recognizable images of Santa Monica. It's been in so many movies and television shows, you will feel like you have been here before. There was once talk of making Santa Monica the port for Los Angeles, but honestly San Pedro and Long Beach seems like a better choice because of the sheltered harbor.

These days no ships come to the pier, but it's a top tourist attraction, full of tourists day and night. There are restaurants and a food court on the pier, but most of the food is terrible and overpriced. At the end of the pier you will often see people fishing, but they never seem to catch anything. If you want to catch fish, it's better to go out in a boat.

The original Santa Monica pier was built in 1909. Many people think it was built to house an amusement park, or for fishing, or as part of a port, but in fact, it was built as part of the municipal sewate system to carry sewage out past the breakwater, so that it would not wash back up on the beach.

A second pier was built in 1916, with the support of Charles Looff -who also built the first Coney Island Carousel in 1876. He's the one who brought the amusement rides. The two piers were combined and today everyone just calls it the Santa Monica Pier.

For many years the largest business on the pier was the La Monica ballroom, which had room for 10,000 dancers. Then, the pier housed various shows, and they constructed a large roller rink that was in operation until the 1960's.

Movies shot on the Santa Monica Pier include "They Shoot Horses, Don't They?", "The Sting" (even though the movie took place in Chicago), "A Night at the Roxbury", "Titanic", "Iron Man" and "The Hannah Montana Movie".

Pier Sign

This sign has been in so many TV shows and so many movies, you will feel like you have been here before when you see it.

Pacific Park

This amusement park has become part of the recognizable image of the Santa Monica pier. The Ferris wheel that is there now isn't the original one. The old one had benchlike seats, while the new one has cuplike round capsules, each one with a roof. The old Ferris wheel was sold on eBay to Humphreys

Real Estate Investments of Oklahoma City, Okla., and half of the proceeds of the winning bid was donated to the Special Olympics.

Sea Lions

Off the end of the pier are a number of buoys that have been taken over by sea lions and seals. You can tell the Sea Lions, they are much larger. Even though the buoys are only a hundred feet or so off the end of the pier, they are hard to see without binoculars.

Santa Monica Pier Carousel

https://goo.gl/maps/pbD4t3DkL712

1624 Ocean Front Walk, Santa Monica, CA 90401

smgov.net

If you have ever seen the movie "The Sting", this merry-go-round will look familiar. It's a classic merry-go-round with carved wood and painted horses and the mechanical organ music. Your adrenaline levels will probably not reach the same levels as they would on a good roller coaster at Six Flags Magic

Mountain, but hey, it's a merry-go-round. Each one of the horses is hand carved, and each one is different. It was built by the same people who built the carrousel on Coney Island.

Pierburger

No frills burger stand. Burger $4.75 $5.75 with cheese, $6.75 with bacon and egg. If you want something quick on the pier this is your best bet. It's nothing fancy, but it's a good solid burger.

Starline

https://goo.gl/maps/dLAW7zihf5y

300 Santa Monica Pier, Santa Monica, CA 90401

starlinetours.com

(323) 785-6740

This is the office where you can book bus tickets and tours. I'm not big on tours, but the double decker busses roaming around town look fun.

Bubba Gump

https://goo.gl/maps/CoFKUeYcGeT2

301 Santa Monica Pier, Building 9, Santa Monica, CA 90401

bubbagump.com

This mediocre restaurant chain is a spinoff from "The World According to Garp", a movie that came out a few years ago.

The location is great. It's set on the north side of the Santa Monica pier, so you can get a great view of the ocean the beach and the skyline of the city.

The menu is standard California restaurant fare: burgers, fish, salads, beer and mixed drinks in big glasses. They also have a big shop selling logo T-shirts and hats.

This is the kind of place that puts a menu outside in front of the restaurant, but doesn't have any prices. Locals don't come here much. It's mostly for tourists.

Ristorante Al Mare

https://goo.gl/maps/sYA7N2L2P572

250 Santa Monica Pier, Santa Monica, CA 90401

ristorantealmare.com

This surprisingly good Italian restaurant is on the pier right across from Bubba Gump. Prices at both are about the same, and this place is vastly better. Pizza, pasta, and salads are all very good.

Rusty's Surf Ranch

https://goo.gl/maps/xhqznAEFwbP2

256 Santa Monica Pier, Santa Monica, CA 90401

rustyssurfranch.com

Another Santa Monica standby that has been here for decades, Rusty's Surf Ranch is a classic surf bar that very often features live music in the evening. They serve beer, burgers, wings, and other sports bar fare. This is a good place.

Pacific Park Food Court

https://goo.gl/maps/kF5EGHXrEjQ2

380 Santa Monica Pier, Santa Monica, CA 90401

pacpark.com

The stands selling pizza, tacos, burgers and other fast food are uniformly horrible and overpriced. It's a food like you would find at a ballpark. However, unlike the ballpark, you're not trapped here. If you want fast food, leave the pier. You will find McDonalds, Subway and Joe's Slice Pizza all less than a block away.

Pier Concert Series

http://santamonicapier.org/twilightconcerts/

(310) 458-8900

All Summer long there are free concerts every Thursday on the Santa Monica Pier.

The pier itself quickly fills up and most people go down to the beach with a blanket and picnic basket to enjoy the show. You may or may not be able to see the band from the beach, but it's good fun anyway. Wine and beer are not allowed on the beach, but this seems to be loosely enforced.

Mariasol

https://goo.gl/maps/TpMUofiRML22

401 Santa Monica Pier, Santa Monica, CA 90401

mariasol.com

Mariasol is the worst Mexican restaurant in Santa Monica.

It's unfortunate, because the location is amazing. They have the perfect spot, right at the end of the Santa Monica pier, with the most incredible views. It's sad that this valuable public property is occupied by a restaurant that is overpriced and terrible. Local people never ever come here. It is only for tourists.

This is another restaurant that has a big menu out front, with no prices. You have been warned.

Montana Avenue

Shopping along Montana tends to be oriented toward high end housewives who live in the multi-million dollar homes north of Montana. There are lots of little shops selling designer clothes and restaurants that serve nice lunches and coffee. This is a great area for coffee, but the shops are expensive.

Subway

https://goo.gl/maps/c4pMAP5bE6r
625 Montana Ave Suite D, Santa Monica, CA 90403
order.subway.com
Located between sixth and seventh on the north side of Montana, Subway offers the usual cold cut sandwiches including the daily $2.99 fresh value menu.

Starbucks

https://goo.gl/maps/1gHSnj2QVRB2
701 Montana Ave, Santa Monica, CA 90403
starbucks.com
One of about a dozen Starbucks within walking distance of my home, the Starbucks offers the usual Starbucks menu and pleasant outdoor seating along Lincoln Boulevard.

Primo Paso Coffee Company

https://goo.gl/maps/JtwaaKBiMjs

702 Montana Ave, Santa Monica, CA 90403

A relatively new addition to the neighborhood, this modern coffee shop with shiny metal chairs and tasty coffee has quickly become a local favorite.

Marmalade

https://goo.gl/maps/4FxvyQjBzWq

710 Montana Ave, Santa Monica, CA 90403

No website

This is one of my absolute favorite restaurants in Santa Monica. It's part of the larger Marmalade chain of a half dozen or so restaurants, but this one is drastically different than the others. Others, such as the branch in Malibu, offer full black tie waiter service, a dining menu, and a happy hour. This one on Montana is just the opposite. It's more of a bakery, and they do a big take out business. They offer a large selection of salads and pastas which are kind of expensive but very good. They also have fantastically good soups and various egg-based breakfasts such as omelets, wave us rancheros, and oatmeal. Locals from the neighborhood will come in here and sit and drink coffee and a bagels or chocolate croissants for hours on end. In the refrigerator cases they have entrees such as lasagna and various fish and chicken based salad items. Everything is good.

You can sit at one of the individual tables or you can join whoever is sitting at the big green picnic table. I usually get a bagel with cream cheese, onions and tomato, with fresh cracked pepper, and a cup of coffee. This Is absolutely one of the best places in town. Open 7am-7pm. When friends come to visit this is where I take them for breakfast.

A sizeable crowsd of regulars gathers here every morning for coffee.

Spumoni

https://goo.gl/maps/wSYBjpxTsgF2

713 Montana Ave, Santa Monica, CA 90403

This nice Italian restaurant offers breakfast lunch and dinner, and often has coupon specials which offer you a free entrée if you order one entrée and a couple beverages. Food is good and reasonably priced. A few years ago, the old restaurant burned down. There was quite a lot of noise, and about five fire engines came to put out the fire. Fortunately it has been rebuilt and back in business.

Angelo's Shoe Repair

https://goo.gl/maps/JNHowpbViBG2

724 Montana Ave, Santa Monica, CA 90403

(310) 394-7237

This is our neighborhood shoe repair shop. Prices aren't that cheap, because they have to cover the rent, but they're honest and do a good job. If you need your shoes fixed, this is the place to go.

Andrew's Cheese Shop

https://goo.gl/maps/zpXJpp2Z5ST2

728 Montana Ave, Santa Monica, CA 90403

andrewscheese.com

Not just the cheese shop they also sell excellent beer and wine. They also have excellent sandwiches made with quality ingredients. We have had them cater a few events and the food was excellent. Their motto is "this place stinks ". Good stuff.

Menchie's Frozen Yogurt

https://goo.gl/maps/FTJN8q6YYfw

732 Montana Ave., Santa Monica, CA 90403

menchies.com

This is a fun by the ounce yogurt place. Fill your cup with however much you feel like eating, take it up to the counter and they will weigh it and charge accordingly. If you are a glutton it will be expensive, but if you eat a moderate quantity it's a very cheap dessert option and quite tasty.

Pavilions Grocery Store

https://goo.gl/maps/ZkZpJbScQNo

820 Montana Ave, Santa Monica, CA 90403

local.pavilions.com

A proud member of the Safeway chain, this is our neighborhood grocery store. The merchandise here is really pretty much identical to what you would find at Vons or Safeway, which have the same owner. Sandwiches, bread, deli items, fried chicken, vegetables, wine, and anything you else you might want from full-service grocery store is available here.

A few years ago, the Safeway chain was involved in a labor dispute with the employees of this grocery store. The store locked the employees out demanding wage and benefit concessions. The objective was to break the union.

Many local people switch the grocery shopping to Trader Joe's or Costco, which while not unionized seem to have better relations with their employees.

Eventually the strike was resolved. Existing employees took some wage and benefit concessions. New employees took a major cut and lost medical care. This is what they call progress in the 21st-century.

All the people that work at this grocery store today or all genuinely really nice people. It is a pleasure to do business with them, but I'm not a big fan of the corporation.

Open 5:30 am-midnight

Panda Express

https://goo.gl/maps/Rah8uPtyYX62

804 Montana Avenue, Santa Monica, CA 90403

pandaexpress.com

Oddly enough, this small stand located in the parking lot of Pavilions grocery store at the corner of Lincoln and Montana is one of the most popular restaurants in town. Around lunchtime you will always see a long line of people waiting to purchase orange chicken combinations with noodles and fried rice for eight or nine dollars. This is where all the local Mexican working guys get their lunches.

Horchata Mexican Food Bakery

https://goo.gl/maps/5X53ZQqBmsM2

804 Montana Ave, Santa Monica, CA 90403

orchatamexicanfoodandbakery.com

At one end of the counter of pioneer bakery, in the parking lot of the Pavilions grocery store at the corner of Montana and Lincoln, they make a wide variety of Mexican combination lunches. It is unusual to hear anyone order in English here, but it's very popular with local Mexican construction workers painters and car repair experts who are not in the mood to have Panda Express for lunch today.

Fox Laundry

https://goo.gl/maps/Dsf7Jo5atFK2

924 Montana Ave, Santa Monica, CA 90403

(310) 394-9418

This is our neighborhood laundromat. Machines range from about two dollars to five dollars, while large dryers are $.25 for about 10 minutes. They also have a fluff and fold service if you want them to wash for you.

Rosti

https://goo.gl/maps/ym4BPyXqa7x

931 Montana Ave, Santa Monica, CA 90403

rostituscankitchen.com

Rosti advertises itself as a Tuscan style take home rotisserie chicken place. Do Tuscans roast a lot of chicken? I have no idea. But this is a good restaurant.

The food especially pizza pasta and salads is generally very good.

They have no corkage fee, so if you're in the mood for a glass of wine you can walk down the block to Pavilions grocery store and get a bottle of your favorite Cabernet, and they will serve it to you at no charge. Very nice. Recommended.

Father's Office
https://goo.gl/maps/4gP6LcJDPkk
1018 Montana Ave, Santa Monica, CA 90403
fathersoffice.com
This hyper trendy hipster beer bar offers all your favorite microbrews and imports at two dollars more than anybody else. Isn't that special. They also have hamburgers with an attitude. The attitude is, "We don't allow any ketchup here, we're just way too hip for that." The decor is plain plywood that seems to have been sealed with floor sealer. It's very popular, with a big crowd most every night of the week.

FATHER'S
OFFICE
A

Esquire Barbershop

https://goo.gl/maps/Hgq5XEBX96R2

1020 Montana Ave, Santa Monica, CA 90403

esquirebarbershop.net

This is a traditional local barbershop with one of those little striped polo things that goes around in the window. Vic, the proprietor, he has been having some health issues that seems to be doing pretty well these days. He will be happy to give you a haircut for $23.

Good place, good man.

Arts Table

https://goo.gl/maps/QygVKL3P1Ak

1002 Montana Ave, Santa Monica, CA 90403

http://www.artstablesm.com

Located at the corner of Montana and 10th St., this trendy restaurant has had a number of incarnations over the years. They serve a month and burgers with the California cuisine twist. That's dishes are in the $16-$18 range. It's fairly popular.

Louise's Trattoria

https://goo.gl/maps/E4Um2kEKFGU2

1008 Montana Ave, Santa Monica, CA 90403

louises.com

The small Louisa's chain has restaurants around Los Angeles offering nice pizza, pasta, Chinese chicken salad and delicious desserts. This is one of Louisa's quieter outposts, but the food is generally good. Sometimes they will have lunch or dinner specials, you have to ask. Open 11 to 10 daily Friday and Saturday open until 1030, Sunday from 12 o'clock until 10 PM.

Caffe Luxxe

https://goo.gl/maps/G8NduDyLL1F2

925 Montana Ave, Santa Monica, CA 90403

caffeluxxe.com

One of about five coffee shops in a three block stretch of Montana, Café Luxxe is probably the best. I really like their coffee. It's not cheap. This is a good place to relax while your laundry is in the machines at Fox Laundry across the street.

The Duck Blind

https://goo.gl/maps/GDX4cLV7Gtj

1102 Montana Ave, Santa Monica, CA 90403

duckblindfinewines.com

Fine wines and spirits. This is a local liquor store. It does not stand out in any particular way but they have beer and wine if that is what you need.

Le Macaron

https://goo.gl/maps/ebt3EcfF9SN2

1301 Montana Ave, Santa Monica, CA 90403

lemacaronsantamonica.com

This nice small bakery specializes in macaroons but offers other French pastries and coffee. A nice shop.

R+D Kitchen

https://goo.gl/maps/dGmxwEyAh7U2

1323 Montana Ave, Santa Monica, CA 90403

rd-kitchen.com

Located in the former Wolfgang Puck's restaurant on Montana, this is considered one of the best and most popular restaurants in Santa Monica this week. The prices are upper mid-range but the food is reliably good and it's always busy. They have burgers and salads and chicken in that kind of thing. It's not cheap, but people like it.

Aero Theater

https://goo.gl/maps/3pmfMrN58Ht

1328 Montana Ave, Santa Monica, CA 90403

americancinematheque.com

One of the two homes of the American cinematheque, the aero theater is big fun. Every night they have a different movie. Sometimes they show classics, sometimes foreign films, and quite often they will have speakers to. Check their website for details, find out what's coming on and if it looks really good you may want to book in advance because the popular shows sell out quickly.

Pete's Coffee

https://goo.gl/maps/LcmhvdUyLvJ2

1401 Montana Ave, Santa Monica, CA 90403

peets.com

A nice coffee shop with delicious coffee.

Whole foods

https://goo.gl/maps/nPVS5abtR462

1425 Montana Ave, Santa Monica, CA 90403

wholefoodsmarket.com

Somehow this Whole Foods seems more organic than the other Whole Foods stores in Santa Monica, and yet not quite as organic as the co-op. Call of the merchandise is generally very good. Whole Foods was recently taken over by Amazon, and a few of the prices were rolled back. There has been much speculation that the Whole Foods stores would be used to support Amazons "Amazon fresh" grocery delivery service, but at the time of this writing nobody's really sure.

Fireside Cellars

https://goo.gl/maps/NrTyHvETSLK2

1421 Montana Ave, Santa Monica, CA 90402

firesidecellars.com

This high-end wine shop has lots of delicious looking ones, though from the pricing you can see that they are not aiming at the same market as Trader Joe's. There's a small door inside that connects to the inside of whole foods. I don't know if there is any financial connection between the two operations. This Whole Foods doesn't seem to have a wine department so maybe there is.

Starbucks 15th in Montana

https://goo.gl/maps/emaH5a8imZ22

1426 Montana Ave #4, Santa Monica, CA 90403

starbucks.com

Yet another nice Starbucks shop, one of many in this neighborhood. Popular.

Margo's

https://goo.gl/maps/2ctQdvpZcqt

1534 Montana Ave, Santa Monica, CA 90403

margossantamonica.com

Very nice looking modern restaurant and bar. I haven't had a chance to try yet. For years this was the Cafe Montana. They have a sign on the sidewalk that says bottomless Mimosas $18. Sounds promising.

Bardonna

https://goo.gl/maps/sU45T84kjYH2

1601 Montana Ave, Santa Monica, CA 90403

santamonica.com

Located at 16th and Montana, this delicious coffee shop is a little on the pricey side but the coffee is very good, and they have a selection of salads and wraps and other healthy-ish lunch options. Inside, barstools line the long handmade cement tables but give it a high tech urban feel, and you will see lots of people working at their laptops. Cover here is very good. But then there's a lot of competition for good coffee on Montana.

William Sonoma

https://goo.gl/maps/j4cvdACZu1m

1600 Montana Ave, Santa Monica, CA 90403

williams-sonoma.com

This is an outpost of the popular kitchen supply store. I want to come in here and look at all the toys.

Pinkberry

https://goo.gl/maps/DKeZGQBEqr42

1612 Montana Ave, Santa Monica, CA 90403
pinkberry.com
Chain frozen yogurt. Generally good.

Montana Library

https://goo.gl/maps/o8KcMUweRCG2
1704 Montana Ave, Santa Monica, CA 90403
smpl.org
This is a smaller local branch of the Santa Monica library system. The main branch is at 6:30 and Santa Monica Blvd. the book collections not all that large but if you need a quiet and comfortable place to read or study this is a good one. Our neighborhood group uses the meeting room in back for our meetings. It's a very nice facility.

Sweet Lady Jane

https://goo.gl/maps/vzvexXW8Mvk
1631 Montana Ave, Santa Monica, CA 90403
sweetladyjane.com
Located at the corner of 17th and Montana this is one of the best cake bakeries in town. The original branch is on Melrose in West Hollywood, and as far as I know this is the only branch.

Sweet Lady Jane makes croissants and breads and other traditional bakery items, but their specialty is really cake.

Chocolate cake, marzipan cake, white cake with lots of fresh fruit. Whatever your favorite cake, they will have it here, and they serve it in slices that are big enough for two people. There's no diet sugar free fat free desserts here.

If you eat a piece of their cake you are probably going to eat about a half pound of butter. You will know that you're not supposed to be eating this kind of food, but your stomach will be very very happy. It's about 9 million calories per slice. It's absolutely the best.

Sweet Lady Jane is not all that cheap. You might spend close to $10 for a slice of cake and five dollars for a little pot of coffee. But you get what you pay for. Seriously this place is the best.

Wilshire/Santa Monica Blvd

There are quite a few businesses and restaurants in the area along Wilshire, east of Lincoln.

Ingo's Tasty Diner

https://goo.gl/maps/ziMx5gNaqPq

1213 Wilshire Blvd, Santa Monica, CA 90403

ingostastydiner.com

(310) 395-4646

This fun bistro has a full menu of things like French Dip Sandwiches and mussels. All the food is excellent, and they have a great happy hour. It's the same management as the Misfit but this is a little more of an eating place with a bar, while Misfit tends to be more of a party.

UKRAINA
DELICATESSEN
CReAM
SKIN CARE
1207
1211

Vienna Pastry

https://goo.gl/maps/aseYowNDRGR2

1215 Wilshire Blvd, Santa Monica, CA 90403

viennapastry.com

(310) 395-6728

Small local bakery making pastries and cakes.

Bagel Nosh

https://goo.gl/maps/YP9uEaegdzr

1629 Wilshire Blvd, Santa Monica, CA 90403

bagelnoshdeli.com

This friendly local bagel shop has been open for many years and is popular with local residents. They actually are a full deli, with soups, sandwiches, bagels, and coffee. The decor is plain functional 1980s with wood chairs and tables. If you want to get away from the hyper trendy new coffee shops where they service coffee that was previously eaten by a civet cat, this would be a good place to have a bagel and read a book.

Staples

https://goo.gl/maps/hq2wGYLatYk

1610 Wilshire Blvd, Santa Monica, CA 90403

stores.staples.com

This is a branch of one of the large national chain of office supply stores. There aren't any more local office supply stores in this area, so if you need paper pens, this is probably the best place to come.

It's interesting to see over the years how Staples has been making the transition from a bix box stationer to a computer store. These days more than half of their floorspace is dedicated to computers.

One nice thing: they will match online prices. So find the price for what you want online and then come get it here and know the price can't be beat.

Open 7am-9pm.

Vons Wilshire

https://goo.gl/maps/tgifnE6E3y92

1311 Wilshire Blvd, Santa Monica, CA 90403

local.vons.com

(310) 394-1414

Grocery store that is a member of the Safeway chain. The Pavilions on Montana, the Vons on Wilshire, and the Vons on Broadway have the same owner and the same prices and merchandise.

Monarca

https://goo.gl/maps/ezt2oHpJWYu

1300 Wilshire Blvd, Santa Monica, CA 90403

lamonarcabakery.com

(310) 451-1114

Excellent Mexican bakery and coffee shop. The cappuccinos and lattes are very good here, as are the ham and cheese croissants and other pastries. Our neighborhood group often buys dinner snacks for our meetings here. Really good stuff. Recommended.

Saint Monica's

https://goo.gl/maps/64QPbq9qRUt

701 California Ave, Santa Monica, CA 90403

stmonica.net

(310) 393-9287

Located a couple of blocks north of Wilshire in a residential area, this church in high school complex uncle Pat occupies a large city block him at the corner of seventh and California doing Saint Monica's high school is famous for the high quality of the education they provide, and they are able to do it on roughly 1/3 the budget per student compared to what Santa Monica high school spends.

Holy Grounds

https://goo.gl/maps/LAxJfMkmHSk

725 California Ave, Santa Monica, CA 90403

stmonica.net

This nice coffee shop, located on the St. Monica's campus, has great coffee as well as place trees, which I believe comes from the nearby earth Earth Café. In the daytime it is often filled with high school students. The coffee is very good.

DK's Donuts & Bakery

https://goo.gl/maps/ikpYAy4mtNt

1614 Santa Monica Blvd, Santa Monica, CA 90404

dksdonuts.com

(310) 829-2512

DK is the best 24-hour donut shop in Santa Monica. Every time my friend Robert visits from Paris, DK is his first stop. They have about 300 different kinds of donuts ranging in price from $.50 to three or four dollars each. It's always filled with extremely stoned people, especially at night. The stoned people buy lots of donuts. If you need donuts, this is the place. Especially after midnight.

Dagwoods

https://goo.gl/maps/zq9JX2JZgwR2

820 Wilshire Blvd, Santa Monica, CA 90401

dagwoods.com

(310) 899-3030

This fun local sandwich and pizza shop started originally in Venice. Good stuff. Happy hour specials on beer and some food items, check for current details.

Pico to Olympic

Wienerschnitzel

https://goo.gl/maps/fVHgJaoofd42

3010 Pico Blvd, Santa Monica, CA 90405

wienerschnitzel.com

(310) 450-7671

I like Wienerschnitzel.

Truth be told, they have no "Wiener Schnitzel", which is actually a breaded veal cutlet, usually served with potatoes. In German, Wiener means Vienna style. Schnitzel is a cutlet, a piece of veal sliced thin and pounded flat.

If you are looking for real Wiener Schnitzel, you will probably have to go to your local Mexican place and ask for "Milanesa", because that's about the only place you can find it.

This Wienerschnitzel is a hot dog stand. Not a pretentious one like Pinks, but a place that is happy to sell you one of their quality food products for about a dollar.

Looking for a corn dog? Chili dog? Looking to pay about a dollar, maybe a dollar and a half? This is your place.

They have a number of other items, like fries, and it's all cheap. Drive through. Fun and basic and no place to hang out at all.

You know already if you will like it or not. It's not for everyone, but I like it.

Santa Monica Animal Shelter

https://goo.gl/maps/uAebsjRHqu32

1640 9th St, Santa Monica, CA 90404

smgov.net

(310) 458-8594

Located on 9th street just off Olympic, the Animal Control Shelter is part of the Santa Monica Police Department.

The nice people at the animal shelter are doing their best to find homes for numerous dogs and cats whose owners have left them to live on the streets.

I can't see why anybody would spend money to buy a dog or can when there are plenty here who desperately need homes. The cute baby ones go quickly, while older ones just look at you with big eyes. They know what happens if nobody chooses them.

Once in a while you see other types of animals. Sometimes they board horses for the police department, or for horse owners in Malibu who are threatened with fires.

One time I saw a mad pygmy goat, who tried to head butt me into oblivion. This would have been a very frightening experience, except that he was only about 14 inches high, and it was about as dangerous as being head butted by a dachshund. I held out a foot and he repeatedly charged the sole of my shoe. A brave effort. He was clearly out of his mind.

I wonder if someone adopted him?

Tacos Por Favor

https://goo.gl/maps/v97TAMAXrCH2

1406 Olympic Blvd, Santa Monica, CA 90404

tacosporfavor.net

(310) 392-5768

This excellent and unpretentious family run restaurant serves all the popular Mexican items.

There is a line at the register where you can choose from a wide variety of traditional Mexican items, tacos, enchiladas, tortas, pollo al diablo, soups, pretty much anything you can think of.

I am particularly fond of the Chilaquiles. Pozole is good too.

Then you can walk over to the other counter and watch the cooks put it all together. If that gets boring you can go over to the sauces stand and fill up some little plastic cups with one of the various colored hot sauces, pepper, carrots, and salsa fresca.

What really makes this place excel is the flavor of their sauces, both the self-serve, and the cooking sauces. I love them all - the red, the green, the mole. The food is just plain tasty.

There are a lot of car repair places in this area, and their main market seemed to be local mechanics on break. More recently, the place has been catching on, and you will often find it full of hipsters from big offices nearby.

The wine list is terrible, and overpriced, but this just isn't the right place for wine. Not really for beer either. This is a lunch place, have some water or a horchata.

Prices used to be pretty cheap, but are slowly inching upwards. It doesn't seem to be hurting their business. One cost plus: there are no waiters, so you save a significant amount right there.

This place is just great, and the people really nice. Highly recommended.

Warning: they close early, check hours if you're coming for dinner.

Tip Top Tow Service

https://goo.gl/maps/EZMEHQsWsf62

1654 12th St, Santa Monica, CA 90404

tiptoptow.com

(310) 314-4040

These guys are thieves.

My next door neighbor's car was stolen. Not towed, but stolen.

The stolen car was recovered a few weeks later by SMPD on the Santa Monica pier. Instead of calling her (she lives within walking distance), they turned the car over to Tip Top Towing.

Tip Top Towing waited a couple of weeks before notifying her that they had her car, then charged her close to a thousand dollars to get her stolen car back.

This is completely dishonest. She had done nothing wrong, she wasn't parked illegally, she had violated no law, she just had the misfortune to have her car stolen and recovered by SMPD and put in the hands of Tip Top Towing.

Legally speaking, Tip Top had no "lien" on the car and no legal basis to hold it. They just charge as much as they can and laugh all the way to the bank. Often their charges are more than the cars are worth, which is why they have so many cars for sale in their lot. A lot of them go to the auction.

Many local residents believe that Tip Top and certain people in the police department are in cahoots and split the profits from this racket. There is no other explanation that makes any sense.

Please do not use Tip Towing ever for any service. As local residents it is the only way we can fight back against this predatory and evil business.

Unurban Cafe

https://goo.gl/maps/isssuCMvagn

3301 Pico Blvd, Santa Monica, CA 90405

unurban.com

This funky coffee shop is a holdover from the days when Santa Monica was an inexpensive and sleepy town by the sea. Inside, the shop is not in the greatest state of repair, but the coffee is good and it's a fun place

Friday nights are open mic. Bring your guitar and five dollars, and for 10 minutes you can be a star. It's big fun. Some of the acts are excellent and some are beyond terrible. A fun time is had by all.

Often, before the shows, you can see the bands outside on the sidewalk getting ready to play.

Trader Joe's - Pico

https://goo.gl/maps/PxrnZzgNbUK2

3212 Pico Blvd, Santa Monica, CA 90405

traderjoes.com

(310) 581-0253

Trader Joe's is famous for discounted cheese, wine, meats, coffee, and frozen food items. Their foods are generally cheaper and better than the big national grocery chains. There are two locations, one on Pico and one on Olympic.

El Texate

https://goo.gl/maps/de6eQ2bCQMy

316 Pico Blvd, Santa Monica, CA 90405

(310) 399-1115

want very much to love this Oaxacan restaurant, but the food is uninspiring. In some communities this restaurant would be top, but in Santa Monica there are so many good Mexican restaurants to choose from. If you are looking for Mole, try Gueleguetza in Hollywood.

Raes Diner

https://goo.gl/maps/37UHuo5uMYL2

2901 Pico Blvd, Santa Monica, CA 90405

places.singleplatform.com

This is a 50s diner. It's not a retro diner, like Café 50s or Johnny Rockets. It's a real 50s diner that was built in the 1950s. It's very cheap and the food is amazing.

The specialty here is breakfast. The menu includes a number of combinations specials with things like eggs, bacon, biscuits and gravy, pancakes, and omelets. All of them are delicious and cost around $6 to $8.

Lunches and dinners are good too. Burgers, club sandwiches, and whatever is on the daily special will usually be good

Saturday and Sunday mornings, you can expect a significant wait.

I'd say it's worth it, but if the line is too long, you can always go over to Lare's next door, which is also pretty good.

This is one of the best places in Santa Monica, especially for breakfast. Strongly recommended.

Lare's Restaurant

https://goo.gl/maps/uzPBdrj23DN2

2909 Pico Blvd, Santa Monica, CA 90405

lares-restaurant.com

(310) 829-4550

Lare's is a popular local restaurant on Pico almost next door to the famous Rae's diner and just up the street from McCabe's. Best known for margaritas and dinners, they also serve excellent and inexpensive breakfasts.

Lare's is on two floors, with the main bar and hostess upstairs. Downstairs is the breakfast area and second bar.

In the evenings the bar is crowded with locals sipping margaritas. Dinners are traditional Mexican restaurant fare, tacos and enchiladas and chips, as well as real dinner items like Mole and various kinds of pork, beef and chicken dishes.

Everything I've ever had there has been good. I'm particularly fond of Mole enchiladas but you will enjoy most anything you order.

Margaritas here are pretty standard - good but not particularly special.

Breakfasts here are great, and in fact it is at breakfast time that we discovered this place. Rae's breakfast had a line out the door, and some clever person at Lare's had put their breakfast special sign out where those in line outside Rae's could see it. So we thought, why not go in and give it a try.

It was really inexpensive and very good. Lare's has become one of the places we go to fairly regularly. It's pretty good.

McCabe's Guitar Shop

https://goo.gl/maps/wWDKBkipWY82

3101 Pico Blvd, Santa Monica, CA 90405

mccabes.com

(310) 828-4497

McCabe's is one of the most famous guitar shops in the world. You can buy stringed instruments, get them repaired, take classes, and even see concerts almost nightly.

As a guitar shop, McCabe's is one of the best.

Why patronize a national chain when you can get pretty much the same thing here, but with sales people that are really expert in what they are doing. Just because another store looks like Costco inside doesn't mean it's cheaper.

McCabe's caters to acoustic players - you can buy electrics here, but it's not the core of their business. They also have a few basses, banjos, and a wall full of funky ukuleles and a bunch of other instruments, many of which I'm not even sure what their names are. The thing that's half harp and half guitar, and has two necks, what is that? I have no idea.

Their sheet music collection is pretty good, though everything is pretty much at list price. You could get it cheaper at Amazon, but at McCabe's you can look at it, touch it, even take it in back to the room full of guitars and try the music out before you buy it. I think it's worth the few extra dollars you would pay.

If you have a broken guitar, I don't know a better place to take it than McCabe's. Their minimum labor charge is about $85, which is either really expensive or a great deal, depending on what they do for you for that amount.

The best thing to do is to get an estimate, then you know what it's going to cost and you can decide whether it's worth the money. They always charge exactly what they estimate - I wish my car repair place would do the same. I won't say it's always the cheapest place but they've done nice work for me at prices I thought were pretty reasonable.

As a concert venue, McCabe's is legendary. Check their schedule for some amazing shows. Surprisingly many famous acts stop here largely due to the hip/cool factor. It only seats about a hundred people. Big acts sell out fast.

If you are looking for fancy electrics, you may prefer Truetone on Santa Monica, but for acoustic guitars, McCabe's is the best place around.

Note: there is also a bar/restaurant named McCabe's. If you see a lot of people drinking and dining, you may be in the wrong place.

Z Garden

https://goo.gl/maps/Qosao3mFpQp

2350 Pico Blvd, Santa Monica, CA 90405

santamonicazgarden.com

You can tell from the architecture that this used to be some kind of fast food hamburger restaurant, that has been transformed into an amazingly excellent Mediterranean restaurant.

This is one of those places where you order at the counter, and they bring the food over to you when it's ready.

Among the delicious favorites here are shawarma, lamb shanks, lemon chicken, and kebabs. I'll dinners come with rice and salad, hummus, pita bread, and some olive oil dip.

And all of these things are great.

Prices range from about $7 from for a pita sandwich to about $16 for the lamb shank, which is huge.

Z garden charges no corkage fee. We frequently go to the drugstore across the street and buy a nice bottle of wine to go with dinner. Nice.

I love this place. Totally recommend it. Two years ago, we went there for my birthday. and it was so fun.

Gilbert's El Indio Restaurant

https://goo.gl/maps/W7W2gtFdEQE2

2526 Pico Blvd, Santa Monica, CA 90405

gilbertselindio.com

(310) 450-8057

This is one of my favorite restaurants.

Situated up the street from Santa Monica College, this unpretentious local favorite has flourished for years by offering good food, reasonable, prices, and friendly service. The interior is a bit dark, filled with booths and the walls covered with pictures.

Food is classic Mexican cuisine. Gilberts makes great tacos, enchiladas, burritos and all your favorite classic Mexican dishes.

The breakfast combinations, such as "machaca" (shredded beef with eggs, served with rice beans chips and coffee) are great.

My personal favorite is the "Super Chicken Burrito" which has lots of chicken and avocado; light on the beans/rice, covered with amazingly good green sauce.

Chips and sauce are good here, so are the pickled carrots (free). Good margaritas. Locally owned by a local family. The logo (picture of an indian) is taken from an obscure brand of Mexican beer.

Lo/Cal Coffee and Market

https://goo.gl/maps/an4YxNZyRtF2

2214 Pico Blvd, Santa Monica, CA 90405

local-coffee.com

(424) 322-2710

This is a very nice small coffee shop on Pico about halfway between SMC and Trader Joe's.

They use Stumptown coffee, which will mean something to you if you are from the Pacific Northwest. Stumptown is a popular local coffee in Portland, and the cups they make here are tasty.

The coffee situation in Santa Monica is generally getting better and better.

Sammy's Cameras

https://goo.gl/maps/ySRsTetggoL2

4411 Sepulveda Blvd, Culver City, CA 90230

samys.com

(310) 450-4551

This famous camera store caters to professional photographers and filmmakers. The prices are competitive with famous stores in New York, and the people here really know their stuff. This is where the pros go. There are branches in Hollywood, Culver City and Pasadena.

Tacos Por Favor

https://goo.gl/maps/DKP1vj1sDJz

1406 Olympic Blvd, Santa Monica, CA 90404

tacosporfavor.net

Located at the corner of 14th and Olympic Boulevard, this excellent Mexican restaurant offers a full range of Mexican cuisine.

Tacos Por Favor was originally popular with the Mexican employees have a number of nearby auto body and repair shops. As the years go by the area has gentrified and some of those places are gone. However Tacos Por Favor just keeps getting more and more popular.

And among the things which I love To order from this restaurant are Pozole, which is big corn soup with chicken and vegetable base; enchiladas con mole, which are enchiladas with chile cheese sauce, torta Cubana, which is a sandwich with chicken, egg, and a hot dog, and pollo al diablo, which is chicken in fire hot red sauce.

This is a very good place, and enthusiastically recommended.

The Counter Burgers

https://goo.gl/maps/HP4hq7SyEGp

2901 Ocean Park Blvd, Santa Monica, CA 90405

thecounterburger.com

(310) 399-8383

The counter serves some really great hamburgers, with lots of special ingredients. Kind of like ordering pizza with lots of toppings to choose from. You can take one of their named burgers or create your own combination.

Fries and sweet potato fries are pretty good. In fact, everything here is good.

The decor is pretty basic. There's a long counter, like something from a diner, and a dozen or so tables.

In this price range they are competing with places like Father's Office, but I think The Counter is much better. Father's Office basically has only one kind of burger, and they have attitude about people who like ketchup or mustard on their burgers. At the Counter you can get whatever you want on your burger, and nobody will give you attitude.

I like The Counter much better than In and Out Burger too, but then you are paying at least twice as much.

The burgers here really are pretty good.

Main Street

Main Street parallels the waterfront, starting in front of the civic auditorium and stretching down to Venice. There are numerous cool restaurants and 20 shops along the way.

Tongva Park

https://goo.gl/maps/Xt9ipnqTf392

1615 Ocean Ave, Santa Monica, CA 90401

tongvapark.smgov.net

(310) 458-8310

This four-acre park lies between Ocean Avenue and City Hall. It was landscaped at a cost of $55 million, not including the land. I’m not sure I’m really in love with the results. It looks fine but there’s nothing to do here. You can’t throw a frisbee and you can’t sail a model boat. Most of it is unsuitable for picnics. The cost was paid for by allowing builders to develop city owned land to the south. This was great for the builders, who made hundreds of millions, but the benefit for residents seems small.

I would have preferred that all the city owned land be used for parks. We don't need the developer money for metal landscaping. Trees and grass are fine.

Rand Corporation

https://goo.gl/maps/bzjMtw2zJSt

1776 Main St, Santa Monica, CA 90401

rand.org

(310) 393-0411

This think tank was originally part of the Douglas company, but is now an independent company. Their business involves doing foreign policy studies, some for the military, some for other branches of government.

Stella Barra Pizza

https://goo.gl/maps/wADMzi7ZcYC2

2000 Main St, Santa Monica, CA 90405

stellabarra.com

This trendy pizza restaurant also has pasta and sandwiches. All are good. Happy hour here is very popular. They have meatball sliders for three dollars, red or white sangria for three dollars, and a selection of good local top beers for four dollars. It's great. The management here is the same as at M Street Café next door.

M Street Kitchen

https://goo.gl/maps/rtB6uDjEV6E2

2000 Main St, Santa Monica, CA 90405

mstreetkitchen.com

And this popular restaurant serves burger, nachos and salads. Happy hour is very popular. The same management owns Stella Barra pizza next-door, and the bakery in between. The bakery has all kinds of amazing looking pastries and cookies as well as a refrigerator full of beer wine and beverages.

Dogtown Coffee

https://goo.gl/maps/GG8k5qAToPo

2003 Main St, Santa Monica, CA 90405

dogtowncoffee.com

(310) 310-3665

Dogtown was once a name for this neighborhood, and there was even a documentary movie about kids that road skateboards in this neighborhood, but I don't think anybody calls it Dogtown anymore. The coffee shop serves good quality coffee, and is popular.

Urth Cafe

https://goo.gl/maps/ReM6bXYjZus

2327 Main St, Santa Monica, CA 90405

urthcaffe.com

Coffee, sandwiches and salads with an organic twist have made this main street café in one of the most popular in the area. Recommended.

The Galley

https://goo.gl/maps/LU6WY2wDWRw

2442 Main St, Santa Monica, CA 90405

thegalleyrestaurant.net

(310) 452-1934

Popular nautical theme restaurant with good burgers, fish and chips, and frequent happy hour specials.

Jinya Ramen

https://goo.gl/maps/R2mKrHYU4gk

2400 Main St, Santa Monica, CA 90405

jinya-ramenbar.com

(310) 392-4466

Fun trendy Japanese ramen shop. They have a nice outdoor seating area too.

Novel Pizza

https://goo.gl/maps/nWjMvUVnLTw

2507 Main St, Santa Monica, CA 90405

novelcafepizzeria.com

The novel café, I'll bookstore a few blocks away, branched out and opened a pizzeria. And they close the original place, and now we have the novel pizzeria. Coffee is good pizza is good at. Nice place.

La Vecchia Cucina

https://goo.gl/maps/Yz8KyhRLTCr

2654 Main St, Santa Monica, CA 90405

lavecchiacucina.com

(310) 399-7979

This popular Italian bistro is best known for their happy hour, with drinks and food items on special. Pizzas and pasta are nice.

Lula Cocina Mexicana

https://goo.gl/maps/bjMLXh1fM5k

2720 Main St, Santa Monica, CA 90405

lulacocinamexicana.com

(310) 392-5711

Lula's on Main offers nice California style Mexican food, with a light and pleasant interior, and a really great Happy Hour. Margaritas and food items at the happy hour are really great, and last I checked, they had happy hour from 1 to 8 pm or something crazy like that. Banana and Mango happy hour margaritas are really excellent. I don't eat dinner here much but I do like the happy hour.

Finn McCools

https://goo.gl/maps/EW1vMgNWk5m

2702 Main St, Santa Monica, CA 90405

finnmccoolsirishpub.com

I've only been to this place on St Patrick's day. It was filled wall to wall with people. They doubled all the prices and cancelled the usual happy hour specials. I guess they need to make as much money as they can when they get the chance.

This place was originally called “Merlin Mcflies”. It had some kind of a Victorian magic theme, that can still be seen in some of the furnishings.

Circle Bar

https://goo.gl/maps/dbpkM6F2Vep

2926 Main St, Santa Monica, CA 90405

circle-bar.com

Circle bar is open really only at night. There is loud thumping music, lots of people dressed for a big night out, and the drinks are a little bit expensive. If you are looking for a late-night dance club feeling, but don’t want to go to one of the giant clubs in Hollywood, this might be the place for you.

Komodo

https://goo.gl/maps/hxGV4Rv6FYF2

235 Main St, Venice, CA 90291

komodofood.com

(310) 255-6742

This nice shop sells tacos with a pan pacific, Indonesian influenced taste. A couple of tacos, a burrito, or a combination plate will cost you $8-$12. Food is good, especially the hot sauces and the Mango lemonade.

Library Alehouse

https://goo.gl/maps/U3g39khyt4H2

2911 Main St, Santa Monica, CA 90405

libraryalehouse.com

(310) 314-4855

Beer is the specialty, but they have good burgers and other food items. The front feels like a saloon, while the seating in the back almost feels like a garden. Good place, popular.

Trader Joe's - Olympic

https://goo.gl/maps/dJ5qGQU73mu

11755 W Olympic Blvd, Los Angeles, CA 90064

traderjoes.com

(310) 477-5949

Trader Joe's is famous for discounted cheese, wine, meats, coffee, and frozen food items. Their foods are generally cheaper and better than the big national grocery chains. There are two locations, one on Pico and one on Olympic.

Rick's Tavern on Main

https://goo.gl/maps/JGukvEoVAzQ2

2907 Main St, Santa Monica, CA 90405

rtavern.com

(310) 392-2772

This tavern has been popular for many years. Karaoke and happy hour.

Enterprise Fish

https://goo.gl/maps/6Jp9o8cpZY22

174 Kinney St, Santa Monica, CA 90405

enterprisefishco.com

This large traditional seafood restaurant serves fish, crab, lobster from a traditional American seafood menu.

The bar is often busy in the evening. Happy hour gives you a couple of dollars off the price of beer and wine, as well as some food specials. I used to be a big fan of the poke, but they've changed the recipe and it's not as good as it used to be.

Three Twins Ice Cream

https://goo.gl/maps/PRYasiwYmEu

2726 Main St, Santa Monica, CA 90405

threetwinsicecream.com

This ice cream stand is run by a locally produced brand of ice cream that is absolutely excellent. You can get a few of their flavors by the carton at Whole Foods, but the selection is much larger here. If they have it, I recommend the chocolate orange flavor. It's so good. This is the best ice cream in town.

Aussie Pies

https://goo.gl/maps/ejjoLYvjAYz

2510 Main St, Santa Monica, CA 90405

forkinpies.com

An Aussie pie is basically a chicken pot pie made by Australians. You can substitute hamburger or some other protein for the chicken. And it's an Australian favorite, and they are generally pretty good.

This restaurant has a variety of pot pie's, and also some good side dishes such as potatoes or vegetables.

Everything is amazingly excellent. It's a little bit expensive, considering the size of the pies isn't all that large, but the quality of the food is very good.

Tsukiji Sushi Sen

https://goo.gl/maps/3AnTawKz7wn

2915 Main St, Santa Monica, CA 90405

eatsushisen.com

(310) 581-3525

Japanese food on Main Street. Food is good, though hard to compare to all the places on Sawtelle.

Sunny Blue Musubi

https://goo.gl/maps/fuv7jq9mPEJ2

2728 Main St, Santa Monica, CA 90405

sunnyblueinc.com

Musubi are Japanese rice balls rolled in seaweed, with some kind of filling inside, such as plums or salmon. This whole in the wall Musubi specialty shop offers various kind, at reasonable prices. They are pretty good. Recommended.

Bareburger

https://goo.gl/maps/NxStfeUgPMy

2732 Main St, Santa Monica, CA 90405

bareburger.com

(310) 392-2122

Heath conscious burgers featuring beef and bison. Has a happy hour too.

Beach

Due to strange zoning laws there are very few restaurants on the beach, but the beach itself is very nice.

Big Dean's

https://goo.gl/maps/7eUQUPDjpsx

1615 Ocean Front Walk, Santa Monica, CA 90401

bigdeansoceanfrontcafe.com

Located right where the bicycle path passes under the pier, this dive beach burger joint has a full bar and is has been here for decades. The floor is sand and they have picnic benches to sit on. The prices are reasonable, but the main reason to come here is the location. This is a good place to have burger and a beverage after visiting the beach.

Hotdog on a Stick

https://goo.gl/maps/gu9bcq3g8372

1633 Ocean Front Walk, Santa Monica, CA 90401

hotdogonastick.com

This small stand serving fresh corn dogs is located on the beach walk just south of the pier. The original "Hotdog on a Stick" was located in the food court in the old Santa Monica mall, but that is long gone. Hotdog on a stick used to be the source of many jokes because of the unusually ugly outfits they made their employees wear, with logo shirts and baseball caps with rainbow colors on them. The menu consists of corn dogs and lemonade. If you're searching for a fresh made batter fried corn dog, this is the place.

Back on the Beach

https://goo.gl/maps/kUpXDvTDkis

445 Pacific Coast Hwy, Santa Monica, CA 90402

backonthebeachcafe.com

Not quite as pricey as Perry's Café, this beach restaurant is not well known but is generally good. It is located on the Annenburg property.

It's cheaper and better than Perry's, but you do pay a couple of dollars extra for the privilege of sitting on the beach.

My biggest complaint here is that the cheap plastic beach chairs they have outside sink into the sand and are unstable to sit on. I wish they would put some kind of floor out so the chairs would have a steady footing.

Perry's Cafe & Bike Rental

North of Pier location:

https://goo.gl/maps/9ksySipW2fm

930 Pacific Coast Hwy, Santa Monica, CA 90403

perryscafe.com

(310) 260-1114

South of Pier location:
https://goo.gl/maps/qYjNjYdPK6M2
2400 Ocean Front Walk, Santa Monica, CA 90405
perryscafe.com
(310) 452-7609

This overpriced gyp joint is home of the $4 regular coffee and the $18 cheeseburger. The quality is about what you would expect at a ballpark. This place is for tourists. They give the burgers fancy names but they are not expecting repeat business.

The city has given them a monopoly in this area of the beach, so they have several shops and they charge anything they want. This is a bad way for the city to manage beach vendors. Vote no with your money.

If you are coming down to this section of the beach I'd suggest bringing your food with you. Go up to Bay Cities or Vons or even Subway and get some sandwiches or drinks and have a picnic on the beach.

There are also a ton of fast food places along the Venice Boardwalk, only a few blocks up the beach path.

Even if you are hungry, I recommend to stay away from Perry's. There are so many good restaurants and so many cheap fast food places in Santa Monica.

Venice

This is the area directly south of Santa Monica. When Abbott Kinney built his housing development here, he put in canals and called it Venice. Unfortunately, this area is an oil field. That's what feeds the La Brea Tar Pits, and that's what feeds the oil well at Beverly Hills High School. As oil seeped into the canals, they began to smell like a chemical dump. Never mind that it was all natural, but it wasn't appealing. Some of the canals were filled in, and they have tried to improve the water flow in the remainder. It's actually a really nice area, and there are many good restaurants and fun shops in this neighborhood.

Venice is an easy walk or a three dollar Uber from Santa Monica. You can also walk or skate along the beach bath to the Venice Boardwalk, then go a block or two inland to get to Main Street. The Boardwalk has minimal parking but is a fun area filled with tourists and little food stands and shops selling T-shirts and marijuana licenses.

La Cabaña

https://goo.gl/maps/vdBPSGHJ1mt
738 Rose Ave, Venice, CA 90291
lacabanavenice.com
(310) 392-7973
This is one of the oldest Mexican restaurants in the area. The look inside is very traditional, with dark vinyl booths and very formal waiters. Everything on the menu is good, from tacos and burritos to salads and entrees like Chile Verde or fish "al Mojo de Ajo". They are open until 3:00, which makes it a good late-night option. Other restaurants in the area all close early. This place used to be cheap but as the years go by the prices have been creeping up. Drinks are kind of small and a little bit expensive.

Casa Blanca

This is the sister restaurant to La Cabana, and is located just across the street, on the other side of Lincoln. The food and style are similar, but Casa Blanca has a seafood theme. "Casa Blanca" means "White house" in Spanish. I'm not sure what the significance of this is, but it's definitely not a reference to Morocco or the famous Humphrey Bogart film. If you are looking for seafood, this will be a good place, otherwise, I usually go to La Cabana. They are both good.

Whole Foods

https://goo.gl/maps/mwY8u6WS3qj
225 Lincoln Blvd, Venice, CA 90291
wholefoodsmarket.com
(310) 566-9480
This is a very large and very successful Whole Foods store. For those not familiar, they are a grocery store that emphasizes organic foods. This one has a particularly large take out food section, with several large bars of hot food items. At lunch they do a huge business. They have everything from salads to pork ribs, and there is plenty of seating. They also have a wine bar, with tastings several times a week.

Rose Café

https://goo.gl/maps/HxHSBawfiDB2
220 Rose Ave, Venice, CA 90291
rosecafevenice.com
(310) 399-0711
This great coffee shop serves pastries, sandwiches, and salads too. Coffee is strong and dark, the way I like it. The feeling is definitely artsy. They have both indoor and outdoor seating. This place has been here for years and is very popular. It's probably the best breakfast place in this end of town.

Venice Boardwalk

https://goo.gl/maps/GG8k5qAToPo
1800 Ocean Front Walk, Venice, CA 90291
laparks.org
(310) 396-6764
This is where all the crazy people skateboard and rollerblade and walk along the beach front. There are tons of small shops and stands, selling lots of t-shirts and souvenirs and fake Rolex watches. There are lots of food stands of varying price and quality. On weekends there are tons of people. It's a little quieter on weekdays. At night the area is totally deserted and feels a little creepy.

The ocean front path goes right along the boardwalk, and it's an easy walk or bike ride from Santa Monica. This is probably one of the most fun things to do in Santa Monica, and should definitely be on your "bucket list". In the morning it's empty, but by lunch time it will be full of people.

On the Waterfront Cafe

https://goo.gl/maps/KEG553dNpgv

205 Ocean Front Walk, Venice, CA 90291

waterfrontcafe.com

(310) 392-0322

This pleasant beach cafe serves beer and Swiss specialties such as Rosti, which is the Swiss version of hash browns. The beers served here are Swiss too. Beers are half price at happy hour, which is a great deal. There is a small beer garden on one side of the shop. Indoors in the back they have a pool table and lots of seating. My German speaking friends like to come here. There is a rumor that they have lost their lease and will be closing soon. Unfortunate.

Sidewalk Cafe

https://goo.gl/maps/s9cVigD4gf82

1401 Ocean Front Walk, Venice, CA 90291

thesidewalkcafe.com

(310) 399-5547

This fun restaurant with a red and white canopy is located right in the middle of the Venice Boardwalk area. They serve sandwiches and salads and other American fare. There is a bar in the back with a full drink menu and happy hour specials. The food is not all that special but it would be hard to find a nicer spot to eat down on the boardwalk. Parking is near impossible. But still, the location makes this one of the best places on the beach.

Small World Bookstore

https://goo.gl/maps/jun454X9CFU2

1407 Ocean Front Walk, Venice, CA 90291

smallworldbooks.com

(310) 399-2360

This excellent small bookstore is almost completely hidden by the Sidewalk Cafe, but if you look over on the right side (south) you will see the entrance. Inside, an excellent collection of books. Bookstores are a rarity these days, especially really good ones like this one.

Groundwork Coffee

https://goo.gl/maps/LcuiNRMawiA2

3 Westminster Ave, Venice, CA 90291

groundworkcoffee.com

(310) 450-4540

This shop serves coffee beverages to early risers along the Venice Boardwalk. They also sell beans by the pound. Quality is very good. There is no place to sit inside, but there are a couple of tables out front. We come here sometimes to practice guitar. The wave sounds from the beach sort of absorb the noise so it doesn't bother anybody and the coffee is good. Groundwork has several other coffee stands in the area.

Food Court

There are several good takeout restaurants in the alley across from Groundwork Coffee. There's slice pizza and Indian food and el Huarique for Peruvian, and several other choices. All are fairly cheap and good. I'm partial to the Indian. If I were on the beach looking for something cheap to eat, this is where I would go.

https://goo.gl/maps/aWxonQpW4GQ2

Food Court

1301 Ocean Front Walk, Venice, CA 90291

(310) 450-5408

Figtree Cafe

https://goo.gl/maps/YvvtV6jn1Wz

429 Ocean Front Walk, Venice, CA 90291

figtreescafe.com

(310) 392-4937

This small cafe serves omelets and other food right down in front of the boardwalk. It's a fun place but hard to reach except on foot, there's no parking here.

Green Doctors

https://goo.gl/maps/fSEHwK6WR562

2007 Ocean Front Walk, Venice, CA 90291

thegreendoctors.com

(310) 985-2233

One of several spots offering medical marijuana along the Venice Boardwalk. I've never bought anything but it's said to be pretty easy. Legalization is coming soon, and licenses will become obsolete.

Venice Alehouse

https://goo.gl/maps/Uq9M5gjf6ZE

22 Rose Ave, Venice, CA 90291

venicealehouse.com

(310) 314-8253

This popular pub on the Venice Boardwalk offers a wide selection of beers in a peasant atmosphere. Excellent location for watching rollerbladers on the boardwalk.

Mao's Kitchen

https://goo.gl/maps/BeNLDgtwypP2

1512 Pacific Ave, Venice, CA 90291

maoskitchen.com

This moderately priced Chinese place has killer lunch combinations. My friend Reinhold says it's absolutely his favorite Chinese restaurant ever.

Taco Trucks

LA is the home of the Taco truck. They have become so popular that they have them in Mexico City now, though they appear to have been imported from California.

Isla Bonita Taco Truck

https://goo.gl/maps/iU8hiuwXJPN2

400 Rose Ave, Venice, CA 90291

(310) 699-8575

This truck parks near the Rose Café. Their tacos are awesome. Shrimp, beef or chicken. They make tostadas and other favorites too. Everything is good.

My friend Rahm had the Isla Bonita truck cater his wedding. They parked the truck in his driveway, and he just told the guests to order anything they wanted, and he'd pay for it. He promised a minimum of about $300. This turned out much cheaper than a regular caterer, and all the food was fresh cooked, instead of delivered in Aluminum trays, the way caterers usually do. It confirmed his opinion that this is the best taco truck in the area.

Bootleg Taco Stand

https://goo.gl/maps/pzWpm1oGuHK2
853 CA-1, Venice, CA 90291
This stand is located on Lincoln near Brooks, about halfway between Rose and Venice.
They have small but tasty tacos for $1. Everybody likes this place. Asada, pastor, they have all the usual choices. Quesadillas and burritos are good. Very good place and very cheap.

La Oaxaqueña Taco Truck

This taco truck is usually found at the intersection of Lincoln and Rose, near Casa Blanca and La Cabana. Their tacos are about $2. They have many types of meat, as well as tortas and burritos. The food seems decent, but they did get a C in their health inspection. La Cabana got an A but it costs twice as much. Your choice.

Leos Taco Truck (Hollywood)

https://goo.gl/maps/MbndX94cuhy
1515 S La Brea Ave, Los Angeles, CA 90019
leostacostruck.com
(323) 346-2001
Solid taco stand in Hollywood. Popular and inexpensive. Open late.

Marina Del Rey

Costco Wholesale (Food Court)

https://goo.gl/maps/48eTbjVY2Ss
13463 Washington Blvd, Marina Del Rey, CA 90292
costco.com
(310) 754-2003
Nothing at Costco Food Court is a home run, and yet, everyone loves it.

The pizza is cheap and hot and fresh and good.
Hot dogs are always a favorite.
Salads are actually pretty great.
Coke is the same as anywhere, but comes in industrial sized cups.
You have to have realistic expectations. This is not Wolfgang Puck.
Ever seen a Costco food court with no line?

Costco Wholesale (Store)

https://goo.gl/maps/48eTbjVY2Ss
13463 Washington Blvd, Marina Del Rey, CA 90292
costco.com
(310) 754-2003

Costco is the original big box store. Everything is delivered in restaurant sized packs. You want toilet paper - you get about a hundred rolls in one package. You want sausages? There will be fifty bratwursts in a pack.

Even though the sizes are large, not everything is cheap. There are a few really good deals however.

Gas is cheaper than anyplace else.

$5 roast chickens are an unbeatable deal.

Prescription glasses, tires and name brand liquors are always inexpensive.

But what really makes this place work is the fact that everything they have is excellent quality.

To top it off, on weekends there are lots of free samples. Can't get enough of those free samples.

Costco Marina Del Rey

https://goo.gl/maps/48eTbjVY2Ss

13463 Washington Blvd, Marina Del Rey, CA 90292

costco.com

(310) 754-2003

I love Costco. The quality of products, brand name or house "Kirkland" brand, is always excellent. The cheeses, the meats, the wines, the ravioli are all fantastic. Everything comes in big containers. Even the shampoo comes in half gallon jugs, a little clumsy in the shower, but hey, that's what it's like if you buy your shampoo at Costco.

Gas at the Costco station is about fifty cents cheaper than any other gas station in the area.

Killer Shrimp

https://goo.gl/maps/udB93APcKEJ2

4211 Admiralty Way, Marina Del Rey, CA 90292

killershrimp.com

This restaurant specializes in New Orleans style shrimp and other similar dishes. It's very popular and the food is tasty. The specialty is shrimp in a soupy sauce with a little bit of pepper kick, suitable for dunking pieces of baguette bread. It's sooo good. Good happy hour too.

Cheesecake Factory Marina Del Rey

https://goo.gl/maps/HE1sAeGDqS82

4142 Vía Marina, Marina Del Rey, CA 90292

thecheesecakefactory.com

This very nice Cheesecake Factory location has a beautiful outdoor eating area with a fire pit, overlooking the Marina.

If you are not familiar with Cheesecake Factory, their menu is about the same anywhere. Almost everything on the menu, from Chinese Chicken Salad to Meatloaf to Cajun Pasta, is excellent. The cheesecake is a heart attack just waiting to happen, but it is so good. Portions are very large. Prices are not all that cheap, but by making good food and giving you a lot of it, they make you feel that you are getting a fair deal. This is a very crafty marketing scheme. Of all the Cheesecake Factories I've been to, this is the nicest one, because of the location.

Summer Concerts in Marina del Rey

https://goo.gl/maps/ThPssEWoook

Burton Chace Park, 13650 Mindanao Way, Marina del Rey, CA 90292

https://www.visitmarinadelrey.com/events/free-summer-concert-series/

The venue isn't that large, just a stage set up in one side of a park, with some small hills and grass around. It's not really laid out as well as it could be if it were a proper concert venue, but this is a park.

Families and friends gathered on blankets with lunches of cheese and bread, and loosely enforced liquor laws meant plenty of wine bottles too. Trader Joe's must do a pretty good business before these shows.

It was kind of like going to something at the Hollywood Bowl, but more informal, and free. The biggest problem is parking. I'd suggest taking a bike or parking someplace a couple of blocks away and walking. Walking half a mile would be a lot faster than dealing with the traffic jam trying to leave after a concert.

Malibu

This city of Malibu stretches on for about half an hour along PCH as you drive north. It's home to beaches, wilderness, and reclusive millionaires.

Cafe Habana Malibu

https://goo.gl/maps/WfzCtSTYCVH2
3939 Cross Creek Rd, Malibu, CA 90265
Located in: Santa Monica Mountains NRA
habana-malibu.com
(310) 317-0300

Fun restaurant and bar in the Malibu outdoor mall near the movie theater. Wednesday nights this place is jumping off, full of people starting around 10 pm for karaoke. Chips and beer are good, but most of the dinner items are a little on the pricy side. The karaoke is fun, but the rotation moves very slowly since the DJ often plays random dance songs in between singers. Which means you get about 4 songs per hour. Which means as a singer you won't get a second song in until the end of the night, if then. But we always have a lot of fun.

Rosenthal Wine Bar & Patio

https://goo.gl/maps/ueF5yCNdKht
18741 Pacific Coast Hwy, Malibu, CA 90265
rosenthalestatewines.com
(310) 456-1392

Great outdoor wine garden on PCH just past Topanga Canyon, across the highway from the beach. Rosenthal makes great wines you can sample indoors at the bar or outdoors in the wine garden. On sunny days best to grab one of the tables with an umbrella. Everyone is very friendly, and sitting outside with a nice glass of wine on a sunny day is really nice.

Dukes

https://goo.gl/maps/sKWhXES3uFG2
21150 Pacific Coast Hwy, Malibu, CA 90265
dukesmalibu.com
(310) 317-0777

This beach front restaurant has one of the nicest view anywhere in the area. Sure, the food is the same as anywhere else, the drinks expensive, and parking difficult unless you opt for valet, but if you are in from out of town this is a place you should not miss. You just can't beat this location.

Moonshadows

https://goo.gl/maps/63swswFZG4C2
20356 Pacific Coast Hwy, Malibu, CA 90265
moonshadowsmalibu.com
(310) 456-3010

Very nice each front bar and restaurant. You don't come here for the food, you come for the view. It's very nice.

Nobu

https://goo.gl/maps/2MLxwxzUEU92
22706 Pacific Coast Highway, Malibu, CA 90265
noburestaurants.com
(310) 317-9140
Fancy California style sushi joint featuring food for the stars, star wanna-be's and those who don't mind paying. Nice view, high prices, doesn't seem very Japanese at all..

Malibu Beach Inn (Restaurant)

22878 Pacific Coast Hwy, Malibu, CA 90265
malibubeachinn.com
(800) 462-5428
The restaurant in this hotel is right up on the beach. They are close to the Malibu Pier. The view is magnificent, the food good, and the prices not too bad, considering it is a tourist destination. We often bring out of town guests here for brunch. Parking can often be found on PCH if you don't mind dodging fast moving traffic as you cross the road.

Malibu Pier

https://goo.gl/maps/awMGgccugFS2
23000 Malibu Pier, Malibu, CA 90265
malibupier.org
If you're driving through Malibu, this park is a good place to stop.

Built in 1905, the Malibu Pier is located in the city of Malibu, about 20 minutes north of Santa Monica off PCH. The pier isn't really used for boats, but is intended as a place for tourists and local residents to walk and enjoy the view and the fresh sea air.

There are a couple of restaurants on the pier, which are good, but generally priced for tourists. The food choices are better than the Santa Monica Pier, but it's still a bit like eating at Disneyland. The "Malibu Pier Cafe" at the end is popular.

The Pier is free, as is the beach all along the coast.

Malibu Country Mart Mall

https://goo.gl/maps/J8GQo5Fqw662
3835 Cross Creek Rd, Malibu, CA 90265
malibucountrymart.com
This low key outdoor mall has some shops, a Starbucks, a small two screen local theater, and restaurants ranging from medium to high priced. We come down here on Wednesdays once in a while for Karaoke at Cafe Habana or to have happy hour at Marmalade. The theaters are fun. The mall is located across PCH from the Malibu Lagoon and a short walk from the Malibu Colony.

Malibu Lagoon Park

https://goo.gl/maps/xv5qsAS2U412
23200 Pacific Coast Hwy & Cross Creek Rd
Malibu, CA 90263

parks.ca.gov

Located across from the outdoor Malibu mall has wetlands, parking, beach access, and public access to the Malibu Colony beach.

Malibu Colony

https://goo.gl/maps/QTuFA2CJwMC2

Malibu Colony Rd, Malibu, CA 90265

This is a swanky gated community on the beach side of Malibu about half an hour north of Santa Monica just past the Malibu Lagoon Park. The houses are not particularly big and the lots are small, so in other areas this would not be considered luxury, but the neighborhood is full of movie stars, so it is super exclusive.

You can't go in the gates, but by state law everyone has the right to walk along the beach. So, you can enter the colony by walking in from either end along the beach.

Article X, Section 4 of the California State Constitution states:

No individual, partnership, or corporation, claiming or possessing the frontage of tidal lands of a harbor, bay, inlet, estuary, or other navigable water in this State, shall be permitted to exclude the right of way to such water whenever it is required for any public purpose, nor to destroy or obstruct free navigation of such water; and the Legislature shall enact such laws as will give the most liberal construction to this provision so that access to the navigable water of this State shall always be attainable for the people thereof.

California law also defines all land below the "mean high tide" line to be public property. In plain English this means you have an uncontestable right to walk on the wet sand anywhere on the beach. Any security guards or barking dogs who tell you different, are in error.

Under Section 30211 of the Coastal Act, the public's right of access is over the sand and beach up to the line of "terrestrial vegetation".

So, if you feel like walking up the beach, you have the law on your side, and if someone puts up a fence, they are violating the law, not you.

Most enter from Malibu Lagoon State Beach.

I've been up and down the beach at Malibu Colony as a guest of one of the residents, and honestly, the beach is better in Santa Monica.

Pavilions Malibu

https://goo.gl/maps/WDmqkWPTF9G2

29211 Heathercliff Rd, Malibu, CA 90265

local.pavilions.com

Located in the Point Dume Shopping Center, this is a good place to stock up on food or beverages if you are headed for the beach.

Point Dume

https://goo.gl/maps/SL98NjmDeCH2

Cliffside Dr. & Birdview Ave, Malibu, CA 90265

ohp.parks.ca.gov

If you have ever seen the original "Planet of the apes" movie, the end, where the hero sees the Statue of Liberty half submerged in the Pacific Ocean, was filmed at Point Dume. I have never really understood how the Statue of Liberty is supposed to have moved from New York to Malibu, but I loved the movie, and it's a wonderful beach.

Point Dume is at the far end of Malibu from Santa Monica. It takes about 45 minutes to drive here along PCH, even if traffic is clear. It's another twenty minutes past the Malibu Pier. On a Saturday or Sunday morning when the weather is nice, the drive will take longer and parking will be difficult.

There are a couple of restaurants with appropriate happy hours along the beach

The beach is absolutely beautiful. It's one of the nicest beaches in Southern California.

There is a misconception among many people that the water at Point Dume or other Malibu beaches is cleaner than the water in Santa Monica. Not true. The reason is that in Malibu they use septic tanks, while Santa Monica has a sewer treatment plant which cleans up water flow.

Picnics are allowed but fire and alcohol are not. You can bring your own food and beverages. There is a small shopping center with a Vons grocery store about a half mile up PCH towards town, where you can buy anything you might want.

There are some nice trails for walking around the point and the hills behind it.

In theory it's open only during daylight hours, but on a practical basis there are no particular opening times or fees required for entrance to this park.

Zuma Beach

https://goo.gl/maps/ZJytYk1YfaL2
30000 PCH, Malibu, CA 90265
ohp.parks.ca.gov
Just beyond Pt. Dume is Zuma Beach, a legendary surfing location and wide sandy beach. It's walking distance from Pt. Dume.

Leo Carrillo State Park

https://goo.gl/maps/eApLemjSsp82
35000 Pacific Coast Hwy, Malibu, CA 90265
parks.ca.gov
This is another place to visit the beach, just past Pt. Dume. Really nice. A great beach, parking, dog friendly zones, and interesting caves to explore.

Rock Store

https://goo.gl/maps/exRnLuBVrxo
30354 Mulholland Hwy, Cornell, CA 91301
rock-store.com
(818) 889-1311
Technically this is close to Malibu. It's located at the far end of Mulholland Drive from Hollywood. It's a popular motorcycle ride. At the end is this little BBQ and beer joint with a few outdoor tables, called the "Rock Store". On a Sunday you will see hundreds of Harleys lined up, with their owners milling around. I have never seen more polished chrome. Fun. People are nice. Motorcycle not required.

West LA

Diddy Riese Cookies

https://goo.gl/maps/S9YVafELmow
926 Broxton Ave, Los Angeles, CA 90024
diddyriese.com
(310) 208-0448
This chocolate chip cookie restaurant in Westwood near the entrance to UCLA, is very popular with students. The cookies are amazingly good and very inexpensive. That's why there is nearly always a line.

When I was at UCLA, cookies were 25 cents. Ice cream sandwiches with two cookies and a scoop were a dollar. I understand everything has gone up to three for a dollar on the cookies and $1.75 for the ice cream sandwich.

One of my friends is convinced they are a front for money laundering. You know, an all cash business. How else could they be making any money with prices like this?

This place is the best cookie shop in town.

Versailles

https://goo.gl/maps/DLbcKTKNeMU2
10319 Venice Blvd, Los Angeles, CA 90034

versaillescuban.com

(310) 558-3168

The specialty of this Cuban restaurant is chicken with fried bananas, rice and beans. Versailles is the name of a palace in Paris, which has nothing to do with the style of the food they serve here. They have other Cuban specialties such as Ropa Vieja, but the chicken is so good you will always wish that is what you had ordered. There are a couple of branches around Culver City and Hollywood.

Galbi King

https://goo.gl/maps/hk7FtKFSHmA2

11267 National Blvd, Los Angeles, CA 90064

(310) 477-6075

Galbi King is the best (onliest) AYCE KBBQ on the westside. If you are not familiar, AYCE is "All You Can Eat" and this means they keep bringing on the plates of marinated meats to throw on the grill.

We come here periodically for Birthdays when it seems too much trouble to drive out to Soot Bull Jeep or Road to Seoul or one of our other K-town favorites.

Recently they bumped the price up from about $17 to $20. The meat improved at the same time so I guess this is ok.

We always have a fun time here.

If you are looking for AYCE KBBQ in Santa Monica/West LA then this is the place to go.

There is a 5% cash discount. They take credit cards, but don't like them much.

Cafe 50's

https://goo.gl/maps/TwMm6dWgtyS2

11623 Santa Monica Blvd, Los Angeles, CA 90025

cafe50s.com

(310) 479-1955

This 50s style diner is part of a chain of about ten similar places, all offering excellent burgers fries shakes omelets and salads. Solid breakfasts.

The shakes are made with ice cream by hand and are very good. That's probably the best thing on the menu. The coffee is like what you get at Denny's, which is not all that great, but pie ala mode makes up for it. Burgers and sandwiches are all great. Good Monte Cristo. The jukebox plays continuous 50 hits; the kind of stuff they had on the soundtrack to American Graffiti. Waiters and waitresses are friendly.

I personally love the 50s music and the crazy posters and articles on the wall. If you like that kind of thing, you'll like this place.

MOD Pizza

https://goo.gl/maps/xJupa7SXwsk

8985 Venice Blvd k, Los Angeles, CA 90034

modpizza.com

(424) 345-9282

MOD offers a thin crust personal pizza, about ten inches in diameter, covered with pretty much whatever you want, for one price, currently $7.17, with no additional charge for toppings. This branch is located on Venice near where it crosses the 10 freeway. There is another branch on Rosecrantz down by the airport.

The great thing is, everyone in your group can get exactly what they want, no more having to negotiate compromise topping choices and no more asking the guys making the pizza if they can make one side vegetarian and the other side Canadian bacon and pineapple. Get your own pizza. No compromise.

They have a number of specialty pizzas, but I mostly ignore these because you can get whatever you want anyway, and the price remains the same.

Last time we went, my brother got a white pizza with tomato and basil and sausage, which was pretty good, though I usually order with tomato sauce instead of white sauce.

My friend Mike got sausage, pepperoni and meatballs, mozzarella and tomato sauce. Very nice.

I ordered every kind of cheese and every kind of pork. It was pretty good, but I think if I got this again I would leave off the blue cheese. I like the parmesan and asiago and mozzarella and I love blue cheese too, but the blue cheese was overpowering. Anyway, it was a nice pizza.

Reasonable prices, inexpensive drinks, comfortable eating area, tasty thin crust pizzas with unlimited topping, what's not to like?

Furaibo

https://goo.gl/maps/fXVxiVd9xCv

2068 Sawtelle Blvd, Los Angeles, CA 90025

(310) 444-1432

This authentic yakitori shop serves skewers, rice balls, noodles, grilled fish and beer. Good stuff. Individual food items are not all that expensive, but the bill can add up quickly. The back door behind the bathrooms is a side entrance into Karaoke Blue.

Karaoke Blue

https://goo.gl/maps/N29P3hZfNSu

2064 Sawtelle Blvd, Los Angeles, CA 90025

karaokebleu.com

(310) 477-4794

Karaoke originally came from Japan, and this is a place where you can try it Japanese style. It used to be that everyone here could speak Japanese, but that's not true any more. The sound system is a little bit funky, so here are some suggestions: don't try to follow the timing queues of the music, they are often a little bit off and can get you very confused. Also, step out of the stage area if you want to get a better sense of what the sound is like. This is a fun place. If you prefer karaoke rooms you can try "Max Karaoke" down the street next to Nijiya.

Tsujita LA Artisan Noodle

https://goo.gl/maps/PeQxEwRSTR82

2057 Sawtelle Blvd, Los Angeles, CA 90025

tsujita-la.com

(310) 231-7373

Located in the middle of a long row of Japanese and other Asian restaurants on Sawtelle in West LA, this restaurant offers some really good Ramen. The specialty here is Ramen with tasty dipping soup, instead of the large bowls of noodles in the soup which is the more traditional style. Many consider it the best in town. My only complaint is that it is a little bit on the expensive side for noodle soup. But it's very good.

Kitchen Story

https://goo.gl/maps/jXCVawyt1C32
2129 Sawtelle Blvd, Los Angeles, CA 90064
kitchenstoryla.com
(310) 444-9955
If you like Kimchee Fried Rice, then this place on Sawtelle is for you. If not, there are about 1500 fun restaurants within walking distance along Sawtelle north of Olympic. You are sure to find something you will like.

Kitchen story specializes in Kimchee Fried rice but they do have a number of other things on the menu. Everything comes with Banchan, the traditional Korean side dishes familiar to anyone who haunts the AYCE spots in Koreatown.

The place is clean and new and friendly and the food is good. What's not to like?

Tatsu Ramen

https://goo.gl/maps/SQW2YLmYzF22
2123 Sawtelle Blvd, Los Angeles, CA 90025
tatsuramen.com
(310) 684-2889
Tasty Ramen on Sawtelle. They have lots of options and a kind of a trendy hi tech vibe. Worth trying if you haven't seen it. Noodles are good. One of many good Japanese places along Sawtelle.

Daiso Japan

https://goo.gl/maps/Gs1UmtSTeVU2
2130 Sawtelle Blvd, Los Angeles, CA 90025
daisoglobal.com
(424) 276-2882
I used to live in Tokyo, and I used to go to the "99 Yen Store". Daiso is the American version of the 99 Yen Store. It's inspired by the original "99 Cent Store", but it's so much cooler.

They have knives and pots and chalkboards and goofy looking plastic fashion accessories. A walk through Daiso will provide at least a half hour of mirth, and you might even find something you like.

Nothing here is expensive. Most things start at about a dollar and a half. I don't think they have anything over about ten dollars.

If you haven't been to Daiso, you owe it to yourself to check it out. There are other branches downtown and in San Gabriel.

Kula Sushi

https://goo.gl/maps/TygptSxTLY22
2130 Sawtelle Blvd #111, Los Angeles, CA 90025
kulausa.com

This is currently one of the most popular restaurants in the Japanese neighborhood on Sawtelle. They serve conveyor belt sushi. You take whatever you like from the conveyor belt, and at the end they count the plates and figure your bill. You can also order specialty custom-made items, and the conveyor belt system shoots in right over to you. Forget places like Nobu, this is the real deal.

If you come anytime in the evening, any day of the week, there is a half hour to an hour wait to get in. That's the sign that it's a good place. Prices are very reasonable.

Nijiya Market

https://goo.gl/maps/oLHpAVfSAT12
2130 Sawtelle Blvd # 105, Los Angeles, CA 90025
nijiya.com
(310) 575-3300
This fun Japanese grocery store has a surprisingly large selection of delicious Japanese food items, from sushi grade fish to ramen. They also often have stands in front selling fresh made squid pancakes, grilled octopus balls, friend noodles, and other authentic Japanese lunch items. There are a hundred or so good Asian restaurants on this block and the next. This is a good place. Recommended.

Marukai Market

https://goo.gl/maps/oJ8k6oEh2eq
12121 W Pico Blvd, Los Angeles, CA 90064
marukai.com
(310) 806-4120
A couple of blocks away from Nijiya is Marukai, a full on Japanese supermarket. Selection and quality are good. They also have a large selection of take-out food. Membership card is free at the cash register, if you ask. Free parking in back. This is a good place. Recommended.

Best Buy

https://goo.gl/maps/o517wk5DT3q
11301 W Pico Blvd, Los Angeles, CA 90064
stores.bestbuy.com
(310) 268-9190
This chain electronics store will be handy if you need anything for your tv, phone, or computer. They also have cameras and games. They will often price match online offers, so do your research before you go in the store.

Tommys Hamburgers

https://goo.gl/maps/REYvM3wxNK82

11289 W Pico Blvd, Los Angeles, CA 90064

(310) 479-0601

Located at the corner of Sawtelle and Pico, this fast food chili burger stand offers good value and tasty food, assuming you like chiliburgers. There are all sorts of chili burger stands all over southern california, often with the name "Tom" in them, though they may or may not be members of one or another chains. This one is good as any. It's a very LA thing. Open 24 hours. This kind of food is best after a late night out.

Tacomiendo

https://goo.gl/maps/YnSQKHNFSEt

11462 Gateway Blvd, Los Angeles, CA 90064

tacomiendo.net

(310) 481-0804

Tacomiendo is bare bones as a restaurant; looks like a fast food place or maybe a Tommy's, but the food is GOOD. You order at the window up front and a little while later they bring the food to you. Tacos, burritos, carne asada sandwiches are all excellent and cheap. I think these folks use a little better meat than a lot of the local taco trucks. Milkshakes and desserts are good too.

I think they rely mostly on a lunch business, people who work in local car repair places and shops come by on their break.

I have been to this place at least a dozen times and it's always been really good.

Gyu-Kaku Japanese BBQ

https://goo.gl/maps/9Hj9KmUwoWu

10925 W Pico Blvd, Los Angeles, CA 90064

gyu-kaku.com

(310) 234-8641.

This is a Japanese chain that makes Korean BBQ for Japanese taste, which means, less spicy, but nice meat and fish. They have gas grills at the table and you cook it yourself. The food is really fantastic.

The restaurant itself is long and narrow, probably only about twelve feet wide, with most of the tables on the sides of a long aisle running the length of the restaurant. Bench seats on one side, chairs on the other, BBQ grills in the middle of the table. It's clean and nice though not terribly fancy.

Gyukaku has "happy hour" specials on many of the meats and drinks. It's almost always happy hour except 6:30-9:30 in the evening. The items seem cheap but they add up quickly and we always end up spending more than we planned to because everything is so good.

Overall, this place is excellent. I have gone there many times and it's always fun

Reservations recommended during happy hour. Sometimes they are pretty full and it's not that big a place and I hate to wait in line.

Casa Sanchez

https://goo.gl/maps/f5CSdChmY892

4500 S Centinela Ave, Los Angeles, CA 90066

casa-sanchez.com

(310) 397-9999

This fun night spot features Mariachi music and good Mexican food. They specialize in in birthdays and "Quinceneras" or wedding parties, but in fact it's fun anytime. The crowd is mostly upscale and much Spanish is spoken.

Fox Studio Commissary

https://goo.gl/maps/WEzZVK3niT62

10201 W Pico Blvd, Los Angeles, CA 90064

foxstudios.com

(310) 369-1000

This is the cafeteria on the Fox movie lot. They have a guard at the gate, but the general public will be admitted for screenings and other occasions.

If you find yourself on the lot, try the commissary. The sandwiches are incredible, especially the club with fries.

There is a good chance for celebrity sightings, but be cool and try to pretend you don't see them, because that's the LA thing, always trying to spot celebrities, and then pretend not to care.

Last time, I was there on the lot to on a Sunday to see "12 Years a Slave", which was great. Chiwetel Ejiofor (the main star) and Lupita Nyong'o (Patsy) where there and spoke afterwards.

I enjoyed the movie immensely.

As to the commissary next door, there was not a soul there, except for a cleaning crew waxing the floors.

If you do hit it on a day when it's open, the Club Sandwich is the best in town.

Records Surplus

https://goo.gl/maps/DgM65exJTTC2

12436 Santa Monica Blvd, Los Angeles, CA 90025

recordsurplusla.com

(310) 979-4577

Fun local used record shop serving Santa Monica and West LA. Lots of good stuff here.

Hollywood

Chateau Marmont

https://goo.gl/maps/A3yRtyQZZVx

8221 Sunset Blvd, Hollywood, CA 90046

chateaumarmont.com

(323) 656-1010

This hotel, located just up the hill from the Sunset Strip, is where John Belushi overdosed and died. It's famous for star sightings, and a bit on the pricey side.

Canter's Deli

https://goo.gl/maps/Duyf1itZEUm

419 N Fairfax Ave, Los Angeles, CA 90036

cantersdelila.com

(323) 651-2030

This Hollywood fixture is probably the most famous of all the local delis. Reliable sandwiches and other traditional deli food. Moderately priced.

El Coyote

https://goo.gl/maps/Qp4bJpuDxjt

7312 Beverly Blvd, Los Angeles, CA 90036

elcoyotecafe.com

(323) 939-2255

The food is mediocre at this Mexican restaurant, but the happy hour margaritas are cheap, and it's a bit of a Hollywood fixture. It's been famous since the 1940's. They say this is where Lana Turner had her last meal before she was killed in an unfortunate car accident.

Los Angeles Zoo & Botanical Gardens

https://goo.gl/maps/L9vkUWvujdG2

5333 Zoo Dr, Los Angeles, CA 90027

lazoo.org

(323) 644-4200
I love the Los Angeles Zoo.
Everyone talks about the San Diego Zoo but I prefer this one. There are lots of animals to see, the setting is informal, and it's much closer too.
The San Diego Zoo is a little too much of a Disneyland experience for my taste. I mean, it's fun too, but we have our own zoo here in LA and it is highly under-rated.
On a typical afternoon it will be filled with families enjoying the animals and quality time together.

Peninsula Hotel

https://goo.gl/maps/YRgrQkUrePn
9882 S Santa Monica Blvd, Beverly Hills, CA 90212
peninsula.com
(310) 551-2888
The bar of this Beverly Hills hotel is famous for overdressed ladies of casual virtue looking to pick up middle eastern millionaires, but still, it's fun. Many people love to come here for afternoon "tea" with snacks. The hotel is very nice.

Magic Castle

https://goo.gl/maps/F7eSGLskvex
7001 Franklin Ave, Los Angeles, CA 90028
magiccastle.com
If you like magic, then you're going to love Magic Castle. It's an old Victorian house at the base of the Hollywood hills, run by a local Magic club.

Inside you can wander from room to room, and see various magic shows, ranging from full on stage shows with theatrical seating, to small demonstrations by individual magicians. All the musicians are amazing, and the entire place is incredible good fun.

They have a restaurant here but that's not really why people come. The food is adequate, but it's the entire experience that makes the trip worthwhile.

Entrances usually by invitation. If you're in Los Angeles, almost everybody knows somebody who is a member of the Magic Castle and can get you tickets. Otherwise, your best bet is to call them well in advance and see what you can arrange. It's usually possible to work something out, though they may offer you a reservation on an off day for an off time.

The Magic Castle a super big fun and is totally recommended.

Cafe Club Fais Do-Do

https://goo.gl/maps/S5v2XFA48a12
5257 W Adams Blvd, Los Angeles, CA 90016
faisdodo.com
(323) 931-4636
Fun venue with lots of crazy and unusual events. Acrobats and jugglers and music. The show varies, so check the schedule. Parts of the building are a little tired and could use some fresh paint, and the beer isn't cheap, but the events are what make this place fun.

Guelaguetza

https://goo.gl/maps/iyYrxqAYdKm

3014 W Olympic Blvd, Los Angeles, CA 90006

ilovemole.com

This Oaxacan style Mexican restaurant specializes in mole.

The standard black mole is a sauce made from chile and chocolate, but it is not sweet at all. There are other kinds of mole too. They have red mole, yellow mole, green mole, and other flavors too. You can even buy mole to take home in jars at the desk in the front of the restaurant by the entrance.

Guelaguetza used to be a very large Chinese restaurant, which explains the exterior with the funky pagoda style tiled roof.

Some evenings they have live music, which can be either really fun or super annoying depending on how you feel about mariachis and Latin music. Once the music starts it's hard to have a conversation.

Food here is very good. If you like mole, this is the place.

Bouchon

https://goo.gl/maps/TQAAMo7Z57y

235 N. Canon Drive, Beverly Hills, CA 90210

thomaskeller.com

Celebrity chef restaurant in Beverly Hills. They are famous for French bistro cuisine, and have a nice happy hour.

Directors Guild of America Cinema

https://goo.gl/maps/tKrZ1rryhBD2

7920 Sunset Blvd, Los Angeles, CA 90046

dga.org

(310) 289-2000

The DGA has a couple of the nicest theaters in town. Comfortable seating, clean, super sound system and the copies they show of films are usually perfect. Plus, nearly always free. What's not to like?

Unfortunately, screenings are often for members only.

I was down there a while ago for a screening of "American Sniper". Bradley Cooper and Clint Eastwood showed up afterwards to discuss the film.

Great fun. Great place.

Merkato Ethiopian Restaurant & Market

https://goo.gl/maps/JPTYV5WoveR2

1036 1/2 S Fairfax Avenue, Los Angeles, CA 90019

merkatorestaurant.com

(323) 935-1775

Merkato is located on Fairfax up the street from Canter's Deli, where Ethiopian restaurants line both sides of the road for several blocks. All of these places are pretty good, but Merkato stands out as one of the best.

Merkato itself is kind of a hole in the wall place, or maybe you could call it a double hole in the wall, since it occupies two small storefronts.

One side is the restaurant. The other side is a little shop selling spices, groceries, bottles of honey wine and various nick nacks. They have espresso and a full bar. You can even buy Awaze hot sauce and raw green coffee, ready for roasting.

Typical Ethiopian food includes various types of stews, grilled or fried items, served on a big kind of a sourdough crepe, called Injera, made from a grain called Tef, which is kind of like buckwheat.

Ethiopians eat with their hands. The food is served on the crepe, and you eat everything. There's no silverware, even if you ask.

Ethiopians like raw beef, but most tourists (that's you and me) usually stick to the cooked stuff.

I did get up my nerve one time and asked a waitress if we could get just a tiny taste of the Kitfo (raw beef).

Our waitress smiled her brightest smile and said "sure".

A moment later she came out with a pork chop sized hunk of strip steak. Mmmm. Raw steak. Dull knife. Chewy chewy. Mmm. :-(

That was pretty funny, but on the whole the food is great.

Tip: If you take a group of four people, get three of the meat type stew dishes and one of the grilled trout. The trout are fairly big and come with a bunch of veggies, so then you have a full meal with the meats and the veggies and everything else.

If you have not been to Merkato, I strongly recommend it. It's one of my favorite restaurants in LA.

Pink's Hot Dogs

https://goo.gl/maps/qSNNQRCdVXr

709 N La Brea Ave, Los Angeles, CA 90038

pinkshollywood.com

(323) 931-4223

Pinks is a hot dog stand that often has a line an hour long.

I like a good hot dogs, but this is out of control. Sure, Pinks makes a good hot dog, really, a very nice hot dog, but I have trouble understanding why people are waiting in line.

Well, if you are in Hollywood and it's late, then Pinks will do just fine. At the end of the day, it is a good hot dog.

Philips BBQ Crenshaw

https://goo.gl/maps/2GA5xMN5Fty

2619 Crenshaw Blvd, Los Angeles, CA 90016

Menuplaces.singleplatform.com

Located on Crenshaw just off the 10 freeway, this restaurant does mainly a takeout business. They only have about two chairs and no tables.

The ribs are amazing. So are the tips, the beef, and the chicken. The sides, like mac, potato salad, and greens are also good.

I think it must have been a paycheck loan place before. The counter has bulletproof glass about 4 inches thick. They open a little glass door to take the money and hand you your barbecue.

Sometimes I also like to get some of their barbecue sauce to go. Then you can cook your own meat on the grill at home, and enjoy the spicy barbecue sauce from Phillips. It is so good.

Roscoe's Chicken and Waffles Manchester

https://goo.gl/maps/HCMR778iPty
621 W Manchester Blvd, Inglewood, CA 90301
roscoeschickenandwaffles.com

This is the iconic Chicken and Waffle restaurant. They have several branches around Hollywood and Inglewood. Lots of hipster places serve chicken and waffles, but this is the real deal. The inside looks like a diner that has slightly gone to seed, but the food is good.

The Grove

https://goo.gl/maps/QBrub8FBYcs
189 The Grove Dr, Los Angeles, CA 90036
thegrovela.com
(323) 900-8080

This very popular mall has provided a model for many other malls. It's always crowded and popular, at a time when many malls are on the decline. In fact, one study estimated that 20% of the nation's malls will close by the end of the decade. The Grove, on the other hand, remains busy. Many credit the open design, that give the mall more of the feel of a walkable medieval village instead of being an enclosed

Amoeba Records

https://goo.gl/maps/LYCiGdAamQN2
6400 Sunset Blvd, Los Angeles, CA 90028
amoeba.com
(323) 245-6400

New and used records, CD's, memorabilia in this enormous legendary music store. Definitely not to be missed, if you like music. Everyone who is anyone at all, or even wishes they were in the music business, they all shop here.

Farmer's Market

6333 W 3rd St, Los Angeles, CA 90036

farmersmarketla.com

(323) 933-9211

The name makes you think of a market where food growers come to peddle their merchandise, but this market is more like a food court, and the stands are permanent installations. It's fun, and many of the stands are quite good. It's adjacent to the Grove mall.

Hollywood Bowl

https://goo.gl/maps/HS3Q9q1wchA2

2301 N Highland Ave, Los Angeles, CA 90068

hollywoodbowl.com

Located on Cahuenga, the main road that runs from Hollywood over the hills up to the Valley, the Hollywood Bowl is a wonderful outdoor musical venue that has hosted famous shows from the Beatles to Monty Python. There is a fun show here almost every night.

Most of the seats in the Hollywood bowl are cement. They're not very comfortable, but it's a fantastic place for a picnic. Usually when we go out there, we swing by Trader Joe's and get a load of cheese, wine and French bread. The picnic will be big fun even if the concert itself is forgettable.

Parking at the Hollywood Bowl is a big problem. There's a big parking lot, with a lot of spaces, but it's expensive, and the biggest problem was at the end of the concert when it takes what seems like an hour or two to get out of the parking lot.

There are several solutions to this.

If you take a motorcycle or bicycle you can park most anywhere, and you can slip through the traffic and get out easily when the show is over.

There are shuttles that come up from several parking lots in Hollywood. This is what we usually do. The parking is cheap and the shuttles are free.

If you're in a hiking mood you could walk from Hollywood up to the Hollywood bowl without too much trouble.

In my opinion visiting the Hollywood Bowl is one of the most fun things you can do while visiting. It doesn't matter who is playing. Check it out. 100% recommended.

Hollywood Sign

https://goo.gl/maps/cpQ3aixF8LN2

Griffith Park, Los Angeles, CA 90068

hollywoodsign.org

(323) 258-4338

Located in the hills in Griffith Park, you can hike right up to the Hollywood Sign. Good photo op.

Beverly Center

8500 Beverly Blvd, Los Angeles, CA 90048
beverlycenter.com
(310) 854-0070
8500 Beverly Blvd, Los Angeles, CA 90048
beverlycenter.com
(310) 854-0070
This is probably the most popular mall in Hollywood. There are lots of shops and restaurants. The mall itself is the traditional enclosed style of mall, though many of the restaurants on the exterior open to the outside. The parking has a novel design where you go up a central track to the floor where you want to park, then look for a spot. This eliminates the continuous traffic jam found in most malls. On the downside, they charge about $1/hour for parking.

Sunset Strip

This short section of Sunset Boulevard in West Hollywood is famous for a small group of Rock and Roll clubs where countless famous bands like the Doors have played over the years. You can go in and check out the bands, or just cruise by in the evening and check out the Rock and Rollers.

Rainbow

https://goo.gl/maps/zxKoJgfVzCq
9015 Sunset Blvd, West Hollywood, CA 90069
rainbowbarandgrill.com
(310) 278-4232

Roxy

https://goo.gl/maps/uwTYLvdMZg42
9009 Sunset Blvd, West Hollywood, CA 90069
theroxy.com
(310) 278-9457

Whisky a Go Go

https://goo.gl/maps/RbvZx9N4YUq
8901 Sunset Blvd, West Hollywood, CA 90069
whiskyagogo.com
(310) 652-4202

Viper Room

https://goo.gl/maps/Cvf717peQF52
8852 Sunset Blvd, West Hollywood, CA 90069
viperroom.com
(310) 358-1881

Hollywood and Vine

https://goo.gl/maps/yLE15KNM6qQ2

This corner is considered unofficially to be the center of the Hollywood neighborhood. Misinformed tourists visit by the thousands every day expecting that they are going to see something of the Hollywood movie industry. There is no movie industry going on in this area. I've included addresses of the main movie studios elsewhere in this book and if you look at them you'll notice that none of them is close to Hollywood and Vine. You would do better in Burbank or Culver City.

When you do find is a gritty urban neighborhood, a nice mall, a big movie theater, frequent tour buses, and a bazillion tourist watering the sidewalks, taking pictures of each other and hoping they'll see somebody famous.

Hollywood Museum

https://goo.gl/maps/YPXe42hyrWC2

1660 N Highland Ave, Hollywood, CA 90028

thehollywoodmuseum.com

Originally this was a costume museum, but they have expanded with new material and so there are many props and other materials. If you like movie trivia then you are going to like this museum. Lots of cool stuff.

Walk of Fame

https://goo.gl/maps/BboUJA1Dqxm

N Highland Ave & Hollywood Blvd, Los Angeles, CA 90028

walkoffame.com

The walk of fame is a tourist attraction that was created in 1958 to fight urban blight and a loss of tourism to the central Hollywood area. There are about 2600 brass stars with the names of Hollywood personalities along 15 blocks of Hollywood Boulevard and three blocks of Vine Street. The initial construction of this site included about 1500 stars who were all installed at the same time. The project was initiated by the Hollywood Chamber of Commerce and paid for by a special tax assessment on businesses fronting the sidewalk. Government participation was challenged by businesses who didn't want to pay the assessment, and by stars such as Charlie Chaplin who were omitted from the list for political reasons. Chaplin eventually did get a star.

Currently, celebrities who wish to have stars on the Walk of Fame are charged $40,000 for installation and upkeep expenses.

Currently the most popular star is that of Donald Trump, at 6300 Hollywood Blvd, north side, between Highland and Orange. If you want to see it, it's free.

Wax Museum

https://goo.gl/maps/wNipoQKxpLz

6767 Hollywood Blvd, Los Angeles, CA 90028

hollywoodwaxmuseum.com

Chinese Theater

https://goo.gl/maps/tZnyK3hXSxC2

6925 Hollywood Blvd, Hollywood, CA 90028

tclchinesetheatres.com

Built in 1927, this famous Hollywood area theater was originally known as "Grauman's Chinese Theatre". As it has changed hands, each owner has enjoyed the opportunity to add their name to the theater. For a while it was called "Mann's Chinese". Now it is the "TCL Chinese Theater". The style is 1920's fake Chinese kitsch, the kind of thing that would probably earn political outrage if it were built today. The theater is famous more for being famous, than for anything in particular that ever happened here. In front are some of the stars of the "Walk of Fame". As you pass by you can cross it off your list, but there isn't really anything to do here unless you would like to see a movie.

Dolby Theater

https://goo.gl/maps/GMmza67tLGz

6801 Hollywood Blvd, Hollywood, CA 90028

dolbytheatre.com

(323) 308-6300

This new theater was built as part of the government funded revitalization of the Hollywood and Vine area. Originally it was called the Kodak Theater, but with their unfortunate bankruptcy in 2012, the name has passed to Dolby, the sound company. The theater is very nice, and is currently the spot used to film the Academy Awards (since 2002). The interior is done in very fancy old Hollywood style, with enclosed boxes along the sides and many curtains and chandeliers and decorations. In additional o the Academy Awards, this theater has also hosted the Cirque de Soleil, America's got Talent, and numerous musical acts on an ongoing basis.

Bar Sinister

https://goo.gl/maps/S82MCWwHRbT2

1652 N Cherokee Ave, Los Angeles, CA 90028

barsinister.net

(323) 462-1934

Goth bar with a whip-me-beat-me theme. Frequent stage shows. Schedule and the nature of the shows varies. If you want to visit something colorful, this might be for you. This club is legendary in certain circles.

The Avalon

https://goo.gl/maps/3s6YVu2rRdt

1735 Vine St, Los Angeles, CA 90028

avalonhollywood.com

(323) 462-8900

Electronic music dance club, open late. It used to be a theater. Lots of people and lots of lights.

Hollywood and Highland Center Mall

https://goo.gl/maps/ptS353YAfhx

6801 Hollywood Blvd #170, Los Angeles, CA 90028

hollywoodandhighland.com

This modest sized mall was built as part of a project to reclaim and revitalize central Hollywood. It has been built in the open style popular today with many other malls such as the Santa Monica Mall. The best thing here is that you can use their parking and ride the shuttle bus up to the Hollywood Bowl for shows.

Koreatown

https://goo.gl/maps/xFxyW4mi5VC2

This is the area directly to the east of Hollywood surrounding streets like Western and Vermont going north south and Melrose Santa Monica and Hollywood going east west. Los Angeles is rumored to have the largest Korean population outside of Korea itself.

Koreatown is actually one of the most ethnically diverse areas of LA, with half the residents being Latino and a third being Asian. Two-thirds of the residents were born outside of the United States, a high figure compared to the rest of the city. Large scale Korean immigration since the 1960's has led to some of the best food in the Los Angeles area, with the AYCE (All You Can Eat) Korean BBQ restaurants becoming a permanent fixture of the LA food scene.

Ambassador Hotel

https://goo.gl/maps/gT5Cvpjwqh52

Corner of Wilshire and Mariposa, Los Angeles C 900101

A landmark hotel it its own right, this hotel on Wilshire hit the national spotlight when Robert Kennedy was assassinated here in 1968. The Academy Awards were here in 1930, 1931, 1932, and 1934. The hotel was demolished in 2005 and is now an elementary school and park.

Wiltern Theatre

https://goo.gl/maps/EckacyY7B8U2
3790 Wilshire Blvd, Los Angeles, CA 90010
wiltern.com
(213) 388-1400
This 12-story, 155-foot (47 m) Art Deco landmark at the corner of Wilshire Boulevard and Western Avenue is one of the top musical venues in the LA area. Clad in a blue-green glazed architectural terra-cotta tile and situated diagonal to the street corner, the complex is an excellent examples of Art Deco architecture.

Soot Bull Jeep

https://goo.gl/maps/9m1yetAkdoE2
3136 W 8th St, Los Angeles, CA 90005
sootbulljeepla.com
This is our favorite KBBQ restaurant. It isn't all-you-can-eat, but the servings are large and you won't go hungry. Just order one meat dish per diner, and then share. My favorite is the spicy pork, but various cuts of marinated beef and ribs are good too. You get plenty of the sides and will be stuffed by the time you are done.

The thing that sets Soot Bull Jeep aside from most other KBBQ spots is charcoal on the grill. Sure, your clothes will come out smelling a bit smoky, but the taste of the food is the best.

Parking is a bit tight here. They do have a parking lot, but it's not huge.

Castle BBQ

https://goo.gl/maps/Rkq32eosEY12
473 N Western Ave, Los Angeles, CA 90004
(323) 467-3813
Castle Korean BBQ is famous for AYCE KBBQ for $11.99, and it's very popular.
You can tell right away when you pull in and see the parking lot stacked three deep with cars, no place to park, and a crowd of people milling around outside waiting to be seated. We came by at 3:00 hoping to beat the lunch and dinner rush, but it was busy even then.

Inside, it's a busy restaurant with maybe 30 grills going and lots of people enjoying really great dinners. A no-speak-English lady at the desk hands you one of those blinking beeper things and then we had some time to pass, looking at what the other tables were eating, waiting for our own seat. What I noticed was that all of the food looked good and everyone in the restaurant seemed to be really into enjoying the dinner.

The meats are more or less the same as you get at most other KBBQ places. Pork Belly, thin sliced beef of various varieties, pork chops, marinated chicken, bulgogi. If you are willing to shell out a couple extra bucks you can upgrade to the 'B' or 'C' plan which includes a few more items like tripe and shrimp. For me, the basic 'A' plan is fine.

Side dishes are great too. Tasty sprouts, kimchee, soup, salad, noodles etc.

Nothing here disappointed. Sure, the pork belly was a bit fatty, but that's the nature of pork belly. I liked that they simply placed the bottles of sauce on the table so you could refill you own dips. Service was great, these guys were really racing to keep up with the customers, but they were doing a heck of a job.

Paris Baguette

https://goo.gl/maps/Ny8NdFytoq62

3470 W 6th St, Los Angeles, CA 90020

parisbaguetteusa.com

(213) 384-0404

Paris Baguette is our go-to place for coffee and a pastry after lunch or dinner in Koreatown.

The pastries here are French style, with an Asian sensibility. Chocolate croissants, various filled pastries, fruit pastries, baguettes, all are reliably good and most under $2. They also make a variety of cakes.

Coffee is generally good, and goes well with the pastries.

This place is always busy, with customers that skew towards college age or young twenties.

If you compare to a place like Kiki bakery, Paris Baguette breads are less sweet and a little harder in texture.

They do a lot of take-out but they also have places to sit.

Located in a very popular strip mall between Wilshire and 6th, they share a crowded parking lot with 7-11 and a number of other restaurants. There's a valet guy out front who can always find you a spot, and the parking charge is only a dollar or so, worth it instead of driving around the block 100 times trying to find parking.

Paris Baguette has locations in a couple of other areas, which I understand are similar.

I've been here quite a few times, and will be back.

Road To Seoul

https://goo.gl/maps/KX3AepZURdq

1230 S Western Ave, Los Angeles, CA 90006l-3108

(323) 731-9292

Road to Seoul is a big noisy all-you-can-eat Korean BBQ place on Western, where there is much competition for the AYCE crowd.

We came in for my birthday on Saturday. It was 6:00 but the place was filling up fast. They had a sign out that said nobody could be seated until everyone arrived, and my friends aren't all the most punctual bunch, at least not for Saturday dinner, so it started to look like it was going to be a problem.

Somehow we talked our way in and started ordering plates of food.

Road to Seoul is decorated in rustic dark stained pine, with long tables and gas fired BBQ where you can cook the food. There are two lists, one for $18 and one for $22. We got the cheaper set, it's way enough.

The waiters were running back and forth, with platters of sirloin and bulgogi and bottles of wine and soju and little bowls of banchan side dishes like kimchi and bean noodles.

Everything was pretty good.

The wait staff seemed to be behind all the time. They were smiling and friendly but we often were looking around trying to find them while they were off in the kitchen or running to the other side of the restaurant. They definitely need more staff.

KBBQ is a great choice for a birthday. Everyone can have whatever they want. Nobody has to compromise and nobody goes home hungry.

By 8:00 the place was jammed and there was an hour wait. We were awfully glad we had made reservations. If there are that many people waiting that long, you know the place is good.

The biggest downside was the noise level. The restaurant is the size of a small gymnasium and everyone was talking and cooking and running around at the same time. If that wasn't loud enough, they also had some really awful hip hop music going. I don't need that for my Korean birthday dinner.

Liquor is a little bit expensive. I think this is their main profit center. You will save a lot if you don't order a lot of soju and beer.

Don't take the complaints too seriously. It's a fun place. The food is good and everyone had a good time. We will be back.

San Ya

https://goo.gl/maps/b652wuN6kEy

2897 W Olympic Blvd #105, Los Angeles, CA 90006

sanya.site.mobi

(213) 383-1144

This is the ultimate AYCE eating experience. They used to charge $10 for all you can eat BBQ, but recently upped the price to $12. It's still crazy cheap, especially if you eat as much as my friends do. Meats include the usuals, plus ribs. There are more expensive menus but they don't make much sense cine the things they add to your AYCE choices are mostly things like intestines, that I would not eat anyway.

While at San Ya, I was amused by some of the signs on the wall warning of the dangers of overeating.

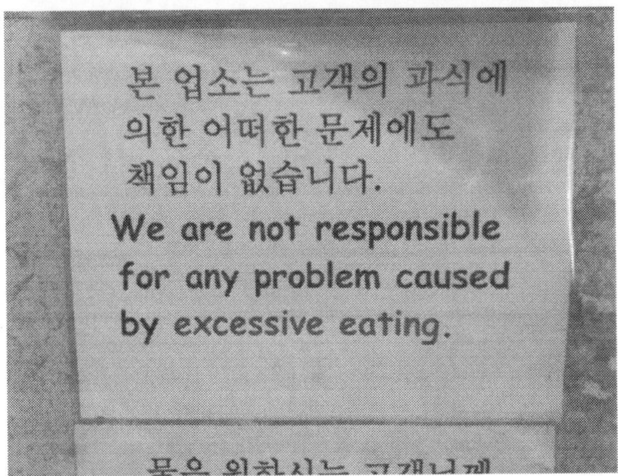

Yook Kal Bap Sang

https://goo.gl/maps/MntHf7xpKmq

861 S Western Ave, Los Angeles, CA 90005

(213) 386-0410

This is an exceptionally good restaurant, clean, nice, with tasty food, though the menu only has about five things on it.

The top choices are the mild broth with beef short ribs, or the spicy soup with meat in a red sauce. Both come with four sides, as well as rice and noodles. They are extremely good, though everyone in our group preferred the spicy one.

They also have some meat pancakes, a large seafood pancake, and perhaps two other things. That's the whole menu.

Prices range from about $8 (short rib soup) to $15 (spicy soup).

This is a very good place and well worth trying.

Vim's Thai Restaurant

https://goo.gl/maps/wP6T3Vd1nCD2
946 N Western Ave, Los Angeles, CA 90029
Vim Thai-Chinese Restaurant
https://goo.gl/maps/7Vm5TFV9db22
831 S Vermont Ave, Los Angeles, CA 90005
(213) 386-2338
vimthai.com

This is a fun and popular restaurant. And it's inexpensive. The lunch specials in particular are a good deal, something like $5 will get you a full plate of tasty food and rice.

The interior is classic red vinyl booths, and well, it feels like a Thai restaurant. It's pretty well known in the area and most everyone seems to like it.

Notice that the other storefronts along Vermont on the same block are mostly all the same restaurant even though they look like separate places.

Hwal Uh Kwang Jang

https://goo.gl/maps/WiiAjdH8kUx
730 S Western Ave, Los Angeles, CA 90005
(213) 386-6688

This modest but clean hole in the wall in a little strip mall off Western serves fantastically good bowls of raw fish and rice, Korean style, for about $7.

The main course is accompanied by a bowl of rice, a cup of miso soup, and hot tea.

Language is a little bit of a problem here. While some of our party were Asian, none spoke Korean and the waitresses, while friendly, spoke close to zero English. Doesn't matter. The menu is pretty self explanatory and almost everyone ordered the same thing anyway.

Two of our group ordered the hot seafood soup, which was also pretty good.

Decor at Hwal Uh Kwang Jang is very clean but basic. If you want some really excellent sushi style fish, in modest surroundings, then this is the place. Strongly recommended.

Chunju Han-il Kwan

https://goo.gl/maps/yQ6Fa8fz1R72
3450 W 6th St, Los Angeles, CA 90020
(213) 480-1799

Located in the corner of the "L" in a strip mall off 6th near Normandy, this friendly place with a rustic wood interior decor gives the feeling of an authentic Korean local family restaurant.
House specialty seems to be a big stew pot with ramen spam and hot dogs, military style. Sounds silly but it's awesome.
Meat dishes noodles soups and the sides. Everything is awesome. Everyone in our group thought it was great. Not dirt cheap, but very reasonable, not expensive.

Feng Mao

https://goo.gl/maps/41fXXhvu1dq
3901 W Olympic Blvd, Los Angeles, CA 90019
(323) 935-1099
Strictly speaking this isn't really a KBBQ, it's more of a Mongolian kebab restaurant. Everything is ala carte, no AYCE here. Some of the lamb kebabs with cumin are particularly good and have an almost Indian flavor. Most everything on the menu is good, even the eggplant, which I normally won't eat. A very good restaurant. Recommended.

Thai Town

https://goo.gl/maps/Pnaf1oKMVLA2
The area around Hollywood Blvd, east of the 101 Freeway, has become an unofficial "Little Bangkok" area. There is more good food here per square foot than in any other part of LA. Stiff competition makes the prices low and the quality high. Almost every restaurant in this area is good.

Torung

https://goo.gl/maps/aMcHZQJ11Rq
5657 Hollywood Blvd, Los Angeles, CA 90028
torung.cafes-world.com
This is the first Thai restaurant I ever tried, many years ago, back when I was a student at UCLA. There are so many other newer places, but the still remains one of the best.
Tom Chi Chi coconut chicken soup is completely pod Thai is delicious. All the curries are super excellent. Everything is just great, and the serving sizes are generally fairly large.
Even better the prices are reasonable, with main dishes averaging only about $7.
The interior of the restaurant is large comfortable final booths. There are three separate rooms and the booths can seat quite a few people.
Torung is open 5pm - 5 am. Around 2 AM the place starts to fill up with people with lots of tattoos and piercings coming in from local clubs. It's a colorful place.
They only take cash. No credit cards.

Thai Patio

https://goo.gl/maps/dcdWrkja5NM2
5273 Hollywood Blvd, Los Angeles, CA 90027
thaipatiorestaurant.com
(323) 466-3894

Located in the Thai Town area of Hollywood Blvd, this has been one of my favorite Thai restaurants for many years. It combines amazingly good food with reasonable prices and seems to be fairly busy all day long, even at off hours. Noodles, curries, fish, main courses and soups, it's all good.

Today I had prik king chicken, sort of a red curry item with string beans, Sea Bass deep fried pieces with ginger spicy sauce, grilled pork salad with lime and chili dressing, and for desert deep fried ice cream with some fried banana rolls. Oh so good. My favorite is the grilled pork salad, but everything was incredibly delicious.

Dishes average about $9 so the cost is reasonable too. I just love this place.

Ruen Pair Thai

https://goo.gl/maps/dexwkhA3xdv
5257 Hollywood Blvd, Los Angeles, CA 90027
ruenpairthaila.com
(323) 466-0153
Located just across the parking lot from Thai Patio, this place offers excellent Thai food, with menu and prices similar to Thai Patio. My friend Ajo feels that this is the best Thai place, and based on how busy they are, many people agree. It's just really hard to go wrong in this neighborhood.

Bhan Kanom Thai Desserts

https://goo.gl/maps/fUwSHy4XU8k
5271 Hollywood Blvd, Los Angeles, CA 90027
Located in: New Hollywood Plaza
bhankanomthai.com
(323) 871-8030
Fantastic Thai desserts. Pastries and shaved ice and various other tasty items as well as a large selection of crackers and munchies. It's a small shop and always crowded. There is no place to sit down so be prepared to eat your desserts standing or take them outside. Incredibly popular. It's located in a U shaped mall along Hollywood Boulevard, next to Thai Patio, Ruen, and several other good Thai restaurants. Highly recommended.

Silom Supermarket

https://goo.gl/maps/h7zGRs8AsvR2
5321 Hollywood Blvd, Los Angeles, CA 90027
Located in: Thailand Plaza
(323) 993-9000
This Thai ethnic grocery store is wonderful. I often come in here and wander around and look at all the tasty items on sale after having dinner at one of the possibly 10,000 excellent Thai restaurants in the Thai Town area, which is roughly between Vermont and the 101 freeway in the general vicinity of Hollywood Blvd. This is a good place for vegetables, mushrooms, ramen, fish sauce, various Thai aluminum and wood cookware, as well as some selection of standard western groceries. From looking at the merchandise you get the impression they sell a lot to local restaurants. They also have an aisle of pre-prepared entree and dessert items, look near the cash register. Sometimes you will also find

vendors with little grills or cook stoves making things in the parking area. Everything is really good and the people here are nice. Highly recommended.

Smog Cutter

https://goo.gl/maps/tdTL5csaVZJ2
864 N Virgil Ave, Los Angeles, CA 90029
This hole-in-the-wall bar has a pool table and Karaoke most every night of the week. Beer is inexpensive. The Thai aunties that run the place are a hoot.

Downtown

Downtown LA is like a big piece of Manhattan plunked down in the middle of the endless suburbs of Los Angeles. In the day, it is the zone of bankers, lawyers, and city staff. There are many homeless people. At night much of downtown becomes a ghost town, but there are some very fun places that are open late. There are lots of interesting things to see downtown, but keep in mind that parking is ALWAYS a problem, and will cost you between $10 to $40 or more. As alternative, consider the train or Uber. Most locals don't go to this area very much because of the parking problems.

The Pantry

https://goo.gl/maps/gfcCGUppToG2
877 S Figueroa St, Los Angeles, CA 90017
pantrycafe.com
(213) 972-9279
This 24-hour diner and steak restaurant is owned by former LA mayor Richard Riordan. The Pantry is a well-known local landmark that has been popular since the 1920's. For many years they have specialized in employing rehabilitated former criminals. Service and food are great, but parking in this area is difficult and there are lines sometimes. It's best at off hours.

Cicada Club

https://goo.gl/maps/VntoJ17MjzC2
617 S Olive St, Los Angeles, CA 90014
cicadarestaurant.com
(213) 488-9488
This downtown deco restaurant is one of the coolest looking buildings in town and worth it just to see the interior. Once or twice a week the have a big band and show. Sometimes they open the rooftop bar which is also amazing. The food is expensive but good. Admission varies depending on the show. Check the website for details.

Clifton's Cafeteria

https://goo.gl/maps/TynfBHPLKhJ2
648 S Broadway, Los Angeles, CA 90014
cliftonsla.com
(213) 627-1673
This cool multilevel restaurant and club serves classic American cuisine such as mac and cheese and meatloaf, and often has live music and dancing. Very cool place.

2nd Street Tunnel

https://goo.gl/maps/4dJ3RdqiAKJ2

620 W 2nd St, Los Angeles, CA 90012

This small tunnel has been featured in countless films, but it's really just a tunnel. It was featured in one memorable driving sequence in "Blade Runner", but there are hundreds of other films and commercials where this location has been used. There isn't much to do here except get a good picture and try to dodge traffic while you are doing it. The tunnel is an active traffic path in downtown LA.

Walt Disney Concert Hall

https://goo.gl/maps/H981ePSG6KA2

111 S Grand Ave, Los Angeles, CA 90012

laphil.com

(323) 850-2000

They say it cost $274 million to build and yet it seats only about 2000 people. It was Designed by famous architect Frank Gehry, who designed the original Santa Monica Mall. The swooshy soft curves of this concert hall raised eyebrows when it was first built, but it's become one of LA's most popular concert venues. It's the home of the LA Philharmonic and hosts various other shows.

Art Walk

https://goo.gl/maps/zJ3JCuNnP4E2

W 4th St, Los Angeles, CA 90013

downtownartwalk.org

This is an event, more than a location. Periodically they will announce a public "Art Walk" with participation from downtown galleries and other businesses. Huge crowds fill the streets. Some take this as a good opportunity show off their skills at body painting. I don't know if they really sell a lot of art, but people seem to have a good time.

Mayan Theater

https://goo.gl/maps/wr6c4xtmS1w
1038 S Hill St, Los Angeles, CA 90015
clubmayan.com
(213) 746-4287
This cool old theater is used mostly for night club events and concerts. It is rumored that they even have Lucha Libre. The architecture itself is amazing. Giant columns and weird wall sculptures. Totally worth seeing just for that. Fridays and Saturdays the crowds are large and the music is loud. Admission is about $10.

The Edison

https://goo.gl/maps/91qPtZqPBP32
108 W 2nd St #101, Los Angeles, CA 90012
edisondowntown.com
(213) 613-0000
This cool restaurant and nightclub was built from a converted electric power plant. Now it is hyper-trendy, often with a line to get in. The interior design is very cool, with parts of the old electric plant integrated into the look. Jacket often required. My friend Barry likes to go there on Thursday nights for the "Leftover Cuties" and other swing and blues bands.

Skyspace/US Bank

https://goo.gl/maps/2JWvJQq68h92

633 W 5th St #840, Los Angeles, CA 90071
oue-skyspace.com
(213) 894-9000
$25 will get you to the top of this very tall downtown tower, and $8 more will get you a ticket to take a ride on the glass slide attached to the exterior of the building. The slide is only 45 feet long, and is supposed to be completely safe, but it sure is a long ways down. Riding this slide is a lot cheaper than a trip to Disneyland, and more exciting.

The Last Bookstore

https://goo.gl/maps/To1LNrMJKao
453 S Spring St, Los Angeles, CA 90013
lastbookstorela.com
(213) 488-0599
Very cool multilevel bookstore selling new and used merchandise. They claim it's the largest bookstore in the US. They certainly have a lot of fun stuff. Very cool, totally recommended.

Grand Central Market

https://goo.gl/maps/SP67duZy9k72
317 S Broadway, Los Angeles, CA 90013
grandcentralmarket.com
(213) 624-2378
This fun food market has vegetable stands and lots of fun little restaurants. It reminds me of the Pike Place Market back home in Seattle. It was used as a location for a number of scenes in "Blade Runner".

Garment District

https://goo.gl/maps/TGP7BhHg77t
210 E Olympic Blvd, Los Angeles, CA 90015
There used to be a lot of garment manufacturing in this area, but Chinese imports have mostly shut them down. There are still a lot of shops selling very cheap clothes, and a few selling knock-offs of designer fashions and watches.

Jewelry District

https://goo.gl/maps/A6Wz3762NnM2
412 W 6th St #1006, Los Angeles, CA 90014
This is one of a large number of Jewelry related malls and shops located in a small district downtown. Rumor has it that a knowledgeable person can save quite a bit of money by purchasing their diamonds and other gems here at the source. There are many shops. Just walk around and look and compare.

Los Angeles City Hall

https://goo.gl/maps/73a2eSnkHZ72
200 N Spring St, Los Angeles, CA 90012
lacity.org
(213) 473-3231

If you are a fan of Dragnet or other old cop shows, this building will look familiar. This 1928 landmark features a ziggurat tower & 27th-floor observation deck. The view from the top over downtown LA is pretty cool. If you want some photos of LA skyscrapers, this would be a good spot.

Los Angeles Superior Court

https://goo.gl/maps/pgVyvhudkkS2
210 W Temple St, Los Angeles, CA 90012
lacourt.org
This is the country courthouse for criminal and civil suits within the State of California. Countless famous criminal trials have happened here.

United States District Court

https://goo.gl/maps/aBNSHrSXRAy
312 N Spring St, Los Angeles, CA 90012
cacd.uscourts.gov
(213) 894-1565
This is the Federal court for this area. It's a boxy glass covered 1970's style tower.

LAPD

100 W 1st St, Los Angeles, CA 90012
lapdonline.org
(213) 486-1000

Chinatown

This area on the far side of the 101 freeway from downtown is the historical tourist Chinatown. There are restaurants here that have pagoda style accents on their strip mal facades and there are los of fun little shops and stands. The real center of Chinese population is further east, in San Gabriel and Alhambra. That's where you find the best food. But still, there are some fun places in Chinatown.

Phillipes French Dips

https://goo.gl/maps/mYUshYQ9mZD2
1001 North Alameda, Los Angeles, CA 90012
philippes.com
This old school French dip restaurant in Chinatown is somewhat of a Los Angeles legend. The sandwiches are good and the prices are so cheap it is completely ridiculous. The downside is that the bread is a little soft, like oversized hot dog buns, but still, it's an excellent sandwich.

Sam Woo Barbecue (三和)

https://goo.gl/maps/nrW8DAzLi7U2
803 N Broadway, Los Angeles, CA 90012
Menuplaces.singleplatform.com
Sam Woo is best known for barbecued pork and roast duck. You can eat it in the restaurant or you can buy it by the pound for take-out. Prices are very reasonable.

They also have a full menu of Cantonese style cuisine. It's generally pretty good though swimming in oil.

I used to always wonder if there was a man named Sam who started this restaurant, but in fact the Chinese character in the name of the restaurant is the symbol for the number three. The name means three harmonies. Actually, according to Wikipedia, the full name is. "Three Harmonies Roast Meats and Noodle House."

We usually go to the Sam Woo in Chinatown, but there are number of other branches, such as next to the 99 Ranch Market in Van Nuys, or on Valley Blvd in San Gabriel.

Sam will is open pretty late. I don't think I have ever been there before midnight.

Little Tokyo

The area around 1st and 2nd street is called little Tokyo. There are quite a number of excellent and often inexpensive Japanese restaurants, a couple of malls, fun shops such as the Kinokuniya Bookstore and U-Space ukulele shop, and other Japanese related shops.

Kinokuniya Bookstore

https://goo.gl/maps/5R2KQUTCeYn

123 Astronaut E S Onizuka St #205, Los Angeles, CA 90012

usa.kinokuniya.com

This is a small branch of the famous multi-story bookstore in Shinjuku, Tokyo. If you read Japanese, you're in luck.

Suehiro Restaurant

https://goo.gl/maps/ae4AnVcH2Hy

337 E 1st St, Los Angeles, CA 90012

suehirocafe.net

(213) 626-9132

There are many good Japanese restaurants in this area, but this modest diner is my favorite. It's kind of the Japanese equivalent of a Denny's. They have curry rice, noodles, soup and other comfort foods. Sushi is NOT a specialty here. Prices are super reasonable. This is my favorite downtown restaurant.

U-Space Ukuleles

https://goo.gl/maps/gYhdtByCtbq

244 S San Pedro St, Los Angeles, CA 90012

uspacela.com

(323) 577-5567

This fun shop on the edge of Little Tokyo has coffee, musical instruments, and lessons. They have a good selection of Ukuleles. My sister bought a really nice one, though it was close to $1000. They said it used to belong to Don Ho. There are many cheaper models available. The people are nice and helpful.

Japan American National Museum

https://goo.gl/maps/hu6Qcs6vsaq

100 N Central Ave, Los Angeles, CA 90012

janm.org

Art, artifacts & historical exhibits exploring over 130 years of the Japanese-American experience.

Long Beach

https://goo.gl/maps/C7xRouGz5212

Long Beach, the port of Los Angeles, is one of the busiest ports in the world, in terms of total tons of shipping and traffic.

As a city is it urban but low key. Rents are much lower here than in areas closer to the center of LA, which is nice for residents.

Downtown Long beach is a pleasant place to walk, has quite a few good restaurants, as well as a few tourist attractions.

It takes about 45 minutes to drive to Long Beach from Downtown LA or Santa Monica, if traffic is favorable.

The Sky Room

https://goo.gl/maps/pLeXaQsrvVR2

40 S Locust Ave, Long Beach, CA 90802

theskyroom.com

This Long Beach restaurant and bar is on top of a hotel overlooking the harbor. The view is amazing.

Terrace Theater - Long Beach Convention Center

https://goo.gl/maps/QXzp3DKmvrB2

300 E Ocean Blvd, Long Beach, CA 90802

longbeachcc.com

(562) 436-3636

We caught the Joe Bonamassa concert here which was big fun. The theater is medium to large size, clean, nice, comfortable. Whether you have fun depends on who you go with and what show you see. Nobody goes just to see a nice concert hall.

Vincent Thomas Bridge

https://goo.gl/maps/5WxoSUKaxDt

The bridge off the freeway coming into town off the 110 freeway is spectacular.

Gerald Desmond Bridge

https://goo.gl/maps/xT4SvXJrXh12

This new bridge should be spectacular too.

Aquarium of the Pacific

https://goo.gl/maps/JfjqwfALRFT2

100 Aquarium Way, Long Beach, CA 90802

aquariumofpacific.org

This fun aquarium is worth at least a couple of hours to walk through. At $30 admission, $17 for kids, it's not cheap, but it's as good an aquarium as you will find anywhere.

Battleship Iowa

https://goo.gl/maps/BQXAEboeV342

250 S Harbor Blvd, Los Angeles, CA 90731

pacificbattleship.com

(877) 446-9261

Built in 1943, the Iowa was one of the most powerful Battleships ever built. It saw action in the South Pacific, including combat at Kwajalein and Okinawa, and was present when the Japanese surrender was signed on the Missouri, which is now at Pearl Harbor. Eventually the Iowa was retired, twice reactivated, and finally retired for good to become a floating museum. It is parked in San Pedro harbor, right next to the cruise ship landing and the dock for the boat to Catalina Island.

Admission is $10-$20 depending on age, with an additional charge of $30 if you want a tour of the lower decks and engine room.

Queen Mary

https://goo.gl/maps/P6AFfph1ziy

1126 Queens Hwy, Long Beach, CA 90802

queenmary.com

(877) 342-0738

In an effort to promote Long Beach as a tourist destination, the city bought the Queen Mary, a retired cruise ship. They use it as a hotel, with restaurants, bars, events, and tours.

You can stay on the Queen Mary (Hotel) for about $170, depending on dates and availability.

Tours start at about $25, which may be higher than the cost of some of the events on the boat that get you in for free.

There are also exhibits that may require an additional fee, such as the Titanic show. Check their website for details.

Other Areas

Mount Wilson Observatory

https://goo.gl/maps/u3MZE8sacVB2

Red Box-Mount Wilson Rd, Mount Wilson, CA 91023

mtwilson.edu

(626) 440-9016

This classic electrically powered telescope represented futuristic technology when it was built around 1900. Now it seems a little bit steampunk, but in a very cool way. The drive up through the mountains is magnificent. My friend Ajo had his birthday party here at the Observatory. How cool is that?

Mount Baldy

https://goo.gl/maps/F8vRs9TpBzK2
6777 Mt Baldy Rd, Mt Baldy, CA 91759
mtbaldylodge.com
(909) 982-1115

What I love about Mt. Baldy is the absence of slickness, the absence of overpriced resorts and overpriced crap restaurants like you find around Mammoth or other more well known ski areas.

Granted they had about ten ounces of snow for the whole mountain this year, and global warming seems to be endangering their season next year.

But there is something charming about this disorganized country town nestled in the mountains just an hour or so from Los Angeles. Next time there is some snow come up and check it out.

Carnitas El Momo

https://goo.gl/maps/EAWNvQGMm1t
2411 Fairmount St, Los Angeles, CA 90033
(323) 627-8540

Taco truck in East LA that sells only pork tacos. You can have shoulder, skin (chicharrons) or pork belly. The servings are huge. My friends really liked the chicharrons and pork belly, but I thought it was kind of cheap meat. I prefer the shoulder. Their specialty is the "Aporkalypse", combining all three kinds of pork. Two tacos are enough, three will put you in food coma.

Porto's Bakery & Café Glendale
https://goo.gl/maps/XuBB3Jm1fN92
315 N Brand Blvd, Glendale, CA 91203
portosbakery.com
(818) 956-5996
This is the go-to bakery for the Glendale area.

Forget the silly sugar bomb pastries from the grocery story, much better to get rolls, cakes, pastries here.

To be honest I know this place mostly from pastries that show up at various events. Someone will ask where the fabulous pastries came from, and again and again the answer will be Portos.

Hotels

There are quite a few hostels and hotels around Santa Monica and nearby neighborhoods. Unfortunately, prices have risen a lot in recent years, so that it's hard to find much under $200.

If you can't find anything reasonable in Santa Monica, there are less expensive places in Venice, Marina del Rey, Mar Vista and Culver City. Always be sure to ask about parking, if you have a car. Airbnb and Hostels are the other option.

Airbnb

Hotels in this area are expensive, so Airbnb is very popular. It's great that Airbnb offers a way for local residents to make a few extra dollars, and a way for visitors to reduce their expenses.

If you stay in Airbnb, be sure to check the reviews of any place you stay. Avoid places that get in fights with guests, or that have fishy requirements like women only, that make them sound like they are looking for dates instead of offering accommodation.

Many places on Airbnb turn out to be not as good as they look online. Reading the reviews helps a lot with this problem.

Location is very important. If you get a great deal on a great place and it's an hour away by car, then it's going to be a problem. LA is a really big place.

Santa Monica recently passed an ordinance officially making Airbnb legal for residents with the following limitations:

1. The person doing Airbnb must be a person, not a corporation. This means apartment buildings run by NMS that offer apartments Airbnb, are illegal, regardless of location or dates or anything else.
2. The person doing Airbnb must be staying (sleeping) at the place being rented. It is not legal to rent out a whole apartment.
3. The person doing Airbnb must get a business license and pay hotel and business taxes.

The law was passed to allow Airbnb, but prevent Apartment owners from running unlicensed hotels in residential areas.

Aside from that, Airbnb offers some excellent alternatives for accommodations in the Santa Monica area. Check the reviews and compare the prices and you are sure to find something you will like.

http://www.airbnb.com

NMS Properties

Please do not patronize Airbnb listings posted by NMS, a large local development firm that seems to be almost continuously in legal trouble. NMS owner, Neil M Schechter, has been convicted of tax fraud, forgery, and perjury; and yet continues to be the largest developer in Santa Monica. He greases the palms of city government, and is able to get the green light for oversize projects when nobody else can. He controls something like 2,000 rental units in Santa Monica. Many of his buildings are active on the Airbnb market. All of his Airbnb units are illegal.

Here's a little more about Schechter:

- http://smdp.com/corruption-case-against-nms-properties-on-hold-but-allowed-to-continue/161354
- http://smdp.com/local-developer-faces-city-scrutiny-amid-fraud-scandal/158945
- http://www.smobserved.com/story/2016/12/12/business/real-estate-developer-nailed-for-evidence-tampering-by-la-superior-court-judge-bruguera/2319.html

Schechter's forgeries were proven, because the version of Adobe Acrobat he used didn't exist when he claimed the contracts were signed. Also, printed copies had conflicting date stamps automatically created by the printers. Oops! Schechter then mysteriously misplaced his hard drive in an attempt to destroy evidence. Oops! The court was not amused.

Santa Monica Hotels

Santa Monica Youth Hostel (AYH)

https://goo.gl/maps/6ow3WUD6qMn

1436 2nd St, Santa Monica, CA 90401

hiusa.org

Even if you're not a youth, this is hands-down the best deal and for accommodations in the Santa Monica Area. The location second street is just steps from the beach, the Mall and the Promenade. It's perfect. Parking will be a bit difficult, but if you're on foot that's not a problem. As far as value for money, for about $32 a night, no other place is even close. On the other hand, if you need a double room, you will need to look elsewhere. Accommodation here is youth hostel style bunks, with lots of people in a room.

Casa Del Mar

https://goo.gl/maps/gysTrfpd6hx

1910 Ocean Way, Santa Monica, CA 90405

hotelcasadelmar.com

This is one of the nicest hotels in town. The big brick building is right on Ocean front walk. The restaurant has a splendid view of the beach. At night there is often live music, and no cover charge.

Barbara Morrison used to play here a lot. Prices for everything a little bit on the expensive side but you are paying for the location, and it is magnificent. Nightly rate around $500.

Shutters

https://goo.gl/maps/HvvSNUMU2Gq

1 Pico Blvd, Santa Monica, CA 90405

shuttersonthebeach.com

This hotel seems like some kind of English Victorian beach resort on the beach in the middle of Santa Monica.

It is considered one of the nicest hotels in town, but prices are through the roof.

The restaurant here is good, but it is also through the roof. Beer is $9 to $12 nine to $12, mac & cheese snack is $15, salmon salad $29, chicken club sandwich $21.

If budget is no issue, then shutters will be a great place to stay.

Nightly rate around $600.

One important note here is that as part of the requirements shutters agreed to when they expanded, the city required the hotel to allow locals to park in the hotel valet parking lot at the same rate as the meters along Pico Boulevard, which cost a dollar an hour.

If you want to take it vantage of this, just pull your car up to the valet and let them know that you want to pay the discounted rate. We do this sometimes when we come down here to go surfing.

Cadillac Hotel

https://goo.gl/maps/VTjXfhemjnu

8 Dudley Ave, Venice, CA 90291

thecadillachotel.com

The Cadillac hotel is a nice backpack or place with hostile space and rooms for tourists. It's not the fanciest place in town, but it's cheerful and the prices are reasonable. If you want to stay right on the beach this is a good option.

Nightly rate around $150.

Hotel Carmel

https://goo.gl/maps/dRZDhuCx4Pt

201 Broadway, Santa Monica, CA 90401

hotelcarmel.com

(310) 451-2469

My parents stay in this downtown hotel sometimes when they come to town. The hotel is an older one and not quite as chic as some of the fancy places, but the location is very convenient. It's across the street from the Mall and just around the corner from the Promenade. The Pier and beach are about two blocks away. Location is the main benefit here. Nightly rates start at around $173.

Fairmont Miramar

https://goo.gl/maps/zRhPAKFXZiA2

101 Wilshire Blvd, Santa Monica, CA 90401

fairmont.com

Located on Wilshire between Ocean and Second Street, this is one of the nicest hotels in Santa Monica.

Like everything else in Santa Monica price just keeps going up and up. You should expect to pay $400 or more to stay here.

My friends who work at Microsoft usually stay here when they visit LA on expense account. Famous people like Bill Clinton show up here regularly.

The hotel is owned by Michael Dell, the computer magnate.

Dell and the management of the Miramar have become politically controversial because of a proposal to erect skyscrapers full of multi-million-dollar condominiums on the property.

The Huntley Hotel

https://goo.gl/maps/7Qf5f7vZTn72

1111 2nd St, Santa Monica, CA 90403

thehuntleyhotel.com

Once upon a time, Huntley was a modest high-rise hotel set back a block or two from the beach, with an amazing view and a Mexican restaurant on the roof that offered a free buffet and cheap drinks during happy hour.

Amazing how times have changed. The hotel has been renovated and re-renovated. Now it is one of the nicest hotels in town. Everything here is nice, and all the food is good, but prices have risen too.

The glass elevator that goes up the side of the Huntley is amazing. This should be on your bucket list of things to do while visiting Santa Monica.

The restaurant at the top is very popular.

Nightly rate $339, which is a good deal compared to many other nearby hotels that aren't as nice and charge even more. I think this is one of the better choices in this price range.

Comfort Inn

https://goo.gl/maps/UNQao4oMerj

2815 Santa Monica Blvd, Santa Monica, CA 90404

choicehotels.com

(310) 828-5517

About a mile from the center, this moderately priced hotel is close to the hospital and Volkswagon Santa Monica. Price is reasonable at $134/night. You could take a lot of Uber rides for the difference in price to one of the places downtown, and it's really not very far.

Courtyard Marriott

https://goo.gl/maps/AMkW4Wnu5yQ2

425 Colorado Ave, Santa Monica, CA 90401

marriott.com

(310) 394-1700

This new hotel is conveniently located across the street from the new train station and the mall, close to downtown and an easy walk to the pier. Nightly rates start at $214.

Ambrose Hotel

https://goo.gl/maps/Dy5Fn4XJww72
1255 20th St, Santa Monica, CA 90404
ambrosehotel.com
(310) 315-1555
This pleasant hotel is located away from the beach, close to St Monica's hospital and the Whole Foods grocery store. If you are visiting someone who is staying at the hospital, or don't mind a short drive to get downtown, the prices are more reasonable and the hotel nice. Nightly rate $245.

Viceroy Hotel

https://goo.gl/maps/vVtkyForJUN2
1819 Ocean Ave, Santa Monica, CA 90401
viceroyhotelsandresorts.com
(310) 260-7500
For a long time this was a dilapidated '70's style hotel, but extensive renovations have brought it up to speed. The pool area is very nice. The location, sort of between the Civic Auditorium, Shutters and the Rand Corporation, is convenient and not too far from the beach. Traffic on Ocean and Pico is busy, and crossing the road will feel like a game of Frogger. Nightly rate around $325.

Georgian Hotel

https://goo.gl/maps/wp55qS68sbv
1415 Ocean Ave, Santa Monica, CA 90401
georgianhotel.com
(310) 395-9945
This used to be a nice retirement home, but investors came in, kicked all retirees out, renovated, and now it's a high-end hotel. Your vote at the ballot box means little, but the vote you make with your

money is the one that they listen to. It's a fun old building and they renovated it nicely. Limited parking. $279.

Cal Mar Hotel

https://goo.gl/maps/qwPMFJIDKDx

220 California Ave, Santa Monica, CA 90403

calmarhotel.com

(310) 395-5555

This used to be an apartment building, and it shows in the design, which is about the same as every other apartment building in the area. There is a center court has a pool, and a couple of floors of apartments around it. It's a residential area, but the location is good, near the Promenade. Having a kitchen is nice. The nightly charge of $159 is low for the area.

Rest Haven Motel

https://goo.gl/maps/SFWeCvLxfPK2

815 Grant St, Santa Monica, CA 90405

resthavenmotel.net

(310) 452-3977

The location behind Lincoln isn't really near anything, but it's very close if you have a car. The beach is about a dozen blocks away. The hotel's main advantage is the price, but it's nothing much to look at and the neighborhood is not particularly interesting. Still, a $4 Uber will get you right into the middle. Prices start at $108 per night.

Ocean Lodge

https://goo.gl/maps/QQkdBZs9YAt
1667 Ocean Ave, Santa Monica, CA 90401
oceanlodgehotel.com
Anywhere else in the world, this would be a total totally low end cheap motel, but the location on Ocean Avenue in Santa Monica puts this motel in the $200 range. Good location, mediocre hotel. It's right on the edge of Tongva park, which is pleasant in the daytime, but sketchy at night.

Ocean Park Inn

https://goo.gl/maps/AxGi9MJAPXU2
2452 Lincoln Blvd, Santa Monica, CA 90405
oceanparkinn.net
(310) 392-3966
Inexpensive model on Lincoln. It's a little bit far to walk, but by car it's very close to the beach and downtown. At $108 per night, it's one of the cheapest places in town.

Palm Motel

https://goo.gl/maps/wT3GzoTQkxo
2020 14th St, Santa Monica, CA 90405
palmmotelsantamonica.com
(310) 452-3861
This inexpensive and tired looking motel is conveniently located across the street from the cemetery, and just a block from Santa Monica College and the public pool. It's too far to walk to the beach or downtown, but a short drive. If you are checking out the college, this could be great. $110 per night means it's one of the least expensive options.

Pavilions Motel

https://goo.gl/maps/nAz4SaWhYiN2
2338 Ocean Park Blvd, Santa Monica, CA 90405
pavilionsmotelsantamonica.com
(310) 450-4044
This ramshackle motel ought to get some special prize for setting the lowest standards in town. It's close to Santa Monica Airport and some office parks, but not near the beach or downtown. Low cost is the benefit. Not to be confused with the grocery store of the same name. $108 per night.

Bayside Motel

https://goo.gl/maps/EcfLhbtt7JC2
2001 Ocean Ave, Santa Monica, CA 90405
baysidehotel.com
(310) 396-6000
Moderately priced motel located on Ocean, just a block from the beach and not far from the Pier and Main Street. Rates start at $166.

Travelodge

https://goo.gl/maps/eBxaaM6hQUy
3102 Pico Blvd, Santa Monica, CA 90405
wyndhamhotels.com
(310) 450-5766
This model is quite a distance from the beach and Promenade, but convenient to Santa Monica College and Trader Joe's. Not fancy at all, but if budget is a concern, this might be an option. Around $150 a night.

Santa Monica Motel

https://goo.gl/maps/4x7a9njg23D2
2102 Lincoln Blvd, Santa Monica, CA 90405
santamonicamotel.com
(310) 392-6806
This inexpensive motel on Lincoln is very close by car, but a bit of a hike from the beach or downtown. The neighborhood is safe but not very interesting unless you are interested in car parts. There is a Starbucks nearby. It's about ten blocks walk to the beach. With prices starting at $121 per night, it's one of the cheapest places in town.

Le Méridien Delfina Santa Monica

https://goo.gl/maps/89baJoUyiMv
530 Pico Blvd, Santa Monica, CA 90405
lemeridiendelfina.com
(310) 399-9344
Located on the hill across the street from Santa Monica High School, his is a very nice hotel, though not all that close to the beach or downtown. Nightly rate around $240.

Hotel Shangri-La Santa Monica

https://goo.gl/maps/g2qCaQZv8w22

1301 Ocean Ave, Santa Monica, CA 90401

slh.com

(310) 394-2791

Nice hotel on Ocean Avenue. Location is conveniently near downtown and a couple of blocks to the pier and beach. The rooftop bar is popular. Nightly rates around $279.

Doubletree Inn

https://goo.gl/maps/Lh2XYpeDeMp

1707 4th St, Santa Monica, CA 90401

doubletree3.hilton.com

(310) 395-3332

Nice chain hotel on 4th street across from the police station and behind Santa Monica College. Easy walk to downtown, a few blocks to the pier. About $250 per night.

Best Western Gateway

https://goo.gl/maps/RbLqUEbhmPR2

1920 Santa Monica Blvd, Santa Monica, CA 90404

bestwestern.com

(310) 829-9100

This nice chain hotel isn't near downtown or the beach, but it's close to the hospital and just a couple of blocks from Busy Bee Hardware and DK Donuts.

Ocean View Hotel

https://goo.gl/maps/Td9Qv2RKPJp
1447 Ocean Ave, Santa Monica, CA 90401
oceanviewsantamonica.com
(310) 458-4888
Basic hotel, inexpensive for the area. Clean, nice, modern, great location near the Pier and Promenade. $189 per night.

Sea Shore Motel

https://goo.gl/maps/Le6xiFgzBH42
2637 Main St, Santa Monica, CA 90405
seashoremotel.com
(310) 392-2787
Small basic motel on Main Street, close to many restaurants and a block from the beach. Inexpensive for the area. $120-$250 per night.

Loews Hotel

https://goo.gl/maps/GRFyazpkVww
1700 Ocean Ave, Santa Monica, CA 90401
loewshotels.com
In my opinion this is about the nicest hotel in Santa Monica. It isn't quite on the beach, but it's so close that it's Alma almost the same thing. There is a very nice pool with the lounge and bar, then are very pleasant. It's a hotel bar so it's not going to be cheap, but if you want to find a good place to sit outside, so the beverage and watch the waves in the distance this could be a good choice.

Loews health club is open to the public, for a daily or monthly charge. Check with them for details.

Loews is not cheap, but it's a great location. This would be one of my top choices in this price range. Nightly rate around $385.

Shore Hotel

https://goo.gl/maps/mxrUvvkeBNP2
1515 Ocean Ave, Santa Monica, CA 90401
shorehotel.com
Located on Ocean Avenue just steps from the pier, this recently built hi-tech looking hotel not cheap but it's a nice location.
The architectural theme features a lot of cement and metal, which to me is a little bit off-putting and. They spice it up with orange umbrellas and a small pool in the courtyard. Most of the rooms have a really great view of the ocean. $300/night.

Oceana Beach Club Hotel

https://goo.gl/maps/4bbc35dNUhn
849 Ocean Ave, Santa Monica, CA 90403-1003
(310) 928-6186
https://www.hoteloceanasantamonica.com/

This recently constructed hotel on Ocean Avenue has a nice location, though not actually all that close to the beach. Room includes bike access, Wi-Fi, and a glass of champagne. $293/night.

Sea Blue (Hotel California)

https://goo.gl/maps/qD6Ctne1vFk
1670 Ocean Ave, Santa Monica, CA 90401
seabluehotel.com
This modest B quality motel has become high and, simply because of the location. It's just a half block from the beach. There are some new rooms down on the beach front which are really nice. The location can't be beat, so it's just a matter of whether the price seems right. Nightly rate around $239.

Palihouse

https://goo.gl/maps/ayeHPc58fhM2
1001 3rd St, Santa Monica, CA 90403
palihousesantamonica.com
Located in a residential neighborhood the owners of this apartment just north of Wilshire somehow convinced City officials to allow them to evict all the residents and convert to a hotel. It's a cool looking building, and very nicely renovated, but they have no parking. Local residents are up in arms that the city lets them park valet cars on local streets. Politically this hotel is very controversial. The location is close to the Promenade but not close to the beach. $275 per night seems a lot for that.

Wyndham Hotel

https://goo.gl/maps/taW8Ukq3LUw
120 Colorado Ave, Santa Monica, CA 90401
wyndhamsantamonicapier.com
Located just in front of the entrance to the pier and across the street from the mall, it's not quite as nice as being right on the beach, but it's still a pretty good location. Like every other hotel in Santa Monica, the prices just keep going up and up and up. The hotel is clean, modern and pleasant. Wyndham has announced plans to put up a larger tower, and while they have city backing, many residents are unhappy about it.

Hampton Inn

https://goo.gl/maps/dPRxzJX39712
501 Colorado Ave, Santa Monica, CA 90401
hamptoninn3.hilton.com
(310) 260-1100
This new hotel is located on 5ht and Colorado near the train station and the mall. Nice clean rooms, convenient location close to the Promenade, though not that close to the beach. Rates around $212.

NMS Leasing Gallery

https://goo.gl/maps/AAoKs8siv732
420 Santa Monica Blvd, Santa Monica, CA 90401
nmssantamonica.com
We are listing NMS as a hotel, since they operate Airbnb on a large scale in Santa Monica.

Named after Neil M Schechter, the zillionaire real estate mogul who is in trouble for fraud and forgery, this company is responsible for much of the real recent high-priced development in Santa Monica.

Schechter has friends inside the city government, and is able to get his projects approved even though they drastically exceed zoning restrictions. Construction quality of his buildings is haphazard, and the size of units is absurdly small, considering the astronomical rents he charges.

This company does a whopping business in Airbnb, basically running unlicensed hotels in residential areas. I like Airbnb, but it's for individuals, not for businesses that don't want to pay hotel tax.

NMS owner Neil Schechter has gotten in legal trouble plenty of times before, for everything from tax evasion to forgery. Tourists who stay in his places may find themselves embroiled in his next legal misadventure.

Not recommended.

Hotels/Hostels - Other Areas

If you aren't able to find something satisfactory in Santa Monica, the other areas to consider are Venice, Marina del Rey, and Culver City, Hollywood and Downtown.

Venice

Staying in Venice can be a very good option. Years ago, Venice used to be a cheaper community, with sketchy areas in Oakwood and cheap run-down houses near the beach. These days it's all gentrified, and is about the same in cost as Santa Monica. There are however a couple of fun hostels near the boardwalk.

Samesun Venice Beach

https://goo.gl/maps/zx74KjEGdoJ2
25 Windward Ave, Venice, CA 90291
samesun.com
(310) 399-7649
This fun hostel is located on Windward, just a half block off the Venice Beach Boardwalk. I stayed here a few times many years ago, when I was coming into town for work. It was always fun and cheerful, and very easy on the pocketbook. In the morning we could look out the window and sea the sunrise and waves. In the afternoon there were crowds of people out on the streets and people juggling chainsaws and other fun craziness. This is a good place. Note that parking is a problem in this area. Dorms start at $42 while single rooms are $120.

Venice Beach Hostel

https://goo.gl/maps/LbwGWAiVaTD2

1515 Pacific Ave, Venice, CA 90291

planetvenice.com

(310) 452-3052

Basic hostel just around the corner from the Samesun on Windward and Ocean. It's a lively area and a short block to the boardwalk and beach. It's a bit cheaper than the Samesun and the location is almost as good. Dorms start at $30 while single rooms are $95.

Venice Beach Suites & Hotel

https://goo.gl/maps/ArTv6RqnJxu

1305 Ocean Front Walk, Venice, CA 90291

venicebeachsuites.com

(310) 396-4559

Beach from hotel on the boardwalk. Great location, but parking may be a problem. Fun location. About $189 a night.

Marina del Rey Hotels

The Marina is nice, and hotels here are a bit cheaper than Santa Monica. There is no real downside, except that it's a little bit less convenient. Often when friends come to town, they will stay in hotels the Marina and drive up to Santa Monica to visit.

Jamaica Bay Inn

https://goo.gl/maps/ERPzokMTmKL2

4175 Admiralty Way, Marina Del Rey, CA 90292

jamaicabayinn.com

(310) 823-5333

Located on Admiralty, right in front of the Marina, this hotel has a pleasant view of the boats and a convenient location. The hotel has lots of parking, which is a big plus. The rooms are clean and large and new, and many have a nice view. It's just a few blocks to the Venice Boardwalk. Killer Shrimp and Cheesecake Factory are just a few steps away. Rooms are about $200 but are a good value.

Ritz Carlton

https://goo.gl/maps/EEYrHpNEtzH2

4375 Admiralty Way, Marina Del Rey, CA 90292

ritzcarlton.com

(310) 823-1700

The Ritz Carlton is very nice. As it should be. Small pool, but very nice interior and nice view of the Marina. For the price, it's nicer than what you would get in Santa Monica. $320/night.

Culver City Hotels

Culver City is decent, and cheaper than Santa Monica. You definitely need a car if you are staying in Culver City because transit connections are poor to other parts of town and it's not near the beach at all. Things have improved recently because of the addition of the train line. Culver City itself is developing quickly, and has many fun restaurants and a few cheap hotels.

Hollywood Hotels

Hollywood is popular with tourists due to name recognition, but there really isn't much to see here, and they would probably be happier at the beach. There are no major movie studios and no beach in Hollywood. There are however a couple of good hostels. Bus to the beach takes 1-2 hours or more depending on traffic. If the cheap places near the beach are full, these places give you a good option. Just be aware that the main thing to see at Hollywood and Vine, is other tourists. There are no movie studios here.

Banana Bungalows Hollywood

https://goo.gl/maps/CukDYZajZE62

5920 Hollywood Blvd, Hollywood, CA 90028

bananabungalows.com

(323) 469-2500

This fun hostel is located on Cahuenga, a little bit up the hill from the center of town, in the direction of the Hollywood Bowl. Formerly a motel. Dorms $35 Single $110.

Melrose Hostel

https://goo.gl/maps/phSTjptrdtF2

646 N Western Ave, Los Angeles, CA 90004

melrosehostel.com

(213) 382-5600

Just a stone's throw from Castle BBQ and numerous other delicious Korean restaurants on Western, this hostel isn't quite in the middle of things, but could make a good base.

USA Hostels Hollywood

https://goo.gl/maps/fVqcHNCDFRB2

624 Schrader Blvd, Los Angeles, CA 90028

usahostels.com
(323) 462-3777
Nice hostel with good location near Metro station. Dorms $38 Single $129.

Orange Drive Hostel

https://goo.gl/maps/pJct3VAb42G2
1764 N Orange Dr, Los Angeles, CA 90028
orangedrivehostel.com
(323) 850-0350
This nice facility located across the street from the Magic Castle and behind the Chinese Theater, is close to the tourist ghetto at Hollywood and Vine. The downside is the cost, which seems a little high for a hostel. $44 dorm $95 single (and up).

Walk of Fame Hostel Hollywood

https://goo.gl/maps/NkUykbPxtME2
6820 Hollywood Blvd, Los Angeles, CA 90028
walkoffamehostel.com
(323) 463-2770
Located across from the Kodak Theater near Hollywood and Vine, the Walk of Fame Hostel is right there in the center, if central Hollywood interests you. For me the area is not very interesting, but if you want to see the "Walk of Fame" and the sidewalk with all the stars, it's right out front. Dorm $40, single $115.

Downtown Hotels

City government and the very busy LA courthouses are located downtown. Local people hardly ever go to downtown LA unless they are lawyers or bankers or in some kind of legal trouble. Downtown is lively during the day but most of it becomes a ghost town after dusk.

Japanese tourists often stay downtown, because that's where the Japanese hotels are located.

Staying downtown makes sense really only if you have business downtown or just want to stay in an area that will remind you of Manhattan. Most of the interesting things to see are in other parts of town. Prices here are much cheaper than you would pay for similar hotels near the beach. Keep an eye on parking charges, which can be very expensive.

Biltmore Hotel

https://goo.gl/maps/oEysJoohHkK2
506 S Grand Ave, Los Angeles, CA 90071
millenniumhotels.com
(213) 624-1011
This classic hotel originally built in 1923, is architecturally one of the coolest hotels ever. It's worth visiting just to see. It is located right in the middle of downtown, walking distance to everything in the area. If I were staying downtown, and had the budget, this is where I would stay. Nothing else is even close. Rooms around $212. Note: parking here is $45 a day. If you have a car you might want to keep it somewhere else.

Omni Hotel

https://goo.gl/maps/9i2yukFfu3u
251 S Olive St, Los Angeles, CA 90012
omnihotels.com
(213) 617-3300
This is a very nice hotel with a great pool and convenient location, if you want to be downtown. Rates start at about $180.

Westin Bonaventure Hotel

https://goo.gl/maps/LNitkVeMQ6M2
404 S Figueroa St, Los Angeles, CA 90071
thebonaventure.com
(213) 624-1000
The huge atrium of this hotel, with glass elevators running up the inside, will look familiar because it's been in so many movies. The hotel is definitely a landmark. View from the top are amazing. With rooms starting at $169, it's very inexpensive compared to what you would pay for something similar near the beach.

Standard Hotel

https://goo.gl/maps/ei2oRwehHsx
550 S Flower St, Los Angeles, CA 90071
standardhotels.com
(213) 892-8080
This sleek modern hotel is famous mostly for the rooftop bar, which has a fun party atmosphere, especially on weekends.

Freehand Los Angeles.

https://goo.gl/maps/xVUBF3R1Giz
416 W 8th St, Los Angeles, CA 90014
freehandhotels.com
(213) 612-0021
This is a new high-end hotel and hostel. Nice rooftop bar and pool, but the cost seems beyond what most are willing to pay to stay in a hostel. $49 dorm/$190 room.

LAX Airport Area

Locals would never consider staying near the airport. It's a sketchy area, there's nothing to see here, and it's far from anything. There are a number of hotels and hostels hear which will be convenient if you are flight crew for an airline, or making an overnight stopover while changing planes, but otherwise you won't want to stay here.

PACIFIC
PACIFIC PARK

Places to Go, and Things to See

Santa Monica makes a great base for visiting attractions from surfing beaches to movie studios anywhere in Southern California. The places listed here make fun outings and are almost all within an hour of Santa Monica.

Museums, Art

Getty Villa

https://goo.gl/maps/EqyCLMQatfx

17985 Pacific Coast Hwy, Pacific Palisades, CA 90272

getty.edu

Located just off PCH about 10 minutes north of Santa Monica, this museum is the former residents of fabulously wealthy oil magnate J Paul Getty. The buildings here were inspired by the Roman palace on the island of Capri, though many liberties have been taken, such as the addition of modern plumbing and bathrooms. The collection here is Getty's personal collection of ancient Roman and Greek statues, pottery and other fascinating relics.

In my opinion it is one of the most interesting and most fun to visit museums in the LA area.

The museum has a café with indoor and outdoor seating. Food featuring things such as salads sandwiches and large glasses of wine, is all excellent, though a bit on the pricey side.

There are all kinds of shows and events and even cooking and drawing classes available at both the Getty Villa and the Getty Center. Popular classes require reservation long in advance. Check their website for details and schedules.

Admission to the museum is free. However, the catch is, you have to pay for parking. People in the neighborhood get really upset about museum guest parking on residential streets, so they were able to force the Getty to refuse admission to anyone who doesn't show up in a car. The assumption here is that if you come on foot, you probably parked in the neighborhood. And they don't allow that.

Bicycles are not allowed, because again the assumption is that you parked your car in the neighborhood and then rode a bicycle to the museum. I personally do not agree with this policy, but it is what it is.

You can also travel to the Getty Villa by public bus from Santa Monica, takes about half an hour, or you can take an Uber, which should be about $10, depending on traffic and surge pricing. You used to be able to park motorcycles for free, but now they charge the same for motorcycles cars.

I totally recommend the Getty Villa. Keep in mind however that it is only open during regular business hours, and is closed in the evening. The restaurant closes even earlier. If you want to have a meal, get in there around lunch time.

If you want to visit the Getty Center, you absolutely must make a parking reservation on their website or you will not be admitted. Print out your reservation and show it to them at the gate when you arrive.

Open 10-5 daily, closed Tuesday. Admission free but parking $15. No admission on foot. Reservation required.

Getty Center Museum

https://goo.gl/maps/DXfxoiSvMu82

1200 Getty Center Dr, Los Angeles, CA 90049

getty.edu

Nestled in the Santa Monica Mountains a couple of miles north of UCLA but on the other side of the freeway, the Getty center is both a wonderful museum and the administrative headquarters of the Getty organization that administers this museum, the Getty Villa, The Getty photo organization, etc.

Getty's collection of ancient Greek and Roman art is down at the Getty Villa at a completely different location. The Getty center contains renaissance to modern European art, as well as various changing seasonal exhibits, and various cultural events.

There are all kinds of shows and events and even cooking and drawing classes available at both the Getty Villa and the Getty Center. Popular classes require reservation long in advance. Check their website for details and schedules.

Like the Getty Villa, admission to the Getty center is free. It is paid for by the end I went from J Paul Getty, a hugely wealthy oil magnate. The catch is that you have to pay for parking. The normal routine is to get off the 405 at Getty Center, Way, and pay about $10 per car to park in the immense underground garage. Then, from the garage you catch a little electric tram that runs up to the hilltop where the museum itself is located.

There is also some parking in Westwood, not too far from UCLA, with bus service up to the museum. This takes more time, but it is cheaper, and it will also allow you to park at times when the Getty Center parking itself is full.

Picnics are permitted at the Getty center. There are lots of tables and outdoor seating and nobody seems to object if you bring your own bottles of wine. It's really nice.

If you want to visit the Getty center you abs absolutely must make a parking reservation on their website or you will not be admitted.

Open daily 10:00-5:30, Saturdays until 7:00, closed Mondays. Admission free but parking $15, no admission on foot. Reservation required.

LA County Museum (LACMA)

https://goo.gl/maps/vc44fxkBuoK2

5905 Wilshire Blvd, Los Angeles, CA 90036

lacma.org

Located in the mid-Wilshire area about halfway between Westwood and downtown, the only county museum is one off time is 1 to 3 or four top organisms in Southern California. It's located in the large park on Wilshire, next to the la Brea tar pits.

The permanent collection includes a wide range of art from all places and periods, including grandmasters objects made by Benvenuto chili me, interesting on furniture, With the strongest part being perhaps 20th century western art.

The also often rotating and servants and visiting exhibits, and these are often even more interesting than the permanent collection.

In the past I have enjoyed exhibits on Picasso, Diego Rivera, and many others.

I also once saw an exhibit of all black canvases, that made me question both the sanity of the modern art movement, and the competence of county staff at judging modern art. The joker who sold that set of "paintings" to the museum must have been laughing pretty hard while counting his money.

But don't let that put you off. There is lots of good stuff here.

Anyone who enjoys art museums should visit the LA County Museum.

There are a couple of cafés in the museum complex. Both are a little bit pricey, but the food is generally good.

In the Summer they sometimes have blues concerts, which are amazing. Check the website for details.

Open 11:00-5)00 weekdays, 10:00-7:00 weekends. Admission $15, free for locals every Mon, Tue, Thu 3-5p and Fri 3-8p (for LA County residents only with id)

Norton Simon Museum

https://goo.gl/maps/KyXFjNKW4pC2

411 W Colorado Blvd, Pasadena, CA 91105

nortonsimon.org

Located in Pasadena, just west of the Old Town area, the Norton Simon Museum is not all that well known, but the collection of art is extremely good. The museum was designed by Frank Gehry. Many consider it superior to MOCA and LACMA, which are much more famous, but this one has a better collection.

There are interesting renaissance, 19th and 20th century European, and modern paintings, as well as a very interesting collection of Indian and Southeast Asian statues.

Popular pieces include ballerina sculptures by Degas, Van Gogh paintings, Andy Warhol pop art, weird stuff by Picasso, random pieces by Rubens, Kandinsky, Manet, Monet, and many others.

I have visited this museum several times and completely recommend it.

Admission $10, free for students.

Museum of Contemporary Art (MOCA)

https://goo.gl/maps/or43YuhCXDp
250 S Grand Ave, Los Angeles, CA 90012
moca.org

Located on Grand Ave. near the Disney Hall, this small downtown museum has rotating exhibits of modern art. It's all a little bit too intellectual for me, or perhaps just too random. It's fun to walk through the exhibits and look at them sideways and try to pretend that I have something meaningful to say about them. Still, it's a fun museum, especially if you are a fan of modern art. Free on Thursday from 5-8 pm.

Hammer Museum

https://goo.gl/maps/Qqg9Np2m6hS2
10899 Wilshire Blvd, Los Angeles, CA 90024
hammer.ucla.edu

Art museum and cultural center associated with UCLA.

Bergamot Station

https://goo.gl/maps/TPnz4EopTen
2525 Michigan Ave, Santa Monica, CA 90404
bergamotstation.com
(310) 453-7535

This is not really a museum, but rather an old train station and surrounding warehouses that have been converted into an arts complex. There are a variety of art galleries that are fun to visit, and many evenings there will be an art opening or two with free wine and snacks and visiting artists.

The station was originally used by the Independence Railroad, then the Pacific Electric trolley system until 1953. Southern Pacific took over the land which it used for a freight depot and for car storage. It also leased parts of the land to various manufacturing enterprises, including a facility for American Appliances. In 1987 the City of Santa Monica purchased the land with the idea that it would eventually be used for a transit station. The purchase was made with transit funds, so the usage in theory is limited to transit.

Since the train was still many years away, the city leased out the land for an arts complex to Wayne Blank, a gallery owner who acted as landlord to the other galleries at this site. He in turn sold his operation, including two acres of his own land, $35 million to RedCar Properties in 2016.

The future of Bergamot Station is up in the air. The 62,000 square feet of office/gallery space are rented at $47,000 a month to RedCar Properties, who subleases to the art galleries. This works out to about 70 cents a square foot, compared to Santa Monica retails property rents which range from $4 to $20 per square foot. Some say it's great to promote the arts, others say it's a sweetheart deal that benefits a few at the cost of Big Blue Bus, who owns the land. They could doubtless get a higher rate if they put the property on the market.

The situation has gotten more complicated lately because one of the stops on the new train is at Bergamot. Instead of using the Bergamot property as a station, the city actually purchased an adjacent piece of land. This allowed Blank to keep his business going and in fact made it more valuable than ever. There are proposed plans for hotels and a mall. Galleries complain that their rents are being raised. Special interest groups and developers are jockeying for advantage as the city discusses the future of this site. As is always the way, large political donations will probably take the day. Some will gain and some will lose in any deal.

In the meantime, while it lasts, Bergamot Station is a fun place to visit. Check the website for gallery listings.

Museums, Culture, Science and Technology

La Brea Tar Pits (Paige Museum)

https://goo.gl/maps/ZUoWpVSWouF2

5801 Wilshire Blvd, Los Angeles, CA 90036

tarpits.org

This small museum is one of the most interesting in the Los Angeles area. It is located on the same piece of property as the LA County Museum. On display are the bones of mammoths, sabretooth tigers and dire wolves that were trapped in the tar pits.

The tarpits themselves can be viewed for free outside the museum, where the smell of asphalt is strong. The ground in the Los Angeles area is permeated with oil and tar. There is enough oil in the ground that Long Beach and Ventura are major drilling locations. Beverly hills has an oil well on campus. But here we see the oil in the form of tar.

Back in prehistoric times, before the ice ages, tar rose to the surface and created the La Brea tar pits. Rainwater would cover them. Animals who came to drink would find themselves stuck, and 20,000 years later, they are now found in this museum.

Admission to the museum is not expensive, and they're also stairways where you can pass through the different layers of the tar pits and see how the fossil animals were trapped. It doesn't take long to see the museum, but it is extremely interesting.

Open 9:30-5:00. Admission $10 kids $17 adults.

Natural History Museum

https://goo.gl/maps/KqAEU2m5jgB2

900 W Exposition Blvd, Los Angeles, CA 90007

nhm.org

Located in Exposition Park, at the south side of the USC campus, near the Memorial Stadium, this fun museum has everything from chocolate plants, to giant squids, to skeletons of prehistoric dinosaurs. It's an old school museum in a giant white building with Greek Columns and big stairs out front. Kids like the T Rex and the insect zoo. I love this kind of stuff too. Recommended.

Parking in their lot is $12 and will be difficult if there is a USC game. You could take the train here from Santa Monica. Entrance costs $5 to $12 depending on age.

California Science Museum

https://goo.gl/maps/RaLiCL3htUH2

700 Exposition Park Dr, Los Angeles, CA 90037

californiasciencecenter.org

(323) 724-3623

The space shuttle "Endeavor" is the most popular exhibit at this science museum, which is located in Exposition Park right next to the Natural History Museum. There are lots of interactive exhibits, which are popular with kids. Admission is free, but there are special exhibits which may have extra charges, and parking in their lot is $12.

Museum of Flying

https://goo.gl/maps/4BWeRMUBSox
3100 Airport Ave, Santa Monica, CA 90405
museumofflying.org
(310) 398-2500
With both McDonald Douglas and Hughes in the area, Santa Monica has played a major part in the nation's aerospace industry, especially during WWII. The airplane factories are gone, but Santa Monica field is left over from that time. This is a small but excellent museum with airplanes, on the north side of Santa Monica Airport. The old McDonald Douglas field was here, so it has some real air history.

Petersen Automotive Museum

https://goo.gl/maps/VpHEjYm6DoD2
6060 Wilshire Blvd, Los Angeles, CA 90036
petersen.org
Located on Wilshire Boulevard across from LA County Museum, the Petersen automotive Museum contains a large collection of beautiful and interesting automobiles It's not a huge museum, but it's a very fun way to spend the afternoon, or even a whole day, depending on your level of interest in vehicles. Admission $15. Open 10:00-6:00.

Nethercutt Auto Collection

https://goo.gl/maps/9WgWFfJfZr62
15151 Bledsoe St, Sylmar, CA 91342
nethercuttcollection.org
(818) 364-6464
This is a truly amazing auto collection, with countless super cool cars. Best of all, it's free. Call ahead to make an appointment for entrance. Reservations absolutely required. Totally worth a trip.

Los Angeles Police Museum

https://goo.gl/maps/gaeq6oBCH372
6045 York Blvd, Los Angeles, CA 90042
(323) 344-9445
Exhibiting the history of the LAPD, with armored cars, radios & badges, plus interactive programs.

Ice Cream Museum

https://goo.gl/maps/uWVKgPbuPTs
2018 E 7th Pl, Los Angeles, CA 90021
museumoficecream.com
(855) 258-0719

A pop art museum of Ice Cream with samples on the way. Expensive but fun. Lots of samples. If you hate ice cream or sprinkles then this place is not for you. Everything sounds great, but the entrance fee of $30 is high. An alternative would be a trip to Three Twins on Main Street, or Fosselmans in San Gabriel, where the ice cream will be amazingly good and quite a bit cheaper. Or maybe do all three.

Museum of Jurassic Technology

https://goo.gl/maps/MJxw8zN3UPJ2

9341 Venice Blvd, Culver City, CA 90232

mjt.org

(310) 836-6131

This Culver City area museum of silliness and obscure knowledge will amuse those who don't take it all so seriously. A small dash of "Ripley's Believe it or not" without quite as much commercialism. Free tea and cookies with admission. $8 entrance.

Cabrillo Marine Aquarium

https://goo.gl/maps/RJZndSzFmUN2

3720 Stephen M White Dr., San Pedro, CA 90731

cabrillomarineaquarium.org

(310) 548-7562

Located on the edge of Cabrillo Beach Park in San Pedro, very close to Long Beach, this small facility is as much a science museum as it is an aquarium. There are touching pools where kids can see the fish up close. It's very much the opposite of the nearby Aquarium of the Pacific. Admission is by donation, suggested $5. There is also a beach park here, so if you get tired of the aquarium you can get some sun or go swimming.

Museum of Death

https://goo.gl/maps/2mYNm7ps1Kx

6031 Hollywood Blvd, Hollywood, CA 90028

museumofdeath.net

(323) 466-8011

For those with a fascination with serial killers and crime, the museum of death will be a fun time. Others will find it horrific. It's certainly not for everyone. Located in the tourist zone of Hollywood Blvd, near the Ripley's Museum and the Walk of Fame. The exhibits are mostly text and photos, with some video. The subject is interesting, and I'm not against it, but you are more likely to find me at Amoeba Records, which is only a few blocks away, or Torung, which is just up the street.

Architecture

Los Angeles has some amazing architecture. Much of the best is found in Hollywood, Los Feliz or Pasadena, which are some of the older parts of town. Architects active in this area include Frank Lloyd Wrights, Greene & Greene, Schindler, and more recently, Frank Gehry. There are certain buildings that are businesses listed elsewhere, that would be interesting to anyone with an interest in Architecture, such as the Biltmore Hotel downtown, Green House in Pasadena, the Bradbury Building downtown, the Masonic Hall in Pasadena, the Getty Villa, the Griffith Observatory, the Cicada Club,

The Mayan theater. There are so many. In this list I am including some architecturally noteworthy buildings that aren't listed elsewhere.

Bradbury Building

https://goo.gl/maps/prXtZkTQqrS2

304 S Broadway, Los Angeles, CA 90013

bradburybuilding.blogspot.in

The movie "Blade Runner" is one of my favorites. Several of the most memorable scenes were filmed in the Bradbury building in downtown LA.

In the movie, this is the big building with the courtyard and the iron frame and the old-fashioned elevator, where one of the genetic designers lives. The building is a disaster, and there is rain coming through the ceiling the entire time. The climactic fight in the movie, between Harrison Ford and one of the replicants, takes place in this building.

In reality, the Bradbury building is meticulously maintained and full of nice offices. It's a stunning example of Victorian iron framed architecture, reminiscent of some of the fantastic old department stores in Paris. Because of the movie association and has become a bit of a landmark.

Ennis House

https://goo.gl/maps/ddcjHEBSDTK2

2655 Glendower Ave Los Angeles, CA 90027

Frank Lloyd Wright's 1924 structure was supposed to be Mayan inspired, though one can only suppose that Wright had never been to Mexico. There is nothing remotely Mayan about it. The building is metal framed with much of it simply cement retaining walls. The most interesting stylistic detail is the use of large abstract sculptured tiles covering walls throughout the building and the exterior. Like many of Wright's buildings, it is short on windows but long on style. The building was used in the film "Blade Runner" as Deckard's apartment. Imagine being able to afford this, on a police salary. Unfortunately, the building is not open to the public, but can be viewed from the street, and it's interesting enough to be worth a visit.

Union Station

https://goo.gl/maps/y4vmQyKsaR

12800 N Alameda St, Los Angeles, CA 90012

unionstationla.com

The train station in Chinatown is the main station serving Los Angeles. Built in 1939, it is something of a Deco legend. The outside is "mission" style, but the interior has huge high ceilings and futurist deco design everywhere. Architecture fans will love it.

Union Station is used for the police station in the film "Blade Runner". The Captain's office was built at one end of the ticketing area, and the rest of the area is filled with smoke, colored lights, and police about their duties.

The station is something you can see for free that is pretty interesting. There is no free parking, but maybe you can find a meter in Chinatown. Alternately, if you got here by train, then take a few minutes to check it out.

Hollyhock House

https://goo.gl/maps/9KqZtcudXG42

4800 Hollywood Blvd, Los Angeles, CA 90027

barnsdall.org

(323) 913-4030

One of the most famous of Frank Lloyd Wright's homes, Hollyhock House is located on Hollywood Blvd, close to countless wonderful Thai restaurants.

The building was built for oil heiress Aline Barnsdall who hired Frank Lloyd Wright to build a house and a public theater, then fired him when he went way over budget of $50,000 (he spent more than $200,000). Rudolph Schindler and Richard Neutra helped finish the house. Like many of right's buildings, it is large and tomblike, with lots of geometrical rectangles, fine wood accents, and few windows. Barnsdall never lived here, and neither did anyone else. Eventually she donated it to the city of LA. The site itself is a park, and the home, one of Wright's most famous. Admission $3-$7, depending on age.

Castle Green

https://goo.gl/maps/SrLrBRNiERm

99 S Raymond Ave, Pasadena, CA 91105

castlegreen.com

(626) 793-0359

Like something out of a Maxfield Parrish painting, the Castle Green is a 1920's apartment building, heavily influenced by imaginative paintings of the Alhambra, with columns and stained-glass windows and orientalist influences everywhere. It's not the middle east, but rather, the middle east as it was seen by Hollywood set builders. Somehow it is completely wonderful.

The Castle Green does a big business in wedding parties. There are apartments inside. I've only been here for events, but I assume if nothing is going on you can probably go in and have a look around.

Gamble House

https://goo.gl/maps/EtU1hZUt8632

4 Westmoreland Pl, Pasadena, CA 91103

gamblehouse.org

(626) 793-3334

Charles and Henry Green designed this huge home in 1908. The client, heir to the Proctor and Gamble business, wanted a large craftsman style home. It combines the frame and structure consciousness of the craftsman style with elements reminiscent of Japanese temples. The uses of woods is amazing. There is much stained glass. The furnishings were all designed by the architects. Tours are available.

Eames Case Study House #8

https://goo.gl/maps/j3jNGZD8X5U2

203 Chautauqua Blvd, Pacific Palisades, CA 90272

eamesfoundation.org

(310) 459-9663

This cubist home in Pacific Palisades was built as part of the Arts and Architecture magazine series of case study homes. It was built 80 years ago, but would be considered futuristic today. Modern buildings are often simply big shoe boxes with metal frames and big windows, but Eames explores how to make this interesting. Exterior self-guided tour is $10, interior is $210. Not surprisingly, many opt for exterior only.

Stahl House

https://goo.gl/maps/RcYfqZkwAgs

1635 Woods Dr., Los Angeles, CA 90069

stahlhouse.com

(208) 429-1058

Why not build a house completely out of glass? You still need a frame, but this building in the Hollywood Hills comes as close as you can. The view is amazing. Admission is expensive, $50-$100 depending on how many people come with you in your car. Most expensive if you come alone.

Masonic Temple

https://goo.gl/maps/8cvBeUzjSAz

200 S Euclid Ave, Pasadena, CA 91101

lindygroove.com

This neo-classical building looks like something you would expect to find in a national monument or maybe on the back side of a coin. It's big and white and cubic and stone. Big columns and stairs at the entrance make it neo-classical, while the huge dance floor let us know that it is here for fun. Every Thursday there's swing with Lindy Groove, which is the best swing dance venue in, well, anywhere. Other nights, it's still a cool building.

Schindler House

https://goo.gl/maps/Md2w9t9deTF2

833 N Kings Rd, West Hollywood, CA 90069

makcenter.org

The incredible house of architect Rudolf Schindler is available for "self-guided tours". The style is not that unusual for modern homes, but put it in perspective that this building was built in the mid 1920's, and you can see why Schindler is considered a visionary. Entrance is free. There are several other Schindler homes in the area which can be viewed. Ask the folks at the Mak Center for more information. Their office is here in the Schindler house.

History

Mission San Juan Capistrano

https://goo.gl/maps/x6wDyqQF5h12

26801 Ortega Hwy, San Juan Capistrano, CA 92675

missionsjc.com

(949) 234-1300

Located in southern Orange County, a little more than an hour south of Santa Monica, this is probably the best preserved of the old Spanish missions in California. The mission was founded in 1776, the same year as the America revolution. The location was chosen to be halfway between San Diego and the mission at San Gabriel.

Mission San Juan Capistrano became the first place in California to produce wine in 1779.

The Spanish built a large stone cathedral here, which was very impressive, but unfortunately it collapsed in an earthquake in the early 1800's, and has never been successfully restored.

For many years Junipero Serra preached at the chapel here on Sundays. He was canonized in 2015.

The mission was nationalized in 1833 and went into a long period of decline. The land was sold off, the Franciscans took all their belongings with them when they left, the Indians left, and the buildings were neglected and fell into disrepair.

Such was the state of things when California became a state in 1850. American president Abraham Lincoln returned the mission to the Catholic Church in 1865. There were attempts to restore the complex, which were completed in the early 1900's.

Today, the complex is still a church, but it is also a major cultural and historical center. The various buildings of the mission have been extensively restored.

This mission is known for the arrival every March of doves from Goya, Argentina, on St. Josephs Day.

In 1984, a modern church complex was constructed just north and west of the Mission compound and is now known as Mission Basilica San Juan Capistrano. Today, the mission compound serves as a museum, with the Serra Chapel within the compound serving as a chapel for the mission parish. Entrance is $9.

San Gabriel Mission

https://goo.gl/maps/jDrCBJDFn4B2

428 S Mission Dr., San Gabriel, CA 91776

sangabrielmissionchurch.org

(626) 457-3035

Founded in 1771, this mission was active as a major cultural and economic center. The largest activity was farming. A number of other missions were administered from San Gabriel, including Los Angeles. In 1834, the Mexican government nationalized all the missions, which resulted in San Gabriel being abandoned. It was used as a church starting in 1862, and then restored in the early 1900's. It is an active church today, and can be visited. It lacks the polish of a commercial attraction like Disneyland, but there is real history here. Today there is an elementary and high school at this location. Visitors can see the church, museum, and the grounds. It is about 15 minutes east of downtown LA, or 45 minutes from Santa Monica.

California Heritage Museum

https://goo.gl/maps/6zA2RFt4Nt12

2612 Main St, Santa Monica, CA 90405

californiaheritagemuseum.org

(310) 392-8537

Small local history museum on Main Street by the Victorian.

Santa Monica History Museum

https://goo.gl/maps/RFJus4jroet

1350 7th St, Santa Monica, CA 90401

santamonicahistory.org
(310) 395-2290
Small museum associated with the library. Ignore the hours posted on the door, they are open when they feel like it.

Chumash Cave Paintings

https://goo.gl/maps/U9CSeGVax332
Hwy 154, Santa Barbara, CA 93105
parks.ca.gov
(805) 733-3713
Located in Santa Barbara, this site has cave paintings done by the local Chumash Indians in the 1600's. It is now a state park. The art is reminiscent of cave paintings found in Europe from Cro-Magnon times.

Southwest Museum of the American Indian

https://goo.gl/maps/TcUJEdPL2yr
234 Museum Dr., Los Angeles, CA 90065
theautry.org
(323) 221-2164
Owned by the Autry Museum in Griffith Park, this museum concentrates on Indian culture and history. Only open on Saturdays, 10-4.

Parks and Gardens

Griffith Park

https://goo.gl/maps/c7i8sLqrVxk
4730 Crystal Springs Dr, Los Angeles, CA 90027
laparks.org
Griffith Park is a huge 4200 acre area of hills and ridges that tower over the los Feliz neighborhood of Los Angeles. It's north of downtown, south of Burbank, and east of Hollywood. There are hiking trails all through the park. Vegetation is sparse, because the LA area is a desert and the park is not irrigated.

Griffith Park is best known for the observatory which is on top of one of the highest hills and has an amazing view out of her downtown and Hollywood

Griffith Park is best observed from an automobile just after dark when you can get the famous view of the city lights. It's free, and it definitely should be on anyone's bucket list for a visit to Los Angeles.

The Greek Theater is a popular outdoor music venue in the southwest area of the park.

The Zoo is also in this park in the northeast corner. See separate listing.

Griffith Park is open 5:00 am - 10:30 pm. Free.

Griffith Observatory

https://goo.gl/maps/AXrjGjchKZF2
2800 E Observatory Rd, Los Angeles, CA 90027
Located in the southern part of the park, the Observatory was made famous in the movie "Rebel Without a Cause" with James Dean, but has been in countless other movies since that time.

The view from the Observatory over Hollywood is amazing. It will seem familiar, because it's been used in movies so many times.

The observatory itself has a small museum and a show of twinkling lights that mimic the night sky. It's an educational device that's used to teach people how to identify constellations.

From the observatory there are windy roads that circle around down to Los Feliz and Thai town on one side, and over in the direction of the equestrian center and the San Fernando Valley in the other.

A trip to the Griffith Observatory is an absolute must for any visitor to the LA area.

LA Zoo

https://goo.gl/maps/AFFQXGBj1MK2

5333 Zoo Dr, Los Angeles, CA 90027

lazoo.org

Located inside Griffith Park, the Los Angeles zoo is a highly underrated attraction. I think it's just fantastic. I think it's really important for kids to learn about animals, not just by seeing them on television or in books, but by seeing them living and breathing.

The best-known zoo in Southern California is the San Diego Zoo, but the one in Los Angeles Zoo seems roughly equivalent and is much closer and much cheaper. It lacks the Disney style commercialization of the San Diego zoo, but I don't really need that.

Open daily 10-5, adults $21 children $16.

Huntington Library and Botanical Garden

https://goo.gl/maps/c1n3Gb8qJiR2

1151 Oxford Rd, San Marino, CA 91108

huntington.org

Open 10-5 most days but check ahead.

This beautiful arboretum and park and is the old Huntington estate. Located just south of Pasadena, it is a huge oasis of green surrounded by urban Los Angeles. There is a library, an art collection, and a wonderful botanical gardens. If you're looking for a place to walk all day long and enjoy the Arboretum, then this is the right place. Good for picnics. There also food available in the park which is OK and not all that expensive, though of course it's much cheaper if you pack your own lunch.

Theme Parks

Universal Studios

https://goo.gl/maps/wgug4p2xLCp

100 Universal City Plaza, Universal City, CA 91608

universalstudioshollywood.com

(800) 864-8377

The basic business premise of Universal Studios is that millions of tourists come to Hollywood and want to see films being made. So they are invited to come and spend money at Universal Studios.

Unfortunately, the basic promise is impossible. Movie studios are a place of work, and absolute silence is required. That's why they film on soundstages with soundproof walls. They need to keep the noise out. Tourists are absolutely not welcome when real movies are being filmed.

Universal Studios instead offers a B grade theme park. You can write on the rides and see fiberglass replications of famous movie sets. But there are no movies being made here.

They used to have a flight simulator thing called "Back to the Future" that had a vehicle on legs that would rock and shake. A 360° movie around it created a great illusion of flying. That was pretty good, but I hear they have retired it.

Most of your time at Universal Studios will be spent waiting in line. If the lines get too short, then they will close some of the lines, to make sure the line is long is long enough. They have done a careful analysis and management feels that waiting in line is a valuable part of the experience when visiting this or any other theme park.

If you were to go on a rainy day when there are no lines, you could see the whole park in about 20 minutes. Considering the amount they charge for admission, management feels this is unacceptable. By forcing you to wait in line they convert 20 minutes worth of rides into an all-day experience.

Food at the Universal Studios theme park is absolutely horrible and very expensive. Even McDonald's seems like gourmet fare compared to what they serve here.

There is also a mall attached, which is fairly decent as malls go, except for the really expensive parking. They're quite a lot of restaurants and bars and blues legend B. B. King has a blues club here. When he was alive he used to turn up occasionally.

I just don't like this theme park. I think you would have a lot more fun to go to the beach and go body surfing. If you want to go to a theme park, go to Six Flags Magic Mountain, which at least has some pretty cool roller coasters. If you want a movie studio go to Paramount or NBC. As far as the mall, there must be a mall in your hometown. It will have all the same stores and probably has free parking. Why fly all the way to Los Angeles to visit a mall?

Disneyland

https://goo.gl/maps/PW6dJMEhifN2
1313 Disneyland Dr, Anaheim, CA 92802
disneyland.disney.go.com
(714) 781-4636

I'm not a big fan of theme parks and I'm not really a big fan of Disney either. I just hate waiting in line. I hate overpriced mediocre food. I hate feeling that I am being manipulated by marketers. Bring all these things together and you've got Disneyland.

Originally the theme park was created to allow the company to promote Mickey Mouse and other characters from Disney's movies and the old Mouse Club show.

If you have a look at Disney's 10k annual report, you will find that Disney has become a theme park chain with a movie studio attached. the movies come and go, but the theme park business is vastly more profitable.

When I was a kid Disneyland had individual tickets for rides with letters like ABC and D. The really good rides where the E Ticket rides, and they cost more than the others.

These days most people get all day tickets, and the concept of E Ticket rides doesn't exist anymore.

You can also buy line passes. It cost a lot of money but it will save you a lot of time. Somehow this seems like cheating. It's just one more way for the company to separate money from guests.

Food at Disneyland is not quite as bad as the food at Universal Studios, but it is still a solid notch below the standard of McDonald's or Hometown Buffet, and it's really expensive.

In Japan they opened a Disneyland near Tokyo which was controversial because they prohibited picnic baskets. Japanese people love to pack up rice balls in a Bento box and take them out on a family outing. Disneyland absolutely prohibits this. They want to force you to buy their super expensive and mediocre food.

There are large number of hotels near Disneyland, some associate with the Disney company, and some independent. In general, you will pay a lot more to stay in the hotels that are officially associated with Disney.

The Anaheim convention center is adjacent to Disneyland and while it is not an attraction by itself, there are trade fairs such as the NAMM show which can be a lot of fun to visit.

Disneyland is about an hour from Santa Monica in clear traffic.

Downtown Disney

https://goo.gl/maps/hSvTAujkkd32

1580 Disneyland Dr., Anaheim, CA 92802

disneyland.disney.go.com

This is an outdoor mall is close to Disneyland and the convention center. There is nothing particularly special about it as a mall, but it's nice enough. On some afternoons they will have rockabilly or swing bands playing in the Central Square which is super big fun and highly recommended.

The biggest problem at downtown Disney is parking. They don't want people avoiding the expensive parking rates for Disneyland by parking here at the mall. So, if you don't have a validation, it's going to cost you about $30 to park for a couple of hours at the downtown Disney mall. I got nailed by this once. It won't happen to me again. You have been warned.

Anaheim Convention Center

There is nothing particularly interesting about the convention center, however, they do have some interesting trade shows, such as the NAMM music show. It's very close to Disneyland.

Hollywood Attractions

Walk of Fame

https://goo.gl/maps/zxsuk9foXJp

N Highland Ave & Hollywood Blvd, Los Angeles, CA 90028

viwright.com

(323) 469-8311

Many famous stars have tiles in the sidewalk here dedicated to them. For me this is a pretty dumb tourist attraction, but if you want to see it, it's found here on Highland and Hollywood. Free. It's a sidewalk, so it is open all the time.

Hollywood Cemetery Movie Screenings

https://goo.gl/maps/7PxV2NK6ba72

Hollywood Forever Cemetery, 6000 Santa Monica Blvd, Los Angeles, CA 90038

cinespia.org

(323) 522-6870

They show movies outdoors at the cemetery. It's gotten to be very popular. Bring lawn chairs, snacks and drinks. Get there early if you want to get a good seat. Check the website to see what is playing. Bring a group and this will be a lot of fun. The cemetery itself is of historical interest – you will find more famous people here than you will on the "walk of fame".

Mulholland Drive

https://goo.gl/maps/rXYVPrKN3F42
8591 Mulholland Dr, Los Angeles, CA 90046
smmc.ca.gov
(310) 589-3200
This long and winding road follows the spine of the Hollywood hills and goes all the way to Malibu, which takes a goo 40 minutes. One of the obligatory Hollywood experiences is driving down this road at night. You can look out over the lights of Hollywood on one side, and the San Fernando Valley on the other. There is one discontinuous spot to the west of the Getty Museum, where Mullholland stops and then starts again, but if you check the map, you can go around.

The Hollywood Museum

https://goo.gl/maps/Qqv3EVRwwUu
1660 N Highland Ave, Hollywood, CA 90028
thehollywoodmuseum.com
(323) 464-7776
Fun exhibit of Hollywood props and costumes, in a building which I believe used to belong to Coco Chanel.

Greek Theater

https://goo.gl/maps/Wv4jXyK6oYA2
2700 N Vermont Ave, Los Angeles, CA 90027
lagreektheatre.com
(844) 524-7335
This wonderful outdoor theater reminds me of the Hollywood Bowl. Concerts here are fun.

Sports Stadiums

Rose Bowl

https://goo.gl/maps/U4jTubBkPus
1001 Rose Bowl Dr, Pasadena, CA 91103
rosebowlstadium.com
(626) 577-3100
This stadium in Pasadena is the location of the Rose Bowl, a college football match between two of the best teams in the country.

Dodger Stadium

https://goo.gl/maps/NyaGKtdpXvr
1000 Vin Scully Ave, Los Angeles, CA 90012
losangeles.dodgers.mlb.com

(866) 363-4377
Located north of downtown in the Silverlake neighborhood, Dodger Stadium is home to baseball's Dodgers, and the famous "Dodgers Dogs".

Staples Center

https://goo.gl/maps/upy3mxr8PEo
1111 S Figueroa St, Los Angeles, CA 90015
staplescenter.com
(213) 742-7100
The Staples Center is a huge sports and concert venue. That seats about 20,909 people. Teams that play here include the basketball's Lakers, the Clippers, and the Kings hockey team.

The arena is home to the Los Angeles Lakers and the Los Angeles Clippers of the National Basketball Association (NBA), the Los Angeles Kings of the National Hockey League (NHL),

Unless you're seeing a professional sports game or a big rock concert, you probably wouldn't have any occasion to visit the staple center.

The venue is named after Staples, the office supply store. I think this is kind of lame, but that's how they do things around here.

Factories

If you are interested in manufacturing, here are some fun places to visit:

Sriracha Factory (Huy Fong)

https://goo.gl/maps/ShQ9pE7e9ux
4800 Azusa Canyon Rd. Irwindale, CA 91706
(626) 286-8328
http://www.huyfong.com/toursnow/
This tasty hot sauce, in the clear squirt bottle with the green top, has taken the world by storm. They have tours and welcome visitors. They are located in Irwindale, about an hour east of Santa Monica

Musical instruments

Never mind Austin, Memphis, Chicago or New York. Los Angeles is the heart of the music industry, for better hours. All the big record companies are here, and this means the music is here too . Bands I would be considered amazing in other cities that are found playing in small unknown bars. and we also found some very good instrument stores

McCabe's

https://goo.gl/maps/kbFgThNwDhK2
3101 Pico Blvd, Santa Monica, CA 90405
mccabes.com
(310) 828-4497
If you like acoustic instruments then this is the place. There are plenty of banjos and ukuleles too, and other more exotic instruments. They also have lessons and do repairs. I've had a number of guitar

repairs done at McCabe's and they did a fantastic job. Whenever you visit, you also get free coffee and McCabe's logo picks too.

McCabe's has concerts too. They move aside the guitars and bring out a hundred or so folding chairs, set up the stage, and put on enormously popular shows of bluegrass, country, and alternative music. In certain circles, McCabe's is quite well known, and they are able to bring in some surprisingly well-known acts for their informal little stage.

If you like acoustic instruments then you should definitely come and check this place.

Truetone

https://goo.gl/maps/NoVcjwTPZL92

714 Santa Monica Blvd, Santa Monica, CA 90401

truetonemusic.com

(310) 393-8232

For the amplified rock and roll crowd, this is the best specialty guitar shop around. Their list of rock and roller customers is second to none.

Truetone does a very large business and repairs, mostly of electric instruments. If you look in the back there's always a huge stack of instruments waiting to be repaired or repair prices are high, but they seem to be good.

I got tubes for my Fender Vibrochamp here. They have everything you need for that tube powered musical device.

U-Space Ukuleles & Coffee

https://goo.gl/maps/gYhdtByCtbq

244 S San Pedro St, Los Angeles, CA 90012

uspacela.com

(323) 577-5567

This fun Ukulele shop located in Little Tokyo (downtown) has both local and Chinese made Ukuleles, as well as nice coffee and sheet music. A good place. My sister bought her Ukulele here. They said it used to belong to Don Ho, who is famous for the song "tiny bubbles".

Fender Guitar Factory

https://goo.gl/maps/iGxQ4zvneqr

311 Cessna Cir, Corona, CA 92880

(951) 898-4000

http://www2.fender.com/features/visitor-center/

The famous Stratocaster guitars are made in Carlsbad, California. Unfortunately, the tour is currently closed. They claim it will open again, but no date has been given.

Taylor Guitar Factory

https://goo.gl/maps/5CsBhFeRfwK2

1980 Gillespie Way, El Cajon, CA 92020

taylorguitars.com

(619) 258-1207

The famous steel string acoustic guitars are made in this high-tech factory just east of San Diego. It's a three hour drive from Santa Monica, but the tour itself is a lot of fun.

Guitar Center

Hollywood Store

https://goo.gl/maps/wxc4gZr4PmL2

7425 Sunset Blvd, Hollywood, CA 90046

stores.guitarcenter.com

(323) 874-1060

Westwood Store

https://goo.gl/maps/aAbD1DwRdUz

10831 W Pico Blvd, Los Angeles, CA 90064

stores.guitarcenter.com

(310) 475-0637

The granddaddy of all big box guitar stores, Guitar Center is bigger and has more branches than most any guitar or music store in the world. They have a wide range of Fender, Gibson, as well has hordes of cheap junk Chinese instruments at generally competitive prices. They also have keyboard, drums, speakers, and anything else you might need to get your rock band started.

Sam Ash

https://goo.gl/maps/ToyaCMfSoJS2
7360 Sunset Blvd, Los Angeles, CA 90046
locations.samashmusic.com
(323) 850-1050
This store has roughly the same merchandise as Guitar Center, with a slight edge on technology. Prices are usually about the same. There is a big Sam Ash store on Santa Monica Blvd across the street from the mothership Guitar Center store.
Sam Ash is particularly strong in computers and electronic music. They also have recording equipment. The staff are very nice and it's a good store.

Companies in Santa Monica

This is a partial list of some well-known companies that have offices in or around Santa Monica and nearby neighborhoods.

Yahoo

https://goo.gl/maps/nduTAiU5utm
11975 Bluff Creek Dr., Los Angeles, CA 90094
yahoo.com
(408) 349-3300
Formerly at: 2401 Colorado Ave, Yahoo had large offices in Santa Monica. They have recently moved to Playa Vista, near Marina del Rey, in search of larger and less expensive office space.

Google

https://goo.gl/maps/fsCZ4mLC7ur
340 Main St, Venice, CA 90291
google.com
(310) 310-6000
Located in a cool building that looks like a giant pair of binoculars on Main Street, Google has long had offices in Santa Monica.

Rand Corporation

https://goo.gl/maps/t6pXA2HBbfp
1776 Main St, Santa Monica, CA 90401
rand.org
(310) 393-0411
This think tank was founded in 1948 as a division of Douglas Aircraft, but has since become independent. They do studies and reports on many subjects many with military/government funding. Friends who have worked there say they are a great employer.

MTV

https://goo.gl/maps/WUpDuhJo6r12
2600 Colorado Ave, Santa Monica, CA 90404
(310) 752-8000
www.mtv.com
MTV has long had facilities in Santa Monica.

Naughty Dog

https://goo.gl/maps/TwinnpPEYWs
2425 Olympic Blvd, Santa Monica, CA 90404
naughtydog.com
(310) 633-9100
Originally located on third street, upstairs from where Everytable is now located, Naughty Dog has moved to a nearby location on Olympic, where they were able to get larger office space. They are makers of some great console games such as "The Last of Us".

Hulu

https://goo.gl/maps/WfefXse1Q5E2
2500 Broadway, Santa Monica, CA 90404
hulu.com
(310) 571-4700
This popular streaming video company has become a market leader. If you want to dump the cable company, these folks offer alternatives.

Microsoft Advertising

https://goo.gl/maps/oJfH8u3jyws
2425 Olympic Blvd #5000w, Santa Monica, CA 90404
advertising.microsoft.com
(310) 449-7400
Microsoft has a large facility in the Watergarden, an office complex on Olympic Blvd.

Riot Games

https://goo.gl/maps/tYhQnmHKbgm
12333 W Olympic Blvd, Los Angeles, CA 90064
riotgames.com
(424) 231-1111
This company's main offices were moved recently from Santa Monica into nearby neighborhood of LA. They specialize in free online games that are financed by in-game purchases. "League of Legends" has been hugely successful, and the company is expanding rapidly. I asked a friend who works there, if many people really make significant in-game purchases, and he said, that a person who becomes truly addicted to a game can spend quite a lot.

Snapchat

https://goo.gl/maps/EvWQ8Fi1yKv

523 Ocean Front Walk, Venice, CA 90291

snapchat.com

(310) 399-3339

New business involving photos and Facebook. They have brought a lot of employee to Santa Monica.

Leaf Group (Demand Media, eHow)

https://goo.gl/maps/FSDQfrYfEok

1655 26th St, Santa Monica, CA 90404

demandmedia.com

(310) 394-6400

Demand Media specializes in writing up articles to match Google searches, and uses these articles to carry advertising. eHow for example, gives solutions to many technical problems that people have, and at times can be helpful. The problems is that some of the answers are quickly written and not in depth. The business model seems to be working. The company was recently rebranded as "Leaf Group".

Edmunds

https://goo.gl/maps/kX87XQxiwy72

2401 Colorado Ave, Santa Monica, CA 90404

edmunds.com

(310) 309-6300

They started with a popular car magazine, but these days it's mostly online. Edmunds gives car ratings and prices and is considered authoritative.

Dollar Shave Club

https://goo.gl/maps/RWgbcfVfA6u

13335 Maxella Ave, Marina Del Rey, CA 90292

dollarshaveclub.com

(310) 975-8528

Located in Venice, this business specializes in selling razor blades by subscription. Since the price of most razors in stores is completely silly, they seem to have found an open market.

Dunn and Bradstreet

https://goo.gl/maps/S19VU2t4hMQ2

22761 Pacific Coast Hwy, Malibu, CA 90265

dandb.com

(800) 700-2733

Located just up PCH in Malibu, Dunn and Bradstreet is a credit agency for businesses. These days they are getting more and more into data mining.

Cornerstone OnDemand

https://goo.gl/maps/tQn5HpKsBNF2
1601 Cloverfield Blvd #600S, Santa Monica, CA 90404
cornerstoneondemand.com
(310) 752-0200
This successful company helps other businesses with their human resources tasks.

RPA (Rubin Postaer and Associates)

2525 Colorado Ave # 100, Santa Monica, CA 90404
rpa.com
(310) 394-4000
Successful advertising agency with clients such as Honda, Southwest Airlines and AM/PM Minimarts.

Universities & Colleges

There are countless universities and colleges in the LA area. We will list only a few here that visitors are likely to encounter.

UCLA

https://goo.gl/maps/QpHukk35PTE2
405 Hilgard Avenue
Los Angeles, CA 90024
http://www.ucla.edu
The University of California at Los Angeles is one of the largest universities in California, with 31,000 undergraduate students and about half that many graduates. It's a state school, so tuitions are supposed to be reasonable, although every year it is getting more expensive. When I attended graduate school there, it was $750 a quarter. Now in-state tuition is $12,918 (2017), while out-of-state tuition: $39,600 (2017). That's just for tuition. Sister schools in the UC system include Berkeley, UCSF, UC San Diego, and UC Santa Barbara.

UCLA is located between Westwood Boulevard and Sunset Boulevard, a few blocks east of the 405 freeway. It's a nice location, though somewhat problematic for students, because it is a very expensive area. The Westwood neighborhood is sandwiched between Bel Air Brentwood and Beverly Hills. You won't find any housing deals here.

UCLA offers strong or at least top 20 rankings in almost all popular subjects, and fields nationally ranked teams in most sports. The best-known departments are medicine, which receives almost unlimited research funding from the federal government, and the film department, which has produced many famous filmmakers. Well known graduates of UCLA include Jim Morrison and etc. theater

University of California, Los Angeles holds the third-most Olympic medals among American universities (233 total medals).

Famous UCLA graduates include Jackie Robinson, Kareem Abdul-Jabbar, Tim Robbins, Rob Reiner, James Dean, Jim Morrison, George Takei, John Williams, Jams Franco, Vint Cerf, Jack Black, Steve Martin, Francis Coppola, Troy Aikman, Bill Walton, Tom Bradley (Mayor), Antonio Villaraigosa (mayor), Alex Payne. 15 people associated with UCLA have won Nobel Prizes.

In 2017-2018, *US News & World Report* ranked UCLA as the #1 public university in the United States in a tie with its sister campus, UC Berkeley.

The UCLA campus is a very nice, traditional university campus and m makes for a very pleasant walk on a summer afternoon. Parking can be a problem, and street parking is totally nonexistent.

There are many good and inexpensive restaurants in the Westwood neighborhood just South of campus. Unfortunately, parking is often an issue.

USC

https://goo.gl/maps/aYLCw3BLmVr

850 W 37th St, Los Angeles, CA 90007

http://www.usc.edu

The University of Southern California is the crosstown rival school to UCLA. A private school, USC has approximately 19,000 undergraduate and 24,000 graduate students.

The campus itself is very pleasant, and it is an excellent school, but the location is a mixed blessing. Only a few blocks away the neighborhoods become completely sketchy and the crime rate goes way up.

There is a joke that USC is the "University of South Central". South Central is the name of the blighted urban neighborhood around USC, guy was which is located just a little bit west of downtown Los Angeles.

The USC sports teams are called the Trojans, by which is a reference to the ancient Greeks, not the popular latex product. Originally the team was called the fighting Methodists, but somewhere along the line they decided to redo their image.

USC offers excellent education in almost every field. Like crosstown rival UCLA, the strongest departments are medicine and the film school. USC consistently ranks in the top 20 in most every field.

Famous USC graduates include Shinzo Abe, George Lucas, Neil Armstrong, Frank Gehry, John Wayne, Clint Eastwood, Judd Apatow, and Mohammed Morsi. If you want to be a film director, actor, or the president of a foreign country, USC could be a good place to study.

The Natural History Museum at USC is excellent and well worth visiting. There are dinosaur bones and rocks and exotic plants and lots of other exhibits that are fun for people of all ages. It is well worth a visit. Exposition Park, a very pleasant green space in the city, and the Memorial Coliseum, a sports stadium, are also at the same location.

Caltech

https://goo.gl/maps/sUQCL34v2ZG2

1200 E California Blvd, Pasadena, CA 91125

caltech.edu

A private school specializing in technical subjects. Caltech is one of the best universities in the country for engineering and technical fields.

The student body is lopsidedly male, and full of nerds ytg. The football and other sports teams are just terrible. However, if you want to study physics or some other field in that general direction, you couldn't really do much better than Caltech.

Caltech's mascot is the beaver. We will pass on jokes on this subject.

Caltech is located in Pasadena. It's notable really walkable from the city center, but it's not far.

The Jet Propulsion Laboratory's is loosely attached to Caltech University. This is one of the leading centers of America is space program. Mars Lander's and deep space probes are designed and built here, and they are also control centers here.

This is a bit separate from NASA's space manned space flights, which, built under President Johnson, were placed naturally in Texas as part of Johnson's pork barrel policies.

The Jet Propulsion Laboratory is at least partially open to the public, and they do have tours and various public events where you can come in and see mars landers and things they're working on at the JPL. It's interesting, and it's free.

Santa Monica College

https://goo.gl/maps/EzFnZUcmaY62

1900 Pico Blvd, Santa Monica, CA 90405

smc.edu

This two-year college offers courses in a wide range of subjects, from music to science. Tuition is roughly a hundred dollars per course per quarter, which makes it extremely affordable. Courses are offered at several locations, including the main campus on Pico, the music campus on 11th and Santa Monica, and the expansion area at the airport, where many entertainment courses are offered.

LA City College

https://goo.gl/maps/rkDVZRvEks42

855 N Vermont Ave, Los Angeles, CA 90029

lacitycollege.edu

This campus on Vermont and Melrose was the original location for UCLA. Like other California junior colleges, it offers excellent courses in a wide range of academic subjects, from computers to electronic music. I teach occasional classes here, in the business and computer science departments.

Film Business

Many people who visit Santa Monica are curious about moviemaking. While Universal Studios and other similar tours are a sham, there are plenty of things to see that are real. Most of the Hollywood Film Studios are around the LA area. There are also many television production facilities. There are many famous locations that have been used in films which you can visit, such as Point Dume (Planet of the Apes), the Griffith Observatory (Rebel without a Cause), or Vasquez Rocks (Star Trek).

If you want to have a firsthand look at filmmaking, skip the theme parks and try signing up to be in the audience of a tv show, or sign up to be an extra with Central Casting.

Audiences Unlimited

http://www.tvtickets.com

This website has become a central location for booking free tickets to many of the ongoing productions in Hollywood. They have tickets for everything from "Dr Phil" to "Big Bang Theory". Participating studios include Paramount and Warner Brothers.

Why pay big bucks for a fake Hollywood experience when you can see the real thing for free?

Book in advance and show up really early. Popular shows sell out long in advance and they give out more tickets than they have seats, so latecomers are turned away.

Extras - Central Casting

https://goo.gl/maps/WWmHezQ278N2
220 S Flower Street, Burbank, CA 91502
818-562-2700
https://www.centralcasting.com/

If you want to see films being made, and get paid for it, here's what to do. Sign Up with Central Casting and become an extra.

Extras of the people wandering around in the background movies and TV shows. Pay is modest generally about 50 or $100, but the work is easy, and you can see the movie making process from the inside.

Most of the time, extras relax, try not to make too much noise, and enjoy the craft services department food which is available all-day long. Some people play cards, sleep in folding lounge chairs, while others tell each other stories about how they are looking for agents and plan to make it big in the movie business.

In my opinion the most fun extra jobs are once that involve dancing. The exercise is fun, dancing is social, and the time passes quickly.

If you want to succeed as an extra, it's fairly easy. Show up on time, smile, and stay out of the way and avoid all drama. A surprising number of people are unable to do this.

If you're interested, got on their website, arrange an appointment, but I don't let them take some pictures and get on the list. Is this going to plan works best for someone who's going to be in town for a while, because it takes a while to get your first gig, and a while longer before they decide whether you can be trusted and start giving your work regularly.

Owning your own reclining foldable chairs for work as an extra is a sign that you have been doing it too long and it's time to look for real job.

Movie Studios

Many who visit Southern California are interested to see famous movie studios. You can't really watch films being shot. When making movies they need absolute silence, or the voices of giggling tourists would ruin the soundtrack, and that would be a mess.

On the other hand, many TV shows do have audiences. I'm going to give a list of the locations of some of the studios and also the talent agencies. I will also give you a couple of ideas of things you can do if you are interested to see movie filming. This includes attending the viewing filming of live television shows, and signing up to be an extra with central casting.

Paramount Pictures

https://goo.gl/maps/v9objZyJ2S72
5515 Melrose Ave, Los Angeles, CA 90038
http://www.paramountstudios.com
Tour information:
paramountstudiotour.com
Located on Melrose just east of the main restaurant and shopping area of Melrose, this movie studio also produces many television shows and is one of your best opportunities to see the real Hollywood of moviemaking fame.

Absolute silence is required for sound recording in real movies, but many television shows have a studio audience to augment the laugh track.

I came in here once to see an episode of "Cheers" being filmed. It was amazing to watch the highly skilled five cameramen moving together like synchronized swimmers in the Olympics catching all the action. These days "Cheers" is gone but maybe you could see "Dr. Phil" or on of the other shows currently in production.

Once in a while they would stop and repeat a section, but it all went by surprisingly quickly. Periodically signs would tell us that it was time to laugh.

If you are interested and seeing the filming of a television show, I think this place is your best bet. Get on the website and reserve in advance, and show up an hour or two early, because they overbook and make people stand in line.

If you are at all into that interested in television or video or movie production, this is a place you absolutely must visit. Forget about Universal Studios, that's a total waste of time. This is the place to come to.

You can purchase tour tickets from their website. Prices start at $58. It's a little pricey, but you get a two-hour tour of a real studio where real shows are being made, much better than what you would get at Universal for twice the money.

If you want to see a production live, check http://www.tvtickets.com.

ABC Productions

http://abc.go.com/tv-ticket-request

ABC shows are filmed at a variety of locations, so there is no map. This website should give you a list of what is available. It might include shows like "Dancing with the stars" or "Jimmy Kimmel". You can be part of the studio audience. Tickets are generally free. I think this is more fun that doing a studio tour. Tickets for dramatic shows are not available (because they don't have audiences.) Be sure to reserve in advance and show up early. While busloads of tourists pay a hundred dollars or more to stand in line to view a fiberglass King Kong model at Universal Studios Theme Park, you will be seeing a real studio in operation. Highly recommended.

Burbank Studios (formerly NBC)

https://goo.gl/maps/hMSJEyGHH7A2

3000 W Alameda Ave, Burbank, CA 91523

theburbankstudios.com

Located in Burbank in the San Fernando Valley, north of Los Angeles, NBC is involved in live television production which offers another good opportunity to view the world of entertainment 1st hand.

The best thing to do is check their website, find out what is being produced, and get on the list way ahead of time. I have seen the Tonight Show being recorded here, which was a lot of fun. These days I think that is mostly filmed in New York, but you might still be able to see something. On the other hand, since many shows have moved, that may no longer be possible.

Gamers will be amused to know that Blizzard has a facility on the lot here.

Other NBC productions may be found at Universal Studios.

Universal Studios

https://goo.gl/maps/xRXSvV2tH2x

100 Universal City Plaza, Universal City, CA 91608

universalstudioshollywood.com

There are three more or less independent businesses going on at this large site: The NBC Universal Studios doing Film and TV production; the Universal Citywalk Mall, and the Universal Studios Theme Park.

Admission to one of these does not necessarily get you into the other two. For example, access to the mall doesn't get you backstage at movie productions, nor does access to the theme park. They are all totally separate.

I have been to the theme park a couple of times, because I was dragged there by people from out of town, or because there was an event, such as the premiere of one of the "Blues Brothers" movies.

I don't like the theme park much, but that is discussed elsewhere.

Admission to the theme park is roughly $100-$300 per day, which is pretty mind-blowing to me. If you buy one of the high-end tickets you can get an annual pass or a backstage tour, but wow, is it really worth that much money?

I totally recommend skipping this theme park. You will be so much happier to do almost anything else.

Sony Studios

https://goo.gl/maps/Nrwu5MFovZQ2

10202 West Washington Boulevard, Culver City, CA

www.sonypictures.com/studios/

This is a major Hollywood studio, though it's actually in Culver City, not Hollywood. All kinds of movies are made here, and there are also popular screening rooms where new features and Oscar contenders are shown. There are entrances on Overland and on the other side, and screening rooms on both sides too, so if you are coming here for a screening check and make sure which entrance to use. There is plenty of parking for invited guests, but the general public is not admitted past the security gates. This is definitely a working studio, it's the old MGM, but tours are actually available. They advertise 'Visit soundstages once home to iconic films like “The Wizard of Oz,” “Men in Black” and “Spider-Man.” Swing by smash-hit games shows “Jeopardy!” and “Wheel of Fortune.”' There is also a museum with props and set items.

They charge $45 and have tours several times a day.

For more information check the tours website http://www.sonypicturesstudiostours.com.

Raleigh Studios

https://goo.gl/maps/cF7Vs4Dhpns

300 Melrose Ave E, Los Angeles, CA 90038

raleighstudios.com

Raleigh Studios is a production facility. They don’t really make any of their own film productions. Rather, they rent out soundstages for rock videos commercials and movie productions. If you were to sneak in here, you might see something really interesting, but in general the public is not admitted.

There are no tours. I have worked on a number of commercials for JC Penney’s at Raleigh studio and always liked it. Productions here are busy filming, so they can’t really have people wandering around and talking in the background.

Fox Studios

https://goo.gl/maps/BvpWUjL35x62

10201 W Pico Blvd, Los Angeles, CA 90064

foxstudios.com

This is the location where Fox movies and TV series such as Living Color and "The Simpsons" are (or were) made. In the administration building you will find the executives who determine the coming year's tv lineup for Fox, as well as offices for many Hollywood personalities.

The main entrance is on Pico, but there is also another entrance up on the Century City side.

There are some outdoor New York style movie sets on the left as you enter, which are fun to look at. There are also a good number of soundstages, where filming is done, and post production facilities, where sound and editing are done.

There are also quite a large number of offices for important people. There is a lot of prestige with having an office on the lot.

I have visited Fox Studios countless times for movie screenings. They have several nice theaters, and screen all the new movies when Oscar time comes around.

In my opinion the Fox Commissary, located in about the middle of the lot, is the best of the Hollywood commissaries. If you get a chance to eat there, I recommend the club sandwich and fries. Really, really good.

Just to the east of the Fox Lot in Century City is the "Diehard Building", also known as Fox Plaza. The address is 2121 Avenue of the Stars. This is where the tax and business sides of Fox are located.

All of Century City used to be part of the Fox Lot. Fox was given an exemption from all kinds of zoning laws by the City so they could build movie sets without special permits. When the studio fell on hard times, this allowed them to sell off the land for construction of skyscrapers and a mall, which was hugely profitable.

Disney studios

https://goo.gl/maps/p6YsVmhL5a62

500 S Buena Vista St, Burbank, CA 91521

waltdisneystudios.com

Located in Burbank in the San Fernando Valley, The Disney studio is the center of Disney's moviemaking empire. It isn't open to visitors and does not offer tours.

Warner Brothers

https://goo.gl/maps/EeEmGnrnaqH2

3400 W Riverside Dr., Burbank, CA 91522

wbstudiotour.com

Located in the Burbank Area, this studio has many sound stages that are used for many popular movies and shows. I spent a week here dancing on "Gilmore Girls", which was super big fun. As you walk through these sets you would think you are in New England. They offer a tour. I have never done it, but it is supposed to be good. This is a real, working studio, so what you would see here is a lot more real than anything at the Universal Studios or Disneyland theme parks. At $60, it is expensive, but it's still much cheaper than either Universal or Disney. It's real, and you don't have to spend the whole day waiting in line.

Western Costume

https://goo.gl/maps/sKhdFZ1dx9K2

11041 Vanowen St, North Hollywood, CA 91605

westerncostume.com
(818) 760-0900
The granddaddy of all costume shops. Costumes here were in every movie you ever saw. If Halloween is coming up you might be able to find something to rent. If you are interested in costumes, this place will be more fascinating than any museum.

Talent Agencies

Every service writer actor or director needs to have an agent to sell their services and negotiate the deals.
Being an agent is basically a sales job. Agents and their assistant so much of their time submitting had jobs or resumes or videos of the clients working hopes of getting interviews or auditions. It's busy, and interesting people are always passing through the office, but the hours are brutal. Back when I was in college I did a lot of temp work, and I have helped out more than a few times at a couple of the agencies listed here. I always thought it was fun.

ICM

https://goo.gl/maps/oM7aaD8EsNy
10250 Constellation Blvd 9th Fl. Los Angeles, CA 90067
http://www.icmpartners.com/

William Morris Endeavor

https://goo.gl/maps/wxvwYiATMQw
9601 Wilshire Blvd 3rd Fl Beverly Hills, CA 90210
http://www.wmeentertainment.com/

CAA

https://goo.gl/maps/KX3dRAWqiHF2
2000 Avenue of the Stars # 100, Los Angeles, CA 90067
http://www.caa.com/

Guilds

The various Hollywood Union have offices around town. I will just list a couple that have events from time to time that are open to the public.

Academy of Motion Pictures

https://goo.gl/maps/dNRZTWdMkek
8949 Wilshire Blvd, Beverly Hills, CA 90211
oscars.org
(310) 247-3049
These are the folks who put on the Oscars each year. They have a very nice theater, but the Oscars ceremony is held elsewhere.

Writers Guild

https://goo.gl/maps/kkQXeTVbBp32
7000 W 3rd St, Los Angeles, CA 90048

wga.org
(323) 951-4000
This is the union that negotiates contracts for writers. They have a very nice theater which shows free movies for members.

Directors Guild

https://goo.gl/maps/UPPq631MNgw
7920 Sunset Blvd, Los Angeles, CA 90046
dga.org
(310) 289-2000
This is the union for Directors and their assistants. They have several very nice theaters and many good moves are shown here every week, which may or may not be open to the public.

Screen Actors Guild

https://goo.gl/maps/KeWNfMvwvn32
5757 Wilshire Blvd, Los Angeles, CA 90036
sagaftra.org
(323) 954-1600

Homes of the Stars

There are several tour companies that will take you out on bus tours to see the homes of stars. Alternately, if you would like to know the address of a particular Hollywood personality, they are often possible to find.

Seeing Stars

This website has home addresses, which you can look up by name. Many of them are old time Hollywood names.
http://www.seeing-stars.com/Live/index.shtml

Curbed

Here's another list, with more current names, that is fun.
https://la.curbed.com/maps/20-hot-celeb-homes-right-now-meet-the-celebrity-heat-map-1

Huffington Post

These celebrity homes are for sale.
https://www.huffingtonpost.com/2013/05/14/celebrity-homes-photos_n_3273244.html

ZUMA-JAY
Jobe
Jobe

Sports and Fitness

Horse-riding

LA Equestrian Center

https://goo.gl/maps/Y9HzbaTYnx72

480 Riverside Dr., Burbank, CA 91506

la-equestriancenter.com

(818) 840-9063

There is a riding ring and a number of horse related facilities here on the Burbank side of Griffith Park. It's probably the best horse related facility in the area. If you are interested in taking a ride in Griffith Park, the rates are reasonable, starting at about $25 an hour.

Malibu Riders

https://goo.gl/maps/Vfza4SLwK2w

2903 Cornell Rd, Agoura Hills, CA 91301

maliburiders.com

(818) 510-2245

This riding facility at the Paramount Ranch up in the hills above Malibu offers guided tours and rides through the ranch and surrounding woods and hills. The area is beautiful. Not far from the Rock Store.

Westside Riding School

1501 Will Rogers State Park Rd, Pacific Palisades, CA 90272

westsideridingschool.com

(310) 459-2545

This riding facility is located at Will Rogers Park, just north of Santa Monica. The park itself is a convenient location for picnics and BBQs.

Swimming

Santa Monica Beach

The entire west side of Santa Monica is the beach, and is open to public swimming. In theory it's only open during daylight hours, but in reality, as long as you are not causing trouble you are free to do as you like.

Food and drinks are allowed on the beach, but alcohol and fires are not.

Some people bring tents and shelters. This is allowed, as long as you don't do any camping. Be aware that trucks plow and clear the beach of garbage every night. Once in a while there are stories of people sleeping on the beach who are injured when they get run over or plowed by the night cleaning crew. It is absolutely not safe to sleep on the beach.

Annenberg Beach House (Pool)

https://goo.gl/maps/nAs1fMUyyR22

415 Pacific Coast Hwy, Santa Monica, CA 90402

annenbergbeachhouse.com

The Annenberg Community Beach House at Santa Monica State Beach is a public beach facility built on the location of a now-demolished 110-room mansion that was built for Marion Davies by William Randolph Hearst. This amazing beach club was a gift from a wealthy philanthropist to the city of Santa Monica. Not too many people know about it, but it's amazing facility.

Admission is about $7. The pool is open daily in the Summer, occasional evenings in the off season, check the website for details. The house itself is open 8:30-5:30 daily. There are shower and locker facilities available. In my opinion, this is nicer than any of the private beach clubs in the area. Recommended.

Santa Monica College Pool (Swim Center)

https://goo.gl/maps/QUfgNUzEx6J2

2225 16th St, Santa Monica, CA 90405

santamonicaswimcenter.org

Swimming facilities you're amazing. It's well hidden from the street, so not that many people know about it, but Santa Monica college has a very nice outdoor pool and it is frequently open to the public. Entrance is just a few dollars, and there are nice shower and changing facilities. Sometime periods are open

Check the schedule before you go. And sometimes are reserved for a swim teams, some for people doing laps, and some time periods are open for families kids and general splashing.

Boats and Water Sports

UCLA Marina Aquatic Center

https://goo.gl/maps/UzvE5k5joxq
14001 Fiji Way, Marina Del Rey, CA 90292
recreation.ucla.edu
(310) 823-0048
This conveniently located facility at the entrance to Marina Del Rey rents kayaks, sailboats, and windsurfers. Their windsurfing classes are great, and the sailing classes are supposed to be good too. Preference is given to students, then alumni, others maybe depending on demand. The best thing to do is just call and ask. I took a windsurfing class here, which was great. About twenty minutes from Santa Monica.

Southern California Jet Skis

https://goo.gl/maps/6SAdBQDMpbq
3600 Harbor Blvd, Oxnard, CA 93035
socaljetskis.com
(805) 910-7257
These folks rent jet skis and other watercraft from their office at Chanel Islands Harbor, in Oxnard, a little more than an hour north of Santa Monica. Rates start at about $100 and up.

Diving

Scuba diving is popular along the coast and off the Channel Islands. Trips usually go out of Oxnard, Marina del Rey, or Long Beach harbor. Sports Chalet used to be the main connecting for booking dive trips, but they are unfortunately out of business.

Scuba House

https://goo.gl/maps/CNVayVHFZFQ2
2501 Wilshire Blvd, Santa Monica, CA 90403
shop.scubahaus.com
(310) 828-2916
This nice local dive shop can set up your dive trip or provide you equipment.

Ocean Adventures Dive Co

https://goo.gl/maps/63AkaPeQKQx
4144 Lincoln Blvd, Marina Del Rey, CA 90292
oceanadventuresdiveco.com
(310) 578-9391
Friendly Marina del Rey area dive shop.

Running

Jogging is a popular activity in Santa Monica. Popular routes are long San Vicente Blvd (on the north side of town), along Palisades Park, and on the beach path from Santa Monica to Venice.

Santa Monica Stairs

https://goo.gl/maps/5V1rCvDinsm

699 Adelaide Dr., Santa Monica, CA 90402

If you want to maximize the intensity of your exercise, you might try running the stairs off 4th street that head down to Santa Monica Canyon. The climb is about the same as going up the stairs of a 15 story building. These are popular with joggers at all hours, and are also a spot for people watching. Free.

Outdoor Ice Rink

https://goo.gl/maps/fBBqaVfh2Y42

1324 5th St, Santa Monica, CA 90401

iceatsantamonica.com

In the season leading up to Christmas, the city of Santa Monica, with the sponsorship of Starbucks and a few other local businesses, opens up this outdoor ice rink for public skating.

There is something anomalous about the idea of ice-skating in Santa Monica in balmy weather, under the palm trees. The location is just about a block off of the third street promenade, between Santa Monica and Arizona on fourth Street fifth Street.

I think it's wonderful. I love it. If this is open when you visit town then I would definitely put this on your list.

Unfortunately, big money developers have got their eyes on this piece of land. The entire block belongs to the city of Santa Monica, and corrupt developers are hoping they will be able to get the city to gift them the land for construction of a large hotel and condominium towers. This is a running political battle in Santa Monica today. Don't be surprised if you come looking for an ice rink and find a giant construction site instead.

YMCA

https://goo.gl/maps/kHENV4rYo9E2

1332 6th St, Santa Monica, CA 90401

welcome.ymcasm.org

If you are a member of the YMCA, then you are in luck. The Santa Monica YMCA has a very nice pool, weight room and work out machines, and everything else you need to stay healthy.

Unfortunately, membership is kind of expensive.

If budget is a concern, you may want to check out the public pool at the Annenberg Center on the beach, or the very nice facility at Santa Monica college on Pico, which is frequently open for public swimming.

Loews Hotel also allows public access to their pool and training facilities, though it's expensive.

Beach volleyball

A surprising percentage of the world's greatest volleyball players, including many Olympic gold-medalists, got their start playing on Santa Monica Beach. There are several spots on the beach where you can play beach volleyball.

This first is close to the pier, on the south side:

https://goo.gl/maps/u9jKLQye2m12

930 Ocean Front Walk, Santa Monica, CA 90403

The second spot is further south:

https://goo.gl/maps/wvxAU9YA1uA2

2400 Ocean Front Walk, Santa Monica, CA 90405

https://www.smgov.net/Departments/CCS/content.aspx?id=31581

They are seldom full, and no registration is required. If you want to play volleyball, just bring a ball, take off your shoes, and start playing.

Beach volleyball is totally free. Check the city website for more details.

Trapeze

Trapeze School of New York
https://goo.gl/maps/rKxA6bg7rFE2
370 Santa Monica Pier, Santa Monica, CA 90401
losangeles.trapezeschool.com
(310) 394-5800

Not many would think to include trapeze lessons as part of a visit to Southern California, but when will you have a better chance? There is a trapeze school right on the Santa Monica Pier, where the excitement of swinging on the ropes is combined with fresh air and an amazing view.

Surfing

Santa Monica has an excellent beach for surfing. The good thing is that the beach is relatively safe, with sandy beaches (no rocks) and mild currents. The downside is that the waves are not all that big and he breaks are short, which means after a very short ride you will reach the beach. The problem is that the wave come straight into the beach. Veteran surfers prefer the beaches up towards Malibu, where waves flow along the beach, which gives a much longer ride.

Surfing is popular year around. The water is not as warm as you would find in Hawaii, so many wear "shortie" wet suits that keep the body warm but are easy to get on and off. These are available at places like Zuma J and Rip Curl, or sometimes at Costco, depending on the season.

Serious surfers like to go in the early morning. If you're not so serious, you may find surfing beaches close to empty in the afternoon, which can be nice.

The city tries to separate surfers from swimmers, for safety reasons. During the summer surfing is limited to the stretch of beach between lifeguard towers 18 and 20 (Pico Boulevard to Bay Street) or between towers 28 and 29 (Ashland Avenue to Pier Street). Before surfing it is best to check with the lifeguards. Or, just look and see what the people are doing in the section of water you are considering for surfing. If nobody else is surfing, you are probably in the wrong place.

Lifeguards

https://goo.gl/maps/YAT4jjqkCRA2

1642 Ocean Front Walk, Santa Monica, CA 90401

310-394-3261

fire.lacounty.gov/lifeguard

Zuma J Board Shop

https://goo.gl/maps/dtXX5aeaxt32

2625 Main St, Santa Monica, CA 90405

zjbh.com

(310) 392-5646

This excellent local surf shop has everything you need for your next surfing expedition from board to clothes to GoPro underwater cameras. I have a board made by this shop and it's great. The people who work here are very knowledgeable. They also rent boards and suits.

Rip Curl

https://goo.gl/maps/noswY2sjyQo

1451 3rd Street Promenade, Santa Monica, CA 90401

ripcurl.com

This Australian-based surf shop has a branch located on the 3rd Street Promenade. Their strength is wetsuits, but they also have T-shirts and sandals and lots of other toys. I have a wetsuit from this shop, and it's great.

Licensed Surf Instructors

The City of Santa Monica licenses surf instructors. Their current list may be found here:

https://www.smgov.net/uploadedFiles/Departments/CCS/Permits_Rentals/Beach-Surf-Instructors.pdf

Surfing Beaches

Surfing was a huge fad in the 1960's, and remains popular today. You can surf right in Santa Monica, though many like other beaches north and south of town.

Santa Monica

The surfing area is a little bit south of the pier. Look for other people surfing.
Surfline gives an online guide to wind waves and tides on a daily basis, for this and other beaches.
http://www.surfline.com/surf-report/santa-monica-pier-southern-california_4886/
This website has surf conditions as well as a beach cam.
https://magicseaweed.com/Santa-Monica-Municipal-Pier-Surf-Report/280/

El Porto

https://goo.gl/maps/zz6zUTSKLPF2
45th St & The Strand, Manhattan Beach, CA 90266
http://www.surfline.com/surf-report/el-porto-southern-california_4900/
El Porto is officially part of the City of Manhattan Beach between Dockweiler State Beach and Manhattan Beach, just south of El Segundo. The best place to park is in the metered parking lot on 45th Street just west of Highland Avenue.

Zuma Beach

https://goo.gl/maps/G4jKLSedji52

30000 Pacific Coast Highway, Malibu, CA 90265

http://www.surfline.com/surf-report/zuma-southern-california_4949/

Located at 30000 Pacific Coast Highway, just north of Malibu, is the famous Zuma Beach. Zuma offers both beginners and intermediate surfers a nice array of waves to choose from. There is paid parking lot and free parking along PCH (it may be a bit of a hike).

Venice Beach

https://goo.gl/maps/mEV5KeCbnqy

3100 to 2700 Ocean Front Walk, Venice, CA 90291

310-578-0478

http://www.surfline.com/surf-report/venice-beach-southern-california_4211/

The surfing at Venice, just south of Santa Monica, is good for all levels. The best swells are located along the famed Venice Breakwater between the Venice and Santa Monica Piers, respectively. Parking can be found in the public lot at the end of Washington Boulevard, or in nearby private lots.

Topanga Beach

https://goo.gl/maps/WJWGWBqsngB2

18700 Pacific Coast Hwy, Malibu, CA 90265

beaches.lacounty.gov

http://www.surfline.com/surf-report/venice-beach-southern-california_4211/

On PCH, just off of Topanga Beach Drive, Topanga Beach has a rocky beach but a long break.

Lunada Bay

https://goo.gl/maps/szrqzRAfGus

2300 block of Paseo del Mar, Palos Verdes Estates, CA 90274

http://www.surfline.com/surf-report/venice-beach-southern-california_4211/

The surfing is very good here. Located about 40 minutes south of Santa Monica, South of Redondo and West of Long Beach.

Redondo / The Breakwater

https://goo.gl/maps/2gU3DPd7fY22

210 Yacht Club Way, Redondo Beach, CA 90277

http://www.surfline.com/surf-report/venice-beach-southern-california_4211/

Popular with advanced surfers. Sandy beach but strong currents. About 30 minutes from Santa Monica.

Fishing

Boats take anglers out to catch Tuna and other fish from Ventura, Marina del Rey, or Long Beach harbor. Fishing from the Santa Monica pier is hopeless, there are no fish. You need to go out into the open ocean to catch anything. Friends who go out in boats often come back with a freezer full of tasty Tuna. If you want to go fishing, ask in one of these shops and they may be able to make some good suggestions.

Lincoln-Pico Sporting Goods

https://goo.gl/maps/NCSgas4ac542
2017 Lincoln Blvd, Santa Monica, CA 90405
(310) 452-3831
Fishing equipment and information.

Joy Fishing Tackle

https://goo.gl/maps/NATrB5rXbC92
4918 Santa Monica Blvd, Los Angeles, CA 90029
(323) 664-0808
Fishing equipment and information.

Marina Del Rey Sportfishing

https://goo.gl/maps/d1cRCqENV7n
Marina Del Rey, CA
(310) 822-3625
Fishing charter service out of Marina del Rey.

Channel Islands SportFishing Center

4151 S Victoria Ave, Oxnard, CA 93035
channelislandssportfishing.com
(805) 382-1612
Fishing charter service out of Oxnard. A bit of a drive but the fishing is good. If you can get to Oxnard this will be your best choice.

Day Trips

There are many other activities that could be combined with a trip to Santa Monica. They are outside the area covered by this book, so we can't give extensive information, but here are some ideas for further research.

Blimps

Goodyear Blimp Operations
https://goo.gl/maps/hE44kPRtgvS2
19200 S Main St, Gardena, CA 90248
goodyearblimp.com
(310) 327-6565
The Goodyear blimp airfield is about half an hour south of Santa Monica.

Balloons

Nobody currently flies hot air balloons over Santa Monica, but flights are available at a number of sites south or east of Los Angeles.

Adventure Balloon Rides

2091 Goetz Road, Perris, CA 9257
(951) 678-4778
www.balloonridesovercalifornia.com

Los Angeles Balloon Rides

198 S. Main St, Los Angeles, CA 90012
(323) 406-8464
www.losangelesballoonrides.com

Balloons Above

Washington St.,Bermuda Dunes, CA 92203
(760) 347-0410

www.balloonsabovethedesert.com

California Dreamin' Balloon Adventures

33133 Vista Del Monte Road
Temecula, CA 92591
(951) 699-0601
www.californiadreamin.com

Catalina Island

https://goo.gl/maps/bGn4b2VxeG72
This small island can be seen from Santa Monica. There is a small town, with a harbor and marina, hotels, restaurants, and camping available. You can go from Long Beach, by boat or helicopter. The helicopter might be fun, if you have never ridden in one before.

Catalina Express Ferry

https://goo.gl/maps/FroHCzydfbK2
Berth 95, 95 Berth, San Pedro, CA 90731
catalinaexpress.com
(310) 519-1212

Island Express Helicopter Services

https://goo.gl/maps/BU2mtu2YzAQ2
56 Pebbly Beach Rd, Avalon, CA 90704
islandexpress.com
(310) 510-2525

Vasquez Rocks

https://goo.gl/maps/LzyKXExQCrC2
10700 Escondido Canyon Rd, Agua Dulce, CA 91350
parks.lacounty.gov
(661) 268-0840
Located at the north edge of Los Angeles County, "Vasquez Rocks Natural Area" is the site where Captain Kirk from Star Trek fought countless hand to hand battles with space aliens, keeping the galaxy safe for the rest of us. Westworld, the fantastic new HBO series, also films here. There isn't a lot more to see in this neighborhood, but the 1000 acre park is nice. The hikes are all super easy. There is camping. Sci Fi fans will love it.

Palm Springs

https://goo.gl/maps/pPVeisGQhxk

Official Palm Springs, California Visitor Info & Travel Guide to Palm Springs

www.visitpalmsprings.com

This desert community located about two hours east of Santa Monica has more golf courses per square mile than any other city in America. It is a popular retirement community. Fun activities include golfing, horse riding, visiting Joshua Tree, and gambling at the nearby Indian casinos.

Joshua Tree

https://goo.gl/maps/49bQ9sx8t6L2

Park Service

https://www.nps.gov/jotr/index.htm

(760) 367-5500

Located close to Palm Springs, this park area offers hiking trails and natural beauty. This is a popular getaway for LA residents.

Big Bear

https://goo.gl/maps/m5oiHDqpcp52

Big Bear Lake CA Official Travel Website

https://www.bigbear.com/

Skiing is available at this location only about 2 1/2 hours from the palm trees of LA. Sure, they often have man made snow, but still, it's amazing that you can ski here at all. Fun.

Lake Arrowhead

https://goo.gl/maps/VCJZfTj9UcL2

Lake Arrowhead California Site

www.lakearrowhead.com

This lake and resort community is located about two hours east of LA. UCLA has a big convention facility here.

Mammoth

https://goo.gl/maps/uBWnAJpt9cC2

Mammoth Mountain Skiing

https://www.mammothmountain.com/

This major ski area in the Sierra Nevada mountains is about five hours from LA. Snow tends to be wet and heavy compared to Utah or other colder deserts, but there always is plenty of snow, and an active community of skiers.

Las Vegas

https://goo.gl/maps/WPiYHNA3qFK2

Las Vegas travel deals on hotels, shows, and things to do in Las Vegas ...

https://www.lasvegas.com/
This resort area is about five hours drive from Los Angeles. This is a favorite getaway from LA residents. You could in theory go there and back in a day, but I've never heard of anyone doing that. There are lots of cheap places to stay in Las Vegas.

San Diego Zoo

https://goo.gl/maps/Ymf9CzbFJfM2
2920 Zoo Dr., San Diego, CA 92101
zoo.sandiegozoo.org
(619) 231-1515
This famous animal collection is in San Diego, about 2 1/2 hours south of LA. It's expensive to get in, and it's so overdeveloped it feels a bit like Disneyland, but it has a very good collection and is fun. You could do this in a day but it's a lot of driving. It might be better to spend the night in San Diego.

Death Valley

https://goo.gl/maps/tffjSRSJ46w
Death Valley National Park (U.S. National Park Service)
https://www.nps.gov/deva/index.htm
This park, with the lowest altitude and highest summer temperatures in the US, is located about 4 hours from LA, about a half hour off the highway to Las Vegas. Best to plan this as an overnight trip, and make sleeping arrangements before you go.

Disneyland

https://goo.gl/maps/FcpyKgw2TJT2
1313 Disneyland Dr., Anaheim, CA 92802
disneyland.disney.go.com
(714) 781-4636
This popular resort destination is located in Anaheim, about an hour south of Santa Monica.

Six flags Magic Mountain

https://goo.gl/maps/4L51k5hfggp
26101 Magic Mountain Pkwy, Valencia, CA 91355
sixflags.com
(661) 255-4100
This roller coaster park is located in Valencia, about an hour north of Santa Monica.

Mexico

If everyone in your travel group has their passports, Mexico could make a great side trip. You don't need the passports to get into Mexico, you need them to get back. California residents are probably OK with a driver's license. You can count on an hour wait on the return through customs, so the minimum trip to TJ and back will be about 7 hours. It's probably better to spend the night.

Tijuana

https://goo.gl/maps/oTgTKFhDiBC2
Tijuana Hotels - Attractions
www.tijuana.com/
This Mexican community is about 3 hours south of LA. The border formalities are minimal as you go south, in fact, the border station is often unattended. On the way back they make you wait in line for an hour or longer for no particular reason. Some recommended places to eat are Sanborns restaurant and mall on Revolución, and Caesars restaurant, which claims to have invented the Caesars salad. Street tacos are fun too. Just look for places that seem to be popular with locals, and you will be fine.

Hotel Lucerna

https://goo.gl/maps/WsBqUD7AUdG2
Paseo de los Héroes #10902, Zona Rio, Zona Urbana Rio Tijuana, 22320 Tijuana, B.C., Mexico
hoteleslucerna.com
+52 664 633 3900
Hotel Lucerna is a very nice and reasonably priced hotel just a little bit outside the tourist zone. For Mexicans this is a high-end business hotel. Not many American's stay here which is odd because it's one of the nicest hotels in town. They have a nice pool, clean rooms and a fantastically good hotel restaurant. If you haven't been to Mexico before, I suggest this hotel for comfort and security. You will like it. About $100 per night.

Sanborns

https://goo.gl/maps/qtqvyJkadxp

Av. Revolución, 1102, Centro, Zona Centro, 22000 Tijuana, B.C., Mexico

sanborns.com.mx

+52 664 685 2644

This fun casual Mexican restaurant is clean, healthy, and the food is great. They often have a buffet, but I would skip that unless the buffet items are exactly what you want. It's usually cheaper to just get what you want from the menu. It kind of reminds me of a super nice Denny's. For those who are food paranoid (like me) this place is super clean. Raw items like orange juice and salads are absolutely just fine. If this is your first time to Mexico and you're nervous about the food then Sanborns is a good place to go.

Sanborns also has a department store attached, which is a good place to get souvenirs. There's no haggling, but the Cuban cigars are real ones and everything is good quality. It's like shopping at Macy's at home.

The Pharmacy here is much cheaper than what you would find in the US, so if you buy any expensive medicines, this is the place.

There are other Sanborns in Tijuana, and in fact all across Mexico, but this is one of the nicest.

Caesars Restaurant

https://goo.gl/maps/hch4kapegYN2

Av Revolución 1059, Zona Centro, 22000 Tijuana, B.C., Mexico

caesarstijuana.com

+52 664 685 1927

This venerable establishment claims to have invented the Caesar's salad. If you order one they will make quite a show of it. A waiter in a bowtie will roll up his cart and do the whole thing, dressing and all, from scratch, while you watch. A bit touristy, but fun.

Crime

The tourist zone around "Revolución" street is a known place for car break-ins and pickpockets. In the daytime it's family friendly, but at night this is an active red-light district. There are many sketchy people here. If you are careful you should be fine, but don't leave anything you value in an unattended vehicle unless it is in supervised parking. Other places in Baja are generally fine but in this one area, you should really be careful. Most hotels have supervised parking.

Rosarito

https://goo.gl/maps/ZiN2XS79DjS2

Located about 45 minutes south of Tijuana on the toll road, this beach town is popular with tourists. We usually stay at the Rosarito Beach Hotel. They often have packages which are a good deal. Food at the restaurants is so-so but the beach front location can't be beat and the pool is nice. El Nido restaurant next door features quail eggs. They put a least a half dozen eggs on your breakfast plate because they are very small. Looks strange, like something from a Dr. Seuss book, but the eggs are good.

Rosarito Beach Hotel

https://goo.gl/maps/ummoXod7wH32

Blvd. Benito Juárez 31, Playas Rosarito, 22710 Rosarito, B.C., Mexico

rosaritobeachhotel.com

+52 800 265 2322

Large traditional resort built in the 1920's, with pool, beach, new and old sections. About $110 a night. The rooms range widely in age, convenience and view, so have a look and make sure you like the one they give you.They often have packages that will throw in some food and drinks, and maybe a fast pass to get through the border on the way back.

El Nido

https://goo.gl/maps/YeKerSWpKZ92

Blvd. Benito Juárez 67, Centro, 22710 Rosarito, B.C., Mexico

+52 661 612 1430

Friendly family restaurant, close to the entrance to the Rosarito Beach Hotel. The name means "the nest". They feature quail eggs, but serve full menus for breakfast, lunch and dinner. It's the best restaurant in the area. Recommended.

Villa Ortega - Puerto Nuevo

https://goo.gl/maps/7ib27vuARjk

Barracuda 77, Puerto Nuevo, 22710 Playas de Rosarito, B.C., Mexico

puertonuevolobster.com

+52 661 614 0706

Stopping for Lobster at Puerto Nuevo is one of the rituals of any trip to Baja. Villa Ortega is the biggest and best known of the restaurants. It's a bit of a tourist trap, but the view is amazing and the food reliably excellent. Other nearby restaurants, such as Casa de las Langostas and Puerto Nuevo Restaurant, are also excellent. Lobster is "Langosta" in Spanish. There is no shortage of lobster in Puerto Nuevo.

Ensenada

https://goo.gl/maps/RK2K77JNpkk

Located about an hour south of Tijuana on the toll road, this port town is a popular spot for fishing and is a regular stop for cruise ships coming down from California. Hussongs Cantina is famous for margaritas and is an obligatory stop for any visitor. There are also fishing and surfing opportunities here if you ask around. The market and stands close to the harbor cater mostly to tourists off the cruise ships. Seafood tacos on the docks are not so good. Walk a couple of blocks, and the food and shopping are better.

Wine Country

https://goo.gl/maps/1e3dHUshx2S2

Just north of town, the Valle de Guadalupe has a couple of dozen wineries, and is the center of the Mexican wine industry. Mexico doesn't have much of a tradition of wine production, so the quality is very hit and miss. Some of the wines here are wonderful, others not. The wineries are all fairly close together so it's easy to drive from one winery to the next.

Hussong's Cantina Ensenada

Avenida Ruiz 113, Zona Centro, 22800 Ensenada, B.C., Mexico
cantinahussongs.com
+52 646 178 3210

This is supposedly the oldest bar in Baja. They claim to be the inventor of the Margarita, in 1941. There are other places that make the same claim, but Hussongs' claim is as credible as any. The cantina, or traditional Mexican bar, is located on one of the main streets near the center of Ensenada, and is busy from late morning on, especially if there is a cruise ship in port.

There are no windows and no view. Mariachis wander through periodically, and the place is noisy and musical. They have no food, but they do have peanuts. The shells all end up on the floor. The margaritas are good, and not expensive considering how famous this bar is. If you come to Ensenada you should come here and have at least one margarita.

In recent years Hussong's has gotten so popular, they started selling their own beer and they have opened a branch in Las Vegas.

SANTA MONICA
66
End of the Trail

Lists

The purpose of this section is to help you find places that are the best in each category.

Best Breakfasts

Marmalade
Rae's
Gilbert's El Indio
Lare's

Best Happy Hours

This is a short list of happy hours in Santa Monica. The scene isn't as good as it was a few years ago, since happy hour favorites like Chan Dara, Monsoon and Wokcano closed, but there are still some good options.

Ingo's
Misfits
Fig
M Street Kitchen
Stella Barra
Monsieur Marcel
Lago
Loews
Lula's
Independence
Shangri La

Best Mexican

California used to be part of Mexico, so it's no surprise that Mexican Food is a specialty here. Some of the best places include:

Gilbert's El Indio

El Cholo

Benny's Tacos

Lare's

La Cabana

Tacos Por Favor

There are also some places to avoid

Mariasol

Cabo Cantina

Taco Bell

Best Dinners

None of these places are cheap, but they will make you a fine dinner.

Ingo's

Santa Monica Seafood

R+D Kitchen

Cheesecake Factory

Huntley Hotel

Pacific Dining Car

Meat

Shutters

Del Frisco's

Best "No Corkage" Dinner Spots

These restaurants will let you bring your own wine, and don't charge extra if you do.

Rosti

Marmelade

Z Garden

Best Dinners if Someone Else is Paying

Price is no object? You can spend plenty of money at these places.

The Ivy

Shutters

Melisse

Casa Del Mar

Midnight Hunger

Most restaurants and stores in Santa Monica close by 10 PM, but these are open all night:

DK Donuts
Izzy's Deli
McDonalds on 2nd and Colorado
Pacific Dining Car
Tommy Burger
Swingers
Ralphs Grocery on Olympic

Best Fast Food

Bay Cities
Tacos Por Favor
Tacomiendo
Chipotle
Baja fresh
Bennys Tacos
Nijiya Market
Marukai Market
Vons Grocery
Wienerschnitzel
Tommys
Slice Pizza
Costco Food Court

Worst Restaurants

Perry's, all three locations
Cabo Cantina
Bubba Gump
Mariasol
Pacific Park Food Court, every restaurant

It is interesting to notice that most of the really bad restaurants are on city owned property.

Best Museums

All of the museums listed in this book are worth visiting, but these are my favorites.

Getty Villa
Getty Center
Norton Simon
Paige (La Brea Tar Pits)
LA County Museum

Best Views

Huntley Hotel

Griffith Observatory

Mulholland Drive

LA City Hall

US Bank Downtown

Sky Room, Long Beach

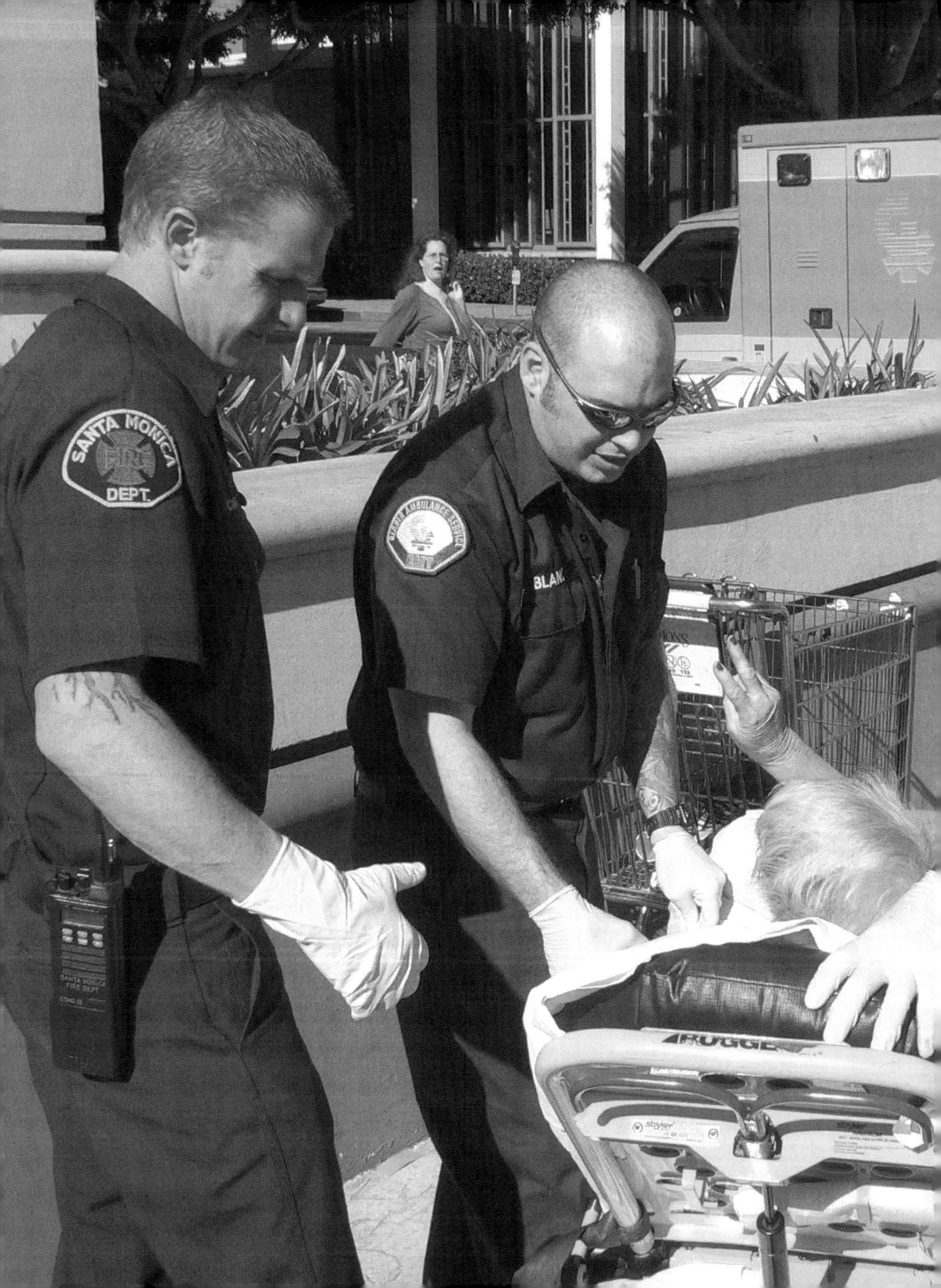
SANTA MONICA
FIRE
DEPT.

Emergencies

For genuine emergencies, pick up the nearest phone and dial 911.
Medical, police, fire, and city government numbers are listed below.

Medical

St. John's Hospital

https://goo.gl/maps/WNhtk8SPR2u
2121 Santa Monica Blvd, Santa Monica, CA 90404
california.providence.org
(310) 829-5511
This is the largest hospital in Santa Monica. They are owned by Providence Health Services, a nonprofit Catholic health care system.

Kaiser Permanents

https://goo.gl/maps/3TdEPed7Tr92
1450 10th St, Santa Monica, CA 90401
kp.org
(800) 954-8000
This small office serves Kaiser patients. It's more convenient than going to their main facilities on Robertson on in Hollywood.

UCLA Hospital

https://goo.gl/maps/L8Kb4epQw4s
1250 16th St, Santa Monica, CA 90404
uclahealth.org
(424) 259-6000
This hospital is associated with Blue Cross, which is convenient for those with that insurance. Getting medical care here is like getting served at the DMV, though the waiting rooms are more comfortable and the staff better paid.

Citizens Medical Group

https://goo.gl/maps/ViHaXF9zGJ82
11560 W Pico Blvd, Los Angeles, CA 90064
citizensurgentcare.com
(310) 477-8285
This cash clinic is an option for those who don't have insurance from Blue Cross or Kaiser. If you want a good clinic with reasonable fees, or if you just want to go to a clinic where you can come in when you want to and not have to make an appointment five week in advance, then I'd highly recommend this place. Doctors are graduates of UCLA and other reputable schools.

Local Government

Police

https://goo.gl/maps/8awLV28eGn12
333 Olympic Dr., Santa Monica, CA 90401
santamonicapd.org
(310) 395-9931

Harbor Patrol

https://goo.gl/maps/D4ycbGZzLcr
200 Santa Monica Pier, Santa Monica, CA 90401
smgov.net
(310) 458-8694

Fire Department

https://goo.gl/maps/U9qt2TrweVF2
333 Olympic Dr., Santa Monica, CA 90401
santamonicafire.org
(310) 458-8652

Courthouse

https://goo.gl/maps/J7gEPSxKjX22
1725 Main St #102, Santa Monica, CA 90401
lacourt.org
(310) 260-1876
Countless famous trials have happened here.

City Hall

https://goo.gl/maps/xbeHPnPW6fJ2
1685 Main St, Santa Monica, CA 90401
smgov.net
(310) 393-9975

todos los clásicos, toda la música,
toda la aventura,
Porrúa
Porrúa
Dividendos
Dentro de la caja
LEY DE AMPARO
COMENTADA

Reading/Viewing List

The following will be useful for further research and inspiration as you plan your visit to Santa Monica.

Books

Santa Monica Bay: Paradise by the Sea

A Pictorial History of Santa Monica, Venice, Marina Del Rey, Ocean Part, Pacific Palisades, Topanga & Malibu

by Fred E. Basten and Carolyn See

It is great fun to compare Santa Monica and the surrounding areas as they are shown in these historical photos, with the way things look today. This is probably the best of the Santa Monica picture books.

Santa Monica: 1950-2010 (Images of America)

by Louise B. Gabriel and the Santa Monica Historical Society

This book is filled with memories of Santa Monica from days gone by. It is one of a series of books about local neighborhoods that are filled with fascinating photos. The originals of many of these photos can be seen at the Santa Monica library.

The Big Sleep (Novel)

by Raymond Chandler

Raymond Chandler set most of his hard-boiled detective novels in Santa Monica, which he renames "Bay City". The books are fantastic good fun to read. characters and the language draw you in and take you on a fun ride. His style keeps the story going even though often when you look back the stories make no sense. The Big Sleep is one of the best of his novels, but they're all good. The movie version is fun too.

The Day of the Locust

by Nathanael West

This well-known novel, later made into a movie, revels in the seedy underbelly of Hollywood

Movies

The Big Sleep

This movie, based on the classic novel by Raymond Chandler, is set in Bay City, which is the name Chandler uses when he writes about Santa Monica. Starring Humphrey Bogart and Lauren Bacall, it is one of the best film noir detective dramas ever filmed. An absolute must see.

The Sting

This classic movie with Paul Newman and Robert Redford is about gangsters and swindlers in Santa Monica. Locations such as the carrousel on the pier will be very familiar. A charming movie, and winner of several Academy Awards. An absolute must -see.

Baywatch

In France they called this show about lifeguards at the beach "Malibu", but in fact it's mostly Santa Monica. The real beach is just as nice as the one in the shows. The show itself is not all that interesting.

Roger Rabbit

This movie mixes live action and animation, with a detective drama involving cartoon characters working at Hollywood studios. The "Red Car" trains that used to connect Santa Monica and LA are featured in various parts of the movie. You can't really take it as history, it's just a movie, but it's a fun one, and well worth seeing. My favorite part of this movie is the song by Jessica Rabbit, and her line, "I'm not bad, I'm just drawn that way."

Chinatown

This film isn't set in Santa Monica at all, it's more Hollywood and the San Fernando Valley, but it gives a flavor of the development mentality that is a driving force in finance and politics in the LA area even today. Starring Jack Nicholson in one of his best performances. It's another absolute must-see movie.

The Author

Jim Pickrell is a native of Seattle. He enjoys traveling, cooking, reading, skiing, diving, computer programming, and playing music. He studied at the University of Washington, the Technical University of Munich, and UCLA. He speaks Spanish, German, French and Japanese. In his spare time teaches computer classes at Los Angeles City College. He can be reached at jim.pickrell@gmail.com.

Index

Printed in Great Britain
by Amazon